Donated
To The Library by

The Frantz Fund

2016

Garth Williams

AMERICAN ILLUSTRATOR

A Life

ELIZABETH K. WALLACE & JAMES D. WALLACE

BEAUFORT
BOOKS

Garth Williams

Library of Congress Cataloging-in-Publication Data On File
Hardcover: 9780825307959
Ebook: 9780825307249

For inquiries about volume orders, please contact:
Beaufort Books
27 West 20th Street, Suite 1102
New York, NY 10011
sales@beaufortbooks.com

Published in the United States by Beaufort Books
www.beaufortbooks.com

Distributed by Midpoint Trade Books
www.midpointtrade.com

Printed in the United States of America
Interior design by Mark Karis
Cover Design by Michael Short

We dedicate this book to the grandchildren—Williams' and our own.

Table of Contents

Introduction

Millions of readers can be forgiven for knowing the work—but not the name—of Garth Williams. After all, as his *New York Times* obituary observed, it was often his fate to remain unrecognized as the illustrator of countless children's classics. By 2004, *Stuart Little* had sold 3,182,566 copies. And this was just one of the more than eighty books done by Williams. His career was prolific and very wide-ranging: for E. B. White, he famously drew Stuart Little, Charlotte, and Wilbur. He illustrated all of the Laura Ingalls Wilder books. He drew many, many other animal books, including innumerable, still cherished titles for the Little Golden Books and several series—George Selden's *The Cricket in Times Square* and all its sequels, four of the Miss Bianca books by Margery Sharp, and Randall Jarrell's *The Gingerbread Rabbit*.

So we could say that, without Williams' contributions, Stuart Little would not have attained his trim, dapper appearance, Laura and Mary Ingalls would not have enjoyed their legacy, the adventures of Chester the Cricket and Harry the Cat would have seemed less vivid, and the travails of Wilbur the pig would not have gained their full existential weight. Miss Bianca would not have possessed her perfectly rendered nutshell chair. Even Frances, eponymous heroine of the series by Russell Hoban, would have been different: it was Williams' idea that she be not a vole, as her author suggested, but a badger.

Yet how many readers would be able to name the artist whose pencil nudged all these famous characters to life? This, however, is the illustrator's destiny: to create indelible characters, often beloved and remembered for generations, and yet to be forgotten by name for his extraordinary contribution. Who, after all, remembers John Tenniel as the illustrator of *Alice's Adventures in Wonderland*? Who remembers that Ernest Shepard limned both Winnie the Pooh and Toad of Toad Hall? Illustration is the bastard child of the fine arts: often the offspring of rigorous artistic training and sheer inspiration, it is rarely perceived as a "legitimate" and freestanding creative art. This issue has received extensive attention in a biography of Norman Rockwell by Deborah Solomon. Especially when an artist draws for someone else, he is seen merely to express, to supplement, or to serve the author's words.

But this is not entirely the case. Great illustrations advance the story. They not only enrich the mood of the text, but they also stress key themes. In the process, they become a kind of ghost writing. In addition, illustrations facilitate the reader's experience of psychological depth by providing visual cues that can be easily read and processed. They fill what one critic has called the "conceptual gap" between the author's expression and the reader's imagination, resulting in experiences that can be broadly disseminated. In Williams' illustration, the tragicomic woe of Wilbur, bewailing a pig's fate, becomes a predicament shared and treasured by millions. Moreover, the ability to illustrate animals is an especially powerful, even visionary talent. Among the best animal illustrators, it is difficult to say where the animal lets off and the human begins—and vice versa. Such artists allow us to see ourselves living not in opposition to, but on a continuum with our animal brothers.

Garth Williams' illustrations accomplish all this and more. Yet his biography is the story of a man—a genius to be sure—who never fully enjoyed the sense of his own accomplishment. Having been trained in Europe, in an old-world setting that privileged highbrow, serious art over the popular, he always thought that one day he would be a "real" artist. Driven by financial exigencies for most of his life, he tended to see himself as a journeyman. Of course, Garth Williams' brilliance did not go completely unnoticed, particularly in the early years of his career. From the beginning, astute critics recognized that his illustrations had the capacity to outstrip the written word and that Williams' contributions frequently assured a book's success. Even in the earliest years, there was an appreciation for his obvious skill. His illustrations could also rescue a failed narrative, like Eva Le Gallienne's *Flossie and Bossie* (1949): "Whatever the faults of the story, there is not a false note in Garth Williams' inspired illustrations," was the assessment in the *New York Times*.[1] Comments like this continued throughout his career, with honors and awards attending him in his later years, and his subsequent reputation as "the great Garth Williams" now seems destined to endure.

Over time, Williams' fans have not needed the critics to tell them the exact nature of his brilliance. Those who knew and loved his illustrations as children remain fiercely loyal to him as adults, making web pages, creating fan sites, and even posting a YouTube video about his art. Though some of his works are no longer in print, there is a brisk trade in second hand copies of books like *A Garth Williams Treasury of Best-Loved Golden Books* (2007)—which is due for a reprint. "His drawings have such magic that anyone who sees them can remember them well after childhood is long gone, and [they leave] them with a hunger to see them again," is a reverent comment from one Williams devotee. But Williams' appeal is not restricted to those of a certain age: in the twenty-first century the tiniest readers, including our own grandchildren, express a palpable enthusiasm for *Mister Dog*, the *Little Fur Family*, or *The Kitten Who Thought He was a Mouse*. Laura Ingalls Wilder enthusiasts form an especially ardent subset of the Garth Williams fan club: they cherish his drawings both as an integral part of the reading experience and as a body of documentary evidence of a life that "really existed."

Scholars and art critics also cite Williams' work for its notable artistic achievement: his black and white drawings are especially appreciated for their energetic use of line and for their classic technique used to capture a dynamic sense of movement. And the commercial world knows the value of Williams' art. His original drawings and sketches, a few still available at auction, have fetched astonishing sums. In one auction held on October 15, 2010, forty-two original drawings for *Charlotte's Web* brought $780, 245. The cover alone sold for $155, 350.[2] At this point, the art is evaluated at even higher prices. Garth Williams' reputation is not limited to the US, either: with editions of his books still appearing regularly across Europe, he is especially beloved to this day in Japan. There his books—and tie-in merchandise—sell briskly.

In short, it is certainly possible to claim—based on an unusually large body of extraordinary art, one that is widely recognized for its precise and telling use of detail sometimes verging on the surreal; its unusually skillful rendering of dynamic and energetic movement; and its ironic whimsy conveying emotion without sentimentality—that Garth Williams was one of the most important illustrators of the twentieth century. Unlike Maurice Sendak, Garth Williams was never really a writer. Also unlike Sendak, he didn't express revolutionary ideas about childhood. Nonetheless, his drawings uniformly capture an original and distinct perspective of the animal world and they provide a unique understanding of the human-animal relation. Taking his cue from the best children's writers, he made visible the secrets of animal life. This dynamic interchange of word and image was at its best in Williams' work with Margaret Wise Brown. Though Brown's best-known book, *Goodnight Moon*, was illustrated by Clement Hurd, she and Garth Williams shared "the closest and happiest kind of collaboration," swapping ideas, criticizing each other's efforts, and provoking each other's best work.[3] The exuberant energy, tender emotion, and domestic harmony of a book like *Wait Till the Moon Is Full* emerge from that collaborative creativity.

But Margaret Wise Brown was only one of the scores of notable individuals who crossed paths with Garth Williams. From the courtly E. B. White to the irascible George Selden, his collaborators included most of the best children's authors of the twentieth century: Laura Ingalls Wilder, Dorothy Kunhardt, Charlotte Zolotow, Margery Sharp,

Randall Jarrell, Russell Hoban, and Jack Prelutsky. Williams' life also intersects with a remarkable series of twentieth-century figures: artists like Rosario Murabito and Mark Rothko, editors like Harold Ross and Ursula Nordstrom, musicians like John Sebastian Junior, of the Lovin' Spoonful, politicians like Winston Churchill, and celebrities like Elizabeth Taylor. Williams' career unfolds in a series of geographic locations, and it encompasses several major twentieth-century events, from bohemian life in London during the Second World War, to the burgeoning art scene of 1940s New York, to the creation of the Little Golden Books in 1950s America, to the first foundations of Aspen as a musical and cultural center, to an artistic community in the suburbs of Guanajuato, Mexico. Thus, to talk about Williams is to evoke major events of the twentieth century, including the two World Wars, the defeat of fascism, the Holocaust, the Civil Rights movement, and the transformation of American youth culture.

This biography explores the full cultural and historical milieu of the major events during Williams' life: what was the New York art scene like in 1942, when Williams first hoped to make his mark? How and why did his European training fail to ensure his success as a sculptor in the postwar years? Conversely, what historical conditions ensured that his talents could be so usefully and lucratively employed in the commercial world of book illustration? What was the status of the publishing world at that time? How did the circumstances of Williams' birth, education, and temperament ensure his becoming one of the most prolific and well-known illustrators of children's books? In a time of rapid suburbanization, Williams' drawings nourished a widespread desire to maintain an intimate, ongoing relation with the animal world. His illustrations often conjure a vanished agrarian lifestyle, tapping into a powerful postwar yearning to connect with a distinctly American past.

Williams' life is also the compelling story of a family man, with all the failures and successes that mark him as indisputably human. He was married four times and fathered six children, the last at age sixty-six. He often did not know how to work out interpersonal differences. He made mistakes, and he could be hard on those closest to him, especially his sons. With his own, sometimes odd, take on the world, he occasionally fell into strange obsessions or enthusiasms that made him a poor manager of his own affairs. Yet he was also forgiving of other people's oddities, generous with his time and energy, and liberal in spirit.

Chapter One

AN UNTYPICAL HUCKLEBERRY FINN (1912-1942)

Illustration from *Charlotte's Web.*

$\mathcal{F}$rom 1960 until almost the time of his death, Garth Williams struggled with the task of writing his autobiography.[4] And for good reason: his was not a life that could be easily summarized. His wide-ranging experiences—including his early promise as a sculptor, his service in London during the Blitz, his four marriages, six children, residences in New York, London, Rome, Aspen, Santa Fe, San Antonio, and Guanajuato Mexico, his innumerable illustrations and other publications, and his long list of notable friendships and acquaintances (and perhaps a few enemies)—defied an orderly narrative. As he aged, his earliest memories tended to become sharper. Various details came and went as he returned, time and time again, to the revised story of his life. In one version of an autobiography published for the Gale Research *Something about the Author Autobiography Series*, while reminiscing about his boyhood, he remembered himself living an idyllic American rural life in New Jersey during the early decades of the twentieth century. He cast himself as Mark Twain's quintessential boy, a youngster who roamed freely in an American wilderness, unfettered by the fussy demands of "sivilization." "I was a typical Huckleberry Finn," he wrote, "roaming barefoot around the farm, watching the farmer milk the cows by hand, or do his other chores."[5]

But Garth Williams never was a quintessential American boy and he never truly knew Huck's freedoms. Instead, he spent his earliest years in New Jersey, followed by a brief time in Canada, until he was taken to England for his schooling. Though he was American by birth, his formative school years shaped him as English and gave him the traces of a British accent he would retain all his life. In fact, the question of his national identity remained unresolved until adulthood. Under the cloud of the Second World War, Williams finally renounced his British citizenship, mistakenly believing that he could later reclaim it.

Still, the image of Huck on the farm is appealing, and it introduces Williams' major accomplishment. Whatever his origins, as an adult he came to create innumerable, deeply memorable images of American life and culture. These images are still cherished by many American readers, beginning with the postwar generation and extending now to their grandchildren. Williams' work includes famous animal characters—Stuart Little, Wilbur and Charlotte, the Sailor Dog, Frances the Badger, Harry Cat and Tucker Mouse—but it also extends to the entire Laura Ingalls Wilder family. Incorporating both creatures and humans, Williams' renditions of classic characters from beloved American children's books populate an American landscape that no longer exists, neither as the unspoiled wilderness of Laura's day, nor as the idyllic farmyard that E. B. White recreated from his memory. There is no small irony in the fact that a man who moved so often and so easily between countries and even continents, only settling toward the end of his life in Mexico, should so irrevocably come to capture aspects of American culture. Yet it may be the case that Williams' complicated status as an inside-outsider allowed him to see and render America so clearly.

Williams' own wanderings and affiliations mirror the experiences of his father, the British-born artist Montgomery John Williams. "Monty" was born August 18, 1884 in London. Trained as an artist, he was a handsome, outgoing, and affable man of considerable ambition. Williams proudly recalled that his father sold a drawing to *Punch Magazine*—then a prestigious British humor publication—when he was only seventeen. As a young man Monty went to America, where he did illustrations for various publications, including sport pages, stories, and miscellaneous humor publications.[6] Later, Monty worked in Paris for *Le Rire*, a French satirical magazine also of considerable stature. Family accounts describe Monty as an active artist who painted landscapes and did oil portraits well into his old age. Yet Williams did not see much of his father during his formative years, since Monty was separated from Williams' mother, Florence Stewart Williams, in 1917, when Williams was only five.

After the First World War, Monty alone returned to Paris, where he met his second wife, Geneviève Merisier, through an artist and mutual friend with whom she was studying design. The couple lived for a time on a barge in the Seine, and then they moved to Majorca, an island off the coast of Spain, where they opened a tea salon. They had their first child, Alain, a half-brother to Garth, in 1933. A half-sister Denise was born 1937 in Seaux and another half-sister, Martine, in Chablis in 1938. When the Second World War began, Monty's second family left France to shelter from the war in Madagascar. They lived there ten years, followed by two years on the island of Mauritius. Monty retired to England for health reasons soon after, while his wife and children returned to Madagascar. The family was reunited in France in 1952.[7]

Through his later childhood, adolescence, and early adulthood, Williams would have known his father mostly from a distance and as a man with a growing second family. Relations appear to have been mostly cordial, though certainly distant, as the two World Wars made communications difficult and contact sporadic. Monty does not seem to have played an active role in major decisions about Williams' upbringing. Nor did he seem to have weighed in on the question of Williams' schooling or education, as such decisions appear to have made solely by Williams' mother.

Williams' autobiography does offer one vivid memory of paternal presence. During the time he lived on the farm, he remembers discovering one day that Monty had left his studio door open. He entered and, upon finding a pile of drawings, added his own "art" to them. But he wasn't punished, he recalls. Instead, his father reportedly said, "I'm afraid he's going to be an artist."[8] This memory establishes the father and son as sharing a vocation, but also introduces the suggestion of a future competition between them.

In 1937, Williams' first wife Gunda (later Gunda Lambton) remembered a trip they took to France so that her father-in-law could meet his son's new bride. Lambton recalled that the second Williams family lived in large, rambling farmhouse near Chablis: "[Monty's] new family, a little boy and a baby girl [Denise], still nursed by her mother were pretty lively." [9] She also records that the relations between the twenty-five-year-old son and his father were "strained": "In a way [Garth] admired Monty's wit, his quality as an entertainer developed with a sense for survival. And Monty admired Garth's achievements within the establishment—his RA [a reference to his having attended the Royal College of Art] and *Prix de Rome*. But he probably saw them as opportunist stepping stones, tedious but necessary; and it was Monty's opportunism that Garth disliked." [10]

Throughout her lifetime, Williams' relationship to his mother was stronger and more consistent, though also, at times, vexed. Williams' mother, Florence Stewart Williams—known as Dé (pronounced "Day")—was born in Australia on May 7, 1877 and grew up among a group of elite Anglican Church officials in Barbados.[11] Her grandfather, William Walrond Jackson (1810-1895) had married Mary Shepherd Pile, a young woman from a prominent Barbados family whose wealth is believed to have come from a sugar plantation, in 1834. In 1860 he was made the Bishop of Antigua. Her parents, Elizabeth Gordon Jackson (1842-1892), and Gateward Coleridge Davis (1833-1882), both born in the West Indies, had been married in Antigua in 1864.[12] One of eleven children, Dé eventually left the Caribbean and went to Paris as a young woman to pursue her dream of studying art.

Florence Stewart "Dé" Williams.

Gunda Lambton, Williams' first wife, greatly respected and loved her mother-in-law, and in her own memoires she reflected frequently on the older woman's accomplishments. She especially admired Dé's politics, which included an early phase as a suffragette. According to Lambton, Dé "had known the Webbs, Bertrand Russell, and was in some way related to Robert Graves and Bloomsbury."[13] Lambton's comments on the time she and Williams accompanied Dé to visit the 1936 World's Exhibition in Paris convey a distinct picture of her

mother-in-law as a worldly, intellectual sophisticate with keen awareness of her surroundings:

> How does one describe goodness? It's what I found in this unpreten-
> tious woman. Dé had no pretensions, but she had a wide circle of
> knowledge. At the World Exhibition, she recognized Henry Miller
> and Anais Nin, who were sitting with young Larry Durrell.

Dé also enthused about the art they saw, which included Picasso's
painting *Guernica* hanging in the pavilion of the Spanish Republic.[14]

Williams' mother had met Monty while studying art in Paris. She
was already in her thirties, while he was younger, still in his mid-twenties.
The couple married in 1910 and honeymooned in France and Spain,
eventually settling on a farm in Caldwell, New Jersey, where the two had
plenty of room to work. Dé gave birth to Garth on April 16, 1912, in
New York City. A daughter, Fiona, followed three years later, in 1915.
These are the happy family years that Williams later tapped in his autobiography, reaching back to remember being taken by their landlord
farmer "on his lap to go harrowing or plowing. Or when we went driving
out in his two-wheel buggy to Peterson or the Passaic River, crunching
along a gravel road or splashing through puddles."[15] In one version of
his autobiography, he recalled his first encounter with an automobile:
"It frightened me—no horse. It was electric I believe, it was silent and the
driver and his wife sat facing the road in front holding a rod—it should
have been a horse, it was the steering rod, no wheel."[16] Before the age
of two, he made his first trip to England with his mother, arriving in
Liverpool from New York on the S. S. *Cedric* on November 15, 1913,
though of course he had no memory of the journey.[17] The family was
still living in Caldwell at the start of World War I in Europe in 1914.
Williams remembered listening to his parents discussing the war, and
he also reminisced he had a plan for escaping a German invasion of the
US, should one occur: "If the Germans came to our house in Caldwell,
I planned to run past the dairy, to the sea. I would look for a boat and
row to England, a few miles out to sea. If the enemy followed, I would

row to the edge of the world, where the water poured over. Fortunately, the enemy didn't arrive." [18]

Garth and Fiona Williams.

In 1917, when Williams was five, his mother left her husband for Canada, taking Garth and Fiona with her. She joined her friends from her suffragette years, Mary Elgood and Jean Ingram, to help them found the school for women known as Ovendon College (now demolished) in Barrie, Ontario, Canada. Young Williams spent the remainder of World War I in Canada. In later years, he recalled many details from this time in his life, including skating on a frozen lake, bobsledding, and sailing. He also recalled quickly learning to swim when he realized he was not wearing the water wings that his mother had fashioned for him out of biscuit tins. In his published autobiography, he recalled airplanes flying over the lake "with boxers [cylinders arranged on either side of the crank shaft] performing on the upper wing." [19]

Shortly after the end of the war, her marriage apparently over, Dé took Garth and Fiona, then seven and five, back to the UK. Fiona tragically died a few years later while attending an English boarding school, possibly of angina that was not treated in a timely fashion, according to Lambton, or perhaps—as Williams recounts—of diphtheria.

Fiona was only twelve, and the impact of her death on her mother was profound, leading Dé (in Lambton's words) "back to the religion that had dominated her childhood until she'd become a rebel."[20] This religious reawakening, with its strict belief in the sanctity of marriage, precluded an actual divorce from her estranged husband. But by now Monty had met Geniviève, whom he was eager to marry. Family lore (repeated by both Williams and Lambton) recounts that Monty once "kidnapped" the teenaged Garth, hoping to force Dé to grant him the divorce he desired. Williams escaped from his father's houseboat on the Seine and made his way back to his mother, who then finally agreed to the divorce.[21]

After the war, in 1922, Dé moved with her son back to Sutton, Surrey, England, where Williams was matriculated at the City of London School, an academy for boys from the British Commonwealth preparing to attend British public schools (that is, private or preparatory schools). Dé, listed as "Mrs. F.S. Williams, Art Mistress, Felpham, Mulgrave Road, Sutton, Surrey" registered her son under the name Garth Montgomery Walrond (Walrond having been a family name). Though the record indicates he started his schooling in September, he appeared in the school magazine for the previous July. He was on track for a university education: he first attended "Old Grammar," and then "Classical First Form," a class designed to prepare boys who had not previously learned Latin to study Classics. Williams progressed rapidly through Classical First Form in 1926 and on to Classical Second Form in 1927. In addition to a prize for Mathematics, he also won prizes for his drawings—two for "Home Drawing" (or drawing done at home), and four more, including one for "Chalk drawing for Cast."[22]

In December 1927, at age fifteen, Williams left the City of London School. He then attended another school in London that has not been traced. In his autobiography he only writes that the school required a fifteen-mile commute by tram or bus. Lambton records that, during this time, Dé was suffering from a form of mental breakdown brought on by Fiona's death, so that Williams was "completely out of touch with his mother" for a while.[23] Dé's mental depression was so severe that she uncharacteristically withdrew from the world, no longer painting or socializing. She also became intensely religious at this point, a shift which might have increased the distance between her and her son.

Dé's withdrawal occurred during a crucial time for her adolescent son, a time when the question of vocation loomed large. Williams appears to have sought—and successfully found—male guidance in the form of an older architect, a man of eighty years with grown daughters, a man who served as his mentor and surrogate father for a while. From the age of eleven—or since they had moved to Surrey—Williams had spent his Saturdays working for the architect, undergoing a training which led him to believe that he himself would follow in the man's footsteps. As Williams remembers, "he taught me how to make architectural drawings, hot-air engines, steam-driven model boats, sailboats, and gliders." He also taught the boy to shoot, a sport at which Williams remembers excelling.[24]

But Williams' skill with a rifle threatened to jeopardize his prized Saturdays, when an official in charge of the Officers Training Corps tried to recruit him for the school shooting team, a commitment which required traveling to different, distant ranges. Williams claims that he then rigged up a fake bullseye, with bullet holes covering his original and accurate shot to evade the responsibilities of the team. As a result, he didn't lose his Saturdays—and happily played a fife in the band instead. As soon as the group had mastered its march, it spent its time playing jazz. Later he learned to play the guitar and the banjo. The portrait that emerges from Williams' adolescence is that of a high-spirited and clever young man with a strong inclination towards amusement and creative expression.

Garth Williams, 1937.

By the time Williams was ready to apply to university at age nineteen in 1931, the Great Depression had begun and his professional aspiration to become an architect no longer seemed viable. When he and Dé visited an architectural firm to explore possible professional opportunities, they learned that fully trained, underemployed architects were reduced to sweeping the floor and making the tea. A seven-year investment in architectural training seemed pointless to both mother and son: "I decided to become an artist, as it required no training."[25] The tone of this comment is perhaps playful, as the path for a professional artist, especially in the UK at that time, did indeed require significant schooling, if not the full seven-year apprenticeship for becoming an architect.

Williams enrolled at Westminster School of Art, then located at 18 Tufton Street, Deans Yard, Westminster. The building has since become Royal Library for the Blind, but in the early twentieth century it was a notable art school with celebrated alumni. Among them was the renowned British cartoonist H. M. Bateman (1887-1970), who described the school's distinctive layout in his 1903 memoire. It was "... arranged on four floors with galleries running round a big square courtyard, the whole being covered over with a big glass roof. Off the galleries were the various rooms which made up the school, the galleries themselves being filled with specimens of architecture which gave the whole place the air of a museum, which of course it was."[26] Dé could only afford to send Garth to the school for one, three-month session. He must have been an exemplary student, however, since he soon won a four-year scholarship to the highly prestigious Royal College of Art, with total remission of fees, round trip "third class railway fare" between school and home once a year, and living expenses of seventy pounds per year. This scholarship placed Williams among an elite group of promising young British artists, and it portended a successful future in the art world. Williams attended the college from 1931-1934, graduating with a diploma in Design.[27] While at the Royal College of Art, he studied "every kind of painting and drawing: etching, lithography, mural painting, [and] theatrical scenery. Life drawing was essential so I joined the Design School."[28]

Why the Design School? The answer lies in a brief history of the Royal College of Art, which by and large, was conservative in its approach to art education. Despite the occasional presence of radical or avant-garde groups who pursued styles now considered influential, the approach at Royal College of Art (RCA) privileged a kind of figurative art with its roots in the nineteenth century. Williams was trained, then, in a school that aimed for a balance between fine arts and decorative painting. He chose not to attend the Painting School, with its mission "to enable the student to 'express himself through disciplined design'." Nor did he choose the School of Sculpture, with its stated mission to study "the Plastic Arts in Ornamental Design, Architecture and the Industrial Arts and Handicrafts based upon the human figure."[29] Both of these schools might have seemed too conservative to Williams, and besides, as he later claimed, he preferred the strong emphasis on life drawing offered by the School of Design.[30] To be sure, the school had fostered sculptors Henry Moore (1921-1924) and Barbara Hepworth (1921-1925), who both studied there under the tutelage of Derwent

Wood. But tensions between progressives and conservatives were high. After graduation, Henry Moore had been hired as a tutor but was soon fired due to questions about the "suitability" of his work. Williams may have found the Design School a more congenial place than other divisions of the RCA.

After he experienced success in portrait drawing, he decided that he wanted to sculpt. He returned to the Westminster School of Art to study in the evenings with the sculptor Eric Schilsky (1898-1974), who was extremely supportive of his young protégé and who acted as another surrogate father-figure. With Schilsky's support, Williams submitted his work to the annual summer exhibition of the Royal Academy of the Arts—a necessary rite of passage for any aspiring British artist. His work was accepted, but he was mistaken for an older, well-known sculptor by the same name.[31] When he graduated in 1934, needing a job, he took a position as an instructor at Luton Technical Institution (now defunct). The original "contract" letter for this job (saved by Williams for his whole lifetime) stipulated that the appointment required him to work four evenings per week from 7:00 to 9:30 pm. During one of those he was to be available for "craft work." The salary was eleven shillings per hour of actual attendance, paid monthly. However, faced with a lengthy commute of two hours each day, Williams soon quit that job. Nonetheless, he left with a letter from the principal of the school, attesting to his status as "a most conscientious and successful teacher of Art."[32]

Schilsky then suggested that Williams prepare work for the 1936 Prix de Rome Competition that would take place in six weeks. This was surely an inspired suggestion, and it speaks to a very high level of confidence in Williams' talent. The British Prix de Rome, as stipulated in its original Royal charter Incorporation of 1912, offered a series of scholarships (available in the categories of painting, sculpture, and architecture and to be held for up to for three years) for artists who would live in purpose-built, live-in studios at what is today called The British School at Rome (Accademia di Archeologicia, Storia, e Belle Arti) on Via Gramsci in Valle Guilia. The promise of a Prix de Rome, with its offer of living and studio space, was extremely enticing to a young artist, as it continues to be today. Williams must have yearned for the opportunity to work, all expenses covered (and this during the Depression), in a city of extraordinary historical and artistic importance. He must have coveted the prestige attached to those who managed to win such a prize. Yet the requirements for submission were extensive, even daunting, as they reflected "the rigid conditions of classical study still firmly established in art schools in Britain at this time." They included:

1. model of nude figure in the round from life, half-size

2. model in bas relief, with two figures at a specified size

3. four drawings from life. Two nude figures, one of drapery, one of hands and feet, also of a specified size

4. some drawings or photographs of original worth

5. "as above but for decorative purposes with Architectural features."

And—"a design for a figure group or relief (as determined by the Faculty of Sculpture) for a given purpose and to a given scale." [33]

With Schilsky's backing, Westminster school generously lent Williams studio space and paid the cost of materials and the Italian casters to cast the sculptures. He worked fast, finishing the toes of one sculpture while the back still was being cast. And he did win the prize. He proudly kept the letter announcing his award, dated 13 January 1936 and signed by the General Secretary of the British School at Rome, for his entire life. Since the scholarship would not begin until October 1st, he spent the summer of 1936 on the continent, taking a canoe trip along the Moselle River in Germany. Accompanying him was Julius Griffith (1912-1997), a Canadian artist of the same age who would later win recognition for his watercolors, landscapes, and linocut prints. It was on that trip that he met his first wife, née Gunda Davidson. By all accounts, Gunda Davidson Williams Lambton, who was born September 9th, 1914, and lived until the 15th of January 2014, was an extraordinary young woman, who would go on to have an uncommon life in Canada.

After her separation and divorce from Williams, she would raise her two daughters alone in Toronto, working long hours at an aircraft plant. Eventually she became a social worker, remarrying and raising a second family beginning in 1949. Much later, at the age of sixty-nine, she received a Bachelor of Arts in English from Ottawa University and then a Master of Arts from Carleton College in 1988. A talented artist and linguist, she published several books under the name Gunda Lambton, including two memoires—*The Frankenstein Room: Growing Up in Germany Between the Wars* (2000), and *Sun in Winter: A Toronto Wartime Journal* (2003). These provide an invaluable perspective on Williams' early adulthood.

Gunda Davidson Williams Lambton.

Lambton's parents were Eduard von Davidson and Maude Lee, née Williams (no relation to Garth). Her father's family, originally from Scotland, had immigrated to Danzig pursuing trade opportunities in the Baltic ports. Her mother was an English teacher and a musician who had left her native Lancashire for Germany as a young woman and had there met her husband.[34] Growing up mostly in southern Germany, Lambton had an extensive set of relatives both on the continent and in the UK, placing her in an especially anxiety-ridden position as the Second World War approached. Her memoire *The Frankenstein Room*, which deals with her life until her departure for Canada in 1940, includes an intimate and vivid account of her first husband as a young man. Seen through her eyes, Williams emerges as a self-assured, talented, yet occasionally immature young artist with an unusual sense of humor. That last quality in particular would continue to characterize Williams for the rest of his life.

Lambton relates the story of how she met Williams in the summer of 1936 while hiking along the Moselle River with her English, Oxford-educated cousin Robert. As the two of them traveled along, they encountered two men, apparently lost, contemplating a sign-laden tree. To Lambton, accustomed as she was to seeing to walkers in sturdy boots and shorts, these hikers "appeared as if they descended from Mars": they wore ordinary shoes, grey flannel trousers, and bulky, striking sweaters intricately knitted in a bold geometric design that she guessed might be African. She judged the two men—Williams and fellow artist Julius Griffith—to be in their early twenties, and noticed especially the shorter, sturdier man with a slightly receding hairline. The two men, with the help of a dictionary, made a belabored attempt at speaking German with Gunda and Robert, only to be answered by the flawless English spoken by the two. Embarrassed and annoyed, the two young men moved quickly ahead. Robert then identified the pattern on their sweaters as belonging to the Cowichan Indians of Vancouver and speculated the hikers were Canadian.[35]

She and Robert next encountered Garth and Julius while on a tour of Burg Eltz Castle, which lies between Koblenz and Trier, Germany. While the guide droned on, the two men amused themselves with a private sign language that seemed to mock the guide's monologue, yet they were stymied by the question of how much to tip at the end. (As Lambton points out, "in the Third Reich tips were a sign of decadence," and unnecessary in any case since the price of admission covered the tip.) The two groups, forced to wait for a train that would not arrive for two hours, traveled on together through a neighboring village. While there,

Williams handled the casual salutation "Hailittler" (a corrupted version of 'Heil Hitler') with a polite and distinct "Great Scot"—which could be mistaken for *Grüss Gott* (God Greet you)—a customary Catholic greeting that evoked confusion from the passers by.[36] The four young people became further acquainted over a meal in a restaurant, where she quickly learned that Williams had been born an American, though Julius was indeed Canadian. She further recorded:

> But—oh glory—both were artists. They carried in their knapsacks sketches they'd made, using nothing more than ink from their fountain pens. They demonstrated how they added tone to these drawings, using their own saliva for wash. The results of this simple method were glorious poignant little sketches of steep-roofed houses, trees, boats, people. [37]

Throughout the meal, Williams and his companion kept up their private sign language, which Lambton feared they were now using to mock Robert's mannerisms or his speech. Nonetheless, impressed by the quality of their art, she took a chance on inviting them for a private tour of her current place of employment, the famous wine cellar in Deinhardt, where the sparkling Moselle wine was produced. She followed the tour with an invitation for a home-cooked meal at her mother's—a detail confirmed in Williams' autobiography with the comment "the free meal was most attractive."[38] Her British-born mother responded especially favorably to the fact that Williams shared her maiden name—and she was suitably impressed by Williams' upcoming residence in Rome as a winner of the Prix de Rome.[39]

Garth and Gunda were engaged by Christmas 1936. Williams records that at the time of their marriage, Gunda spoke five languages—and indeed her job at the wine cellar was that of translator. While Williams began his residency in Rome in September, she stayed behind, working at Deinhardt until she had saved enough money to join Williams. Then, to be closer to him in Rome, and against her parents' objections, Gunda quit her job at Deinhardt and took a position as a governess to a family in Florence, with responsibility for teaching an eight-year-old English and German boy named Paulo, who had a form of hepatitis that made it difficult for him to go to school. To get married in Italy, Gunda, as a German national, needed a German "certificate of fitness." She was still waiting for the certificate in summer of 1937, and when it finally arrived, the couple realized that it would expire before the end of Williams' residence. They married secretly in Florence in late March of 1938 at a registrar's office in "one of the two most famous buildings in Florence, the Signoria"—that is, the Palazzo de la Signoria, now known as the Palazzo Vecchio. The ceremony was anything but sentimental:

> Two young American friends, a couple not connected with the British Academy, or any of our families, were our witnesses. An official, wrapped in the Italien [sic] flag as a gigantic cummerbund, rattled off the marriage vows. We didn't understand a word. He was a little hunchback, which, our friends assured us, was a lucky omen.[40]

The marriage went undetected by the officials at the British Academy who, Williams and Lambton rightly reasoned, were more likely to read British than Italian newspapers: Lambton believed Academy rules at the time stipulated that Williams was not allowed to be married.[41] But Gunda's employers did read her wedding announcement in the small official notices in their local newspaper and she was fired because they assumed she was pregnant. The couple traveled to Capri and Sicily, where, Gunda remembered, "thousands of wild irises spread a carpet around the Greek temple of Segesta." Gunda took another job with a family, but when the wife of the new family met the mother from the previous family in Florence, she was fired again.[42] When Williams' residency was over in 1938, he and Gunda returned with a plan to live with Dé in Sutton, Surrey, a town approximately ten miles southeast of London.

As an aspiring artist with a prestigious residency in Rome behind him, Williams must have believed that his future as an artist was promising. Yet his return to London in 1938 came at a most inauspicious time. Years later, Williams would remember how he had tried his hand at a beautiful poster that he took to the Shell Oil Company, hoping to tap the commercial potential of his art. But he remembers being told, "Alas, we don't have any gasoline for sale; it now belongs to the government and it is called Pool Petrol."[43] Eventually he did manage to find well-paid work on a newly proposed women's magazine for Pearson Publications, only to lose that opportunity once Hitler had attacked Poland and it became clear that Britain would soon enter the war as well. (The original job letter found among Williams' archive stipulated that he would have been paid ten pounds a week.) The newlywed couple soon discovered that Gunda possessed better prospects in London, as her talents could be put to use easily. She quickly found a well-paying job typing and translating German correspondence for the Shell Mex House, which still stands near the Strand. Williams remembered that "she spent less than an hour per day on the phone and read one or two novels and knitted a sweater every day at work. Her pay was very good and mine was next to nothing."[44] In her version of events, Lambton also remembered that the work "was not very demanding." She also recalled the tedium of her one hour commute back to Sutton, especially after she found herself pregnant.[45]

The couple left Dé's house and went to London, moving first to a single room near the Gloucester Road Tube station, where Gunda struggled to make herself nutritious meals on a gas-ring. Soon, however, a better living opportunity presented itself. Several of Williams' old friends, including Julius Griffith and the sculptor Ralph Roberts, as well as a new friend, an archeologist from Rome, decided to pool their resources and rent a house in South Kensington. There, a number of large properties had recently become available for cheap rent as a result of what Lambton called the "Czech crisis" (or the Nazi invasion of Czechoslovakia in March 1939), which had sent their occupants fleeing London for the safety of the countryside.[46] The group of artists took a lease on a house at 23 Brechin Place, still standing today in a quiet residential area not far from Gloucester Road, where they established a co-operative living arrangement.

While Williams acted as organizer, Griffith was able to provide the money to take the house. Later Williams reminisced:

> Auctions in Glocester (sic) Road. My first experience. As I arrived a perfect Chippendale cabinet for china went for £8.00. I bid on everything. After lunch we all came to bid. I borrowed the V & A hand cart to move my purchases into my new home. Curtain were raised, our neighbors peeked. We were furnished. This was one day before Mussolini moved into Yugoslavia.[47]

The artists agreed to use the downstairs space as living rooms and studios, with rooms upstairs and in the basement serving as bedrooms. The basement kitchen became a communal dining room. Additional income came from three rooms rented out to others, including an anthropologist whom Williams had met in Rome, and an Austrian singer. The group shared household expenses—one pound per week went into the kitty for groceries, soap, and other necessities—and they divided up the household chores. Williams cooked. (Lambton remembers him as being very good.) Lambton helped her husband and did some of the cleaning. Foremost on her mind, however, was the approaching birth of her child, which required that she save whatever money she could to purchase what the baby would need—furniture, diapers, and a little rubber bath that could double as a traveling crib.[48]

During 1939 and 1940, the artists took resourceful measures to sell their art, using Brechin Place itself as their exhibition space. Lambton remembers seeing the clay of Williams' unfinished works, covered with cloths daily, "shrouded... mysterious, like ghosts" so it is clear that he continued to make art during the war years.[49] The co-op invited well-heeled friends and relatives, including a cousin of Dé's who had become a Member of Parliament, to see their work. Lambton's memoir describes a lively, exciting time, as the artists supplemented their income with guitar lessons and filled their evenings with jazz and flamenco. The house was visited and photographed by reporters from the *Picture Post* (a British version of *Life* magazine). The reporter was especially interested, she recalls, in the "Bloomsbury people" who had attended one of the house parties, and the musical instruments and sculptures on the premises.[50] Sadly, the archive holds no record of the reporter's visit. Yet the war did impinge on their bohemian lifestyle. Lambton later recalled how "crouching in a damp air raid shelter, waiting for the all clear" was worse than any deprivation she later suffered after she had made the difficult crossing to Canada. She further recalled dragging a heavy stirrup pump (a hand-operated, reciprocating pump) from the bathroom to the attic to help the neighbors put out a fire on their roofs.[51]

When Gunda went into labor one morning in early June, Williams was skeptical, believing that the child was not due for three weeks. It took the frustrated wife half an hour to convince her sleepy husband otherwise. Williams' first daughter was born at 11 o'clock on a Sunday morning, June 4, 1939. She was named Fiona, after the sister whom Williams had lost as a child. The baby's mother remembers that, being premature, Fiona was a "little red crimpled thing," who did not even open her eyes for photographs.[52] Lambton's memoir from the summer of 1939 is understandably replete with her perspective as a young mother living during an especially trying time: the summer was very hot, and she struggled with illness and the demands of nursing a newborn. Momentous changes were occurring in the city around her, as she soon discovered when she tried to take her mother to visit the roof of the Shell Mex building, only to discover that anti-aircraft equipment had been installed there. When Britain declared war on Germany in September, Gunda and the baby were evacuated for the first time to Wales. They would be evacuated three times before Fiona turned one. Eventually, they would be sent to Canada for safety.[53]

Williams' autobiography from the same time omits any memory of the birth of their first child or the struggle to raise a baby in wartime conditions, though he would eventually play a significant role in Fiona's childhood and upbringing, even after the parents divorced. Perhaps it is merely typical of the age that his memory of the time would focus on a more masculine perspective, including his concerns about being an artist during a time of war and his subsequent wartime role as a non-combatant participant. About the first topic, he wrote, "I had stopped reading newspapers, as it seemed that the end of the world was about to happen every day—not the best climate in which to paint a portrait or poster, or sculpt a portrait, or engage in any other peaceful occupation." On the second subject, he recalls that one Sunday morning in September 1939, he "pushed the drawings off his desk, walked out, and joined the British Red Cross Civilian Defense and St. John's Ambulance Organization, a non-military civilian defense group."[54]

Like other male members of the household, Williams became a member of the Air Raid Precautions, or ARP—an organization charged with protecting civilians from the danger of air-raids, as well as responding to the devastation afterwards.

Lambton testifies that her husband, who was paid three pounds a week for his labor, worked hard on the ARP, and she recalls taking up the tasks normally belonging to her housemates when they were too busy working on the mornings after an air raid. Williams himself remembers being in charge of the cars and drivers at the Chelsea Polytechnic, with the

Garth Williams (left) and Ralph Roberts, ARP Stretcher Bearers outside the Royal Academy with their exhibits These models they have sculptured in their spare time after ARP duties.

specific task of getting drivers to memorize the street names, since these were soon to vanish in the hopes of confusing the Germans, should England be invaded. Later, in his published autobiography, when he arrived at the description of what lay in store once the ARP was in action, he was terse: "I think about two hundred civilians had been killed or wounded in Chelsea during 36 hours. We were busy. I drove the first squad out to the bomb incident, as I had to know what reality was like, I found out."[55] Other documents that Williams kept in his files give a fuller sense of how profoundly he had felt the war years.

For instance, for his whole life he kept a typewritten account of the information for ARP drivers for a single day: September 18th, 1940. Three categories describe the perilous state of the streets of South Kensington: "Blocked," "Debris," or "Dangerous Structures," and "Unexploded Bombs," the third being the largest. In a handwritten, undated document (one that he appears to have written years later), he recalls encountering a young woman, in labor, lying in a dug-out hole in a garden, with a corrugated tin roof:

> She was lying in eight inches of water. It had rained hard for hours, and at least eight other people had been crowded into that home-air-raid shelter. I ordered everyone out except her father and mother. Then God took over. The baby appeared and we raised the mother above water onto a stretcher. We tied the cord and the baby was ready, cut the cord, wrapped the baby and attended to mother and wrapped her in blankets.[56]

In this instance, he was much luckier than Raymond Peat, of Hull, who remembered being handed a dead baby his very first night on patrol.[57] Yet there must have been a great deal more, for Williams immediately followed this memory of life preserved with this bleak assessment: "However one's whole life is destroyed. Pieces of people, burnt people, boiled people, crushed people. People with long slivers of glass in them, invisible in the out flowing blood. We looked for missing limbs, heads..."[58]

Williams' hand-written memoir also reveals the extent to which he was continuously terrified that the worst might happen: "Every time the air-raid warning sounded my stomach turned over and I said 'if it's me let it be just my legs blown away, or all of me—not my eyes, not both my arms or hands.'" And then the worst did occur:

> One night, after about fifteen months of the war, I was walking in a pleasant square in Chelsea while on duty in the Red Cross when a bomb landed by my side. There was no noise, just a blast of air and my eyes were squashed as though in someone's fingers. Next I found myself running about a quarter of a mile from where the bomb had landed. . .The following morning I couldn't sit up in bed. I felt something had injured me, perhaps a piece of the bomb. I had to pull myself up out of bed by the bedpost. Once standing, I felt broken in half.[59]

When he went to seek medical help, the doctor could not find evidence of any wound. In later years Williams would prepare a "Dedication" for his autobiography in which he thanked (among others) the "Guardian Angel" who "shielded me when a bomb blew up at my side." At the time, the trauma led to his resignation from the ARP, followed by several weeks of rest.

Shortly afterwards, in March of 1940, Williams applied to become part of the American Field Service, only to be gently reminded that a) he appeared to be of British citizenship, and therefore ineligible and that b) the all-volunteer organization would be unable to offer him any salary. Still, in those days before America entered the war, he went to volunteer at the American headquarters and asked for an American commission. When an American general told him to go to Washington, he scorned the very suggestion:

> That seemed ridiculous—go to Washington to get a commission and return to England. I had officially been through thirty-six thousand air raids (actually only about two thousand over my head) and I knew much more about the war than the Americans, who came to

England for a week and then returned as "experts." What was worse, the Americans, being at peace, could not help me cross the Atlantic.[60]

The last comment suggests that Williams saw enlisting as a commissioned US officer as a means to escape war-torn London. His tone suggests as well an understandable resentment of the U.S. military members who wore their American privilege with ease.

At this point, it becomes somewhat more difficult to discern what happened. But once again, Williams left a clear paper trail. In the published autobiography, Williams recalls that, in an effort to get his American commission, he met with Winston Churchill.

"We talked about painting (he was also a painter)," writes Williams, "and then he said, 'I am going to give you a letter of introduction to Eleanor and Franklin D. Roosevelt.' He did, and I felt very pleased."[61] At first blush the memory seems implausible, and indeed no official record of the meeting exists.[62] Yet Williams' cousin, Roger de Vere, had been a secretary to Churchill, and so he might have arranged an informal meeting between the two men. In any case, a few years later in 1942, Williams apparently did take a letter of introduction from Churchill to Mrs. Roosevelt's residence in Greenwich Village in 1942, as can be proven by a still-existing response, written on White House stationary, and signed by Mrs. Roosevelt's secretary. Though she had not been there to personally receive him, Mrs. Roosevelt in her letter thanks Williams for his offer of help in the Office of Civil Defense, but regrets that she lacks the necessary authority to assist him. This letter came to Williams once he had moved to New York. There, as we will see, Williams was desperate to make the kind of contacts leading to the appropriate employment of his talents.

In the meantime, the story of Williams' eventual relocation to North America demands to be told against another unfolding story—namely the growing tension between him and his first wife and, even more dramatically, the first appearance of a Jewish refugee who would eventually become Williams' second wife. Dorothea Dessauer, born October 28, 1924 in Vienna, was a young Jewish girl sent by her family to London to escape the persecution in Europe. An Orthodox family had agreed to take her in. They had expected to accommodate "a wispy fourteen year old." But Dorothea was a statuesque fifteen-year old who resembled a film star—or perhaps a beautiful Italian woman named Giannina who had served as Williams' model when he was in Rome.[63]

The glamorous young woman arrived in London with trunks full of beautiful clothes. As "the daughter of a wealthy and enlightened family who'd given her every freedom to travel, who went skiing in winter and to summer resorts in season," Dorothea chafed under the rules and restrictions that her Orthodox foster family placed upon her, so she went to live with a family of fur-traders named

Dorothea Dessauer.

Weigalls.[64] Eventually she made her way to Brechin Place, where, according to Gunda, she offered her assistance with the baby or other household chores. Lambton records:

> Fiona was a small baby then, and we were glad to find someone who could help with the chores at the co-op household, since most of its members were now on the air raid patrol. So we took over the sponsorship for this girl. She came to live with us some months before I left. During the Blitz we sent her back to our friends in the country. But she was bored there, and shortly after my departure, she returned

to our house. She fell in love with my husband. The way he tells the story, she seduced him.[65]

In his autobiography, Williams recalls that Gunda quipped that Dorothea would make him a perfect wife. "'Then don't bring her into the house,' I had replied. But she did and she was correct. Dorothea would have been a possible wife *if* I were a bachelor. At the time, however, I was still married to Gunda and had no intention of getting a divorce."[66]

Lambton's comment on what would soon become her husband's affair suggests a growing rift in her marriage. It could not have been easy for her to observe her husband's continuing freedoms, his ability to socialize and work, while she was weighed down with the responsibilities of motherhood. Her own artistic aspirations would have to wait. Williams' expectations that she tend to his needs must have seemed unfair, even burdensome, in a marriage where she had expected to be an equal partner, not a traditionally submissive wife. Williams' comment suggests that indeed Dorothea had caught his eye and further intimates his attraction for her.

Williams' autobiography includes one further memory of Dorothea as a young woman. As recorded, the incident suggests her troubled state of mind, and it foreshadows a psychological instability that would shadow her all her life:

> Dorothea went out during an air raid to walk in the snow. I was annoyed (and said so) that several doctors who were sitting with us all had watched her leave... I stopped playing flamenco guitar with two friends and followed her. She came back after half an hour, and I met her and pointed out that she was walking in the snow in open sandals with no socks or stockings. I took her back home, and, with my two guitar-playing friends from the Red Cross, put her to bed, gave her a hot drink, and rubbed her feet and legs with snow, which was the frostbite cure at that time.[67]

What Williams does not mention is that, under the "Internment of Aliens Policy (KV 4/361-368)," beginning in 1939, Dorothea had to appear as an Austrian national in front of the Local Enemy Alien Tribunal. UK Government records indicate that she was processed under one of three possible categories: "B: loyalty suspect but able to remain at liberty, subject to various restrictions." Her brother, Franz Dessauer, who had come to the UK before her—and who was later to adopt the name Davenport—was not so lucky and was interned under category A: "risks posing potential security threat, to be interned at once." (A third category, C, was granted to those who "posed no risk.")[68] Franz was among a large population of men, women, and children, mostly of German and Italian nationality, who were interned for the duration of the war. By one count, as many as 40,000 individuals were held in detention camps, the largest of which was on the Isle of Man.[69] While his place of internment is not clear, records indicate that Franz was released in September of 1940.[70] Franz was later to serve as an interpreter for the Allied Forces, and he was among those who liberated Buchenwald, in the postwar period, not long after his own father, Dr. Heinrich Dessauer (Garth's father-in-law), perished in Auschwitz in 1944.[71]

As the bombing of London intensified, Garth and Gunda decided that she would take Fiona and go to Canada, where she could stay in Barrie, Ontario, at the school which Dé had taught and where Williams had lived for a while as a boy. This decision was surely motivated first and foremost by concern for Gunda and Fiona's safety, but the couple must have known that it would leave Williams at home in London with Dorothea. Indeed, it is difficult to know exactly when Williams' affair with Dorothea began, as neither he nor Gunda records this clearly. Nonetheless, writing in retrospect in 1942, Gunda was to mention that Dé found shelter in Ovendon from a wrecked marriage—"and now mine is going the same way"—so shortly after her arrival in Canada she recognized that circumstances were against her marriage continuing.[72]

In 1940, as she prepared to leave England, Gunda was pregnant for a second time: a daughter, Bettina (named after the wife of Eric Schilsky, Williams' mentor), was to be born March 21, 1941 in Barrie, after she and Fiona had safely crossed the Atlantic. If immigration officials had known that she was pregnant, Gunda would not have been allowed to travel. She remembered being scolded on board by an angry nurse, who told her that, had her condition been known, "Didn't I know that they would never have allowed me on board."[73] Gunda and Fiona arrived in Canada in November 1940 on what she remembered as "the last government sponsored boat carrying evacuees out of Britain."[74] Once in Canada, she did not have to clear customs, but all passengers were greeted with surprise: those awaiting the boat had been told that it had been torpedoed. In fact, one of their convoy had been taken down. Further, the boat crossing the Atlantic just before them, the "City of Benares," a steam passenger ship put into service for the evacuation of war refugees that was also carrying ninety child evacuees bound for Canada, had also been sunk, resulting in the death of seventy-seven children and the cancelation of an official British plan to relocate British children abroad.

Given the extraordinarily dangerous circumstances, Williams' level of concern for the safety of his family was very high during their transit. He later recalled his relief as "indescribable" when he received a call from Ovendon telling him of their safe arrival.[75] At some point, Williams learned that, having left school at age eleven in Austria, Dorothea had not completed her education. Williams then paid for her to take a secretarial course near Kensington, where she worked hard to improve her English and finished the two-year course in only eight months. With her training, she was able to find well-paid work in a private bank in the stock exchange.[76] The investment in Dorothea's schooling paid off for the couple, since Williams did not have any employment at this time. Garth and Dorothea would eventually marry in New York in 1945. However, before Williams could start over again, he would need to face the complication of his marriage to Gunda. Williams continued to take very seriously the idea that he should provide financial support for his wife and two small girls. When compounded with his distressed physical state and his weariness from living under nightly bombardment, his ongoing anxiety about his inability to make money was too much. He decided to return to the country of his birth and to try his luck there.

Chapter Two

A MOUSE IN NEW YORK (1941-1945)

Illustration from *Stuart Little*.

On November 21, 1941, Garth Williams returned to New York. In the later years, he would often tell the story of the trip, for it marked a major transition in his life. When he officially "made declaration of alienage" from Britain on July 1, 1941, he not only severed his ties with England, he was also consciously choosing to embrace his

American heritage and all the promise it seemed to offer. Although he could not have foreseen his future, the next few years would mark a fortuitous turn of events—his successful attempt to obtain a commission for the illustrations of *Stuart Little*; his highly skillful and much lauded execution of that commission; and the eventual resolution of his relationship with Gunda, which made it possible for him to move forward with Dorothea. By the end of the 1940s he would be well on his way to becoming a major American illustrator, even if illustrator was not quite the career he had envisioned for himself, a graduate of the Royal Academy and the winner of a Prix de Rome.

Once again, Williams' autobiographical account can be read against Gunda Lambton's memoirs. As she makes clear, though the marriage was not officially over, neither she nor Williams was especially inclined to make it work. Gunda, now aware that Williams and Dorothea had started their affair, had begun to make a new life for herself and the girls in Canada. Looking back over her years with Williams, she reflected upon the difficulties that her marriage to Williams, with his demanding personality, had presented. Later she came to understand that a continual sense that he was the more accomplished artist had "overwhelmed" her.[77] In addition, she was beginning to enjoy her independence among a new circle of friends in Toronto. In her memoir, she compared herself to Williams' mother, Dé, taking some comfort in her mother-in-law's example of striking out for Canada to live independently of her husband, Monty. Yet economic circumstances were extremely difficult in wartime Canada. As Gunda struggled to find employment providing sufficient resources for rent, childcare, and other necessities, it was clear that she and the girls would need economic support from Williams.

This necessity must have weighed heavily on Williams' mind as he traveled back to North America. Once in New York, Williams aspired to test his ambitions and abilities as an artist, and he might have hoped that the memory of his father, Montgomery, would quicken interest in and open doors to his own work, allowing him to send money to Gunda. New York also presented another advantage over Canada, which—already in 1941—was a belligerent in the war. After the Canadian National Resources Mobilization Act of 1940, every man in Canada had to register for the draft, and men eligible for military service were barred from holding jobs not considered essential to the war effort—conditions too much like those in London.[78]Perhaps also public pressure to do one's patriotic duty would have made Canada a difficult place for Williams to settle, even if it had been his choice to do so. As Gunda remembers, when she, Fiona, and Bettina first arrived as refugees from the blitz, they were warmly welcomed in the small Canadian town that served as their haven, but once Williams had passed through Canada and gone to New York, the welcome chilled: "The fact that he had renounced British for American citizenship did not go down well among Barrie's patriotic citizens, who had until then supported us in every way."[79] Later Gunda wrote about a couple who refused to take and pay for a bust done by Williams and that she had carried to Canada with her—perhaps because it had been damaged—or "most probably because Williams didn't join the army and gave up his British citizenship."[80] Yet having escaped the violence and carnage of the Blitz in London, Williams was most likely reluctant to return to a war environment: the still-neutral United States, and New York in particular, offered a better promise of refuge.

Reminiscing in 1989, Williams recounted his passage to the United States in October of 1941 in a convoy of fifty ships. He traveled in the *Ville de Tamatave* that had been a French refrigeration ship, but was repurposed to serve as a Commodore's ship for the British Navy. He shared a cabin with two American flyers and sat with the Captain for meals. He also recalled stormy weather during the passage, claiming that, since he was never seasick, he volunteered to sit in the crow's nest.[81] The ship's drinking water, stored in an open vat on deck, was tainted with oil, and the tea he tried to make with a combination of the oily water plus seawater proved impossible to drink. Upon his arrival in New York, Williams was surprised that the American city did not yet display any of the deprivations characteristic of war-torn London: "all lights were on at night. There were no searchlights. Food was stacked in the shops."[82] From New York Williams traveled to Canada to see Gunda and his daughters, remembering that he looked "as if I had crawled out of a concentration camp"—an anachronistic simile, given that the full details of the camps' survivors would not be widely known until after the war. The reunion with his daughters, at least, was joyous, and for a few days he did little but sleep and ski, but then news of the attack on Pearl Harbor made its way to him as he lodged in a back-woods log cabin that had been lent to him by a friend, and he hurried back to New York.

There, eager to do whatever he could do not only to survive but also to send money to his daughters, he tried to obtain employment through a number of different avenues. A curriculum vitae discovered among Williams' archive lists his age as thirty—in other words, it records the state of his intentions in early 1942. Listing his draft status as 3A (that is, not eligible for the draft as a result of having dependents), Williams included his education, travel experiences, and languages—including some lessons in Russian. He detailed his past employment in an architectural firm, as an art editor, illustrator, sculptor, and teacher. He mentioned as well that he had designed murals for the Duke of Norfolk's ballroom. Indicating photography as his "hobby" at this point, he clearly stipulated his ambition to be of assistance now that the Americans had entered the war:

> Suggest that my knowledge of the British and Britain might be of use. Have traveled extensively in England. Possibly the connections I have might be of some advantage.
>
> Had two years in school of O.T.C., had basic training only, played in band.[83]

As mentioned in the previous chapter, though he was unable to personally deliver his letter of introduction from Churchill to Mrs. Roosevelt, he did get it into her hands. And he eventually received a response from her office, in which he was urged to file an application for a Civil Service appointment with the office in New York. He appears to have had in mind that he could help with the project of locating buildings in Manhattan that would be suitable as air raid shelters.[84] But this plan too failed to come to fruition. Meanwhile, friends of his maintained that there was an FBI file on him, and that the US government's plan was not to permit him to go back to Europe, but to send him to the Pacific. Years later Williams would unsuccessfully attempt to track down that file. In 2013, the US Department of Justice files reveal only that, for unstated reasons, records which may have been "responsive" to a request for information were destroyed February 1, 1991—in other words, no proof that the FBI had a file on Williams exists either way.[85] Nonetheless, there is a great deal of credibility to the idea that Williams would have been of interest to the FBI in 1942, both because he had renounced his British citizenship and because he was, at that time, leading what appeared to be a marginal, "artistic" lifestyle.

By August of 1942, Williams' "hobby" of photography had become a major source of livelihood. In the meantime, he pursued yet another war-related means of making a living: working as a camoufleur. He completed a course in "Civilian Camouflage" (as approved by the Office of Civilian Defense) at the Pratt Institute in August of 1942 and promptly offered his service to the War Department Engineer Office, believing that he could put his skills to work painting ships to camouflage them.[86] However, nothing seems to have come of this. Also, sometime during 1942 or early 1943, he worked as lens grinder in a war plant called Hauer and Company on 4th Avenue. This job entitled him to his first Social Security card.[87]

Compounding Williams' difficulties locating lucrative work was a persistent social unease concerning U.S.-British relations. A few months before his arrival in 1941, before the bombing of Pearl Harbor and American entry into the war, there had been mass rallies across the nation of the "America First Committee." "Britain Jeered By Crowd" ran the subhead in a *New York Times* report of an anti-war rally in Chicago.[88] In New York on April 23, Charles Lindbergh, one of the best-known and most popular Americans alive, had spoken to a mass rally and warned against joining Britain in "the fiasco of this war":

I do not blame England for this hope, or for asking for our assistance. But we now know that she declared a war under circumstances that led to the defeat of every nation that sided with her from Poland to Greece. We know that in the desperation of war England promised to all these nations armed assistance that she could not send. We know that she misinformed them, as she has misinformed us, concerning her state of preparation, her military strength, and the progress of the war.[89]

At Lindbergh's rallies it was common to hear chants of "Down with the British!"—which must have been disconcerting for a British refugee from the London blitz.

The art scene was, however, less fractious, and Williams slowly began to make progress toward establishing himself there. When he arrived in 1941, American scene painting still dominated: this naturalist style was best exemplified by the work of Grant Wood, but it also took the form of Regionalism and Social Realism, both of which had been promoted and produced under the New Deal of the 1930s. Abstract Expressionism, which would become ascendant during the 1950s, was still on the horizon; though the American Abstract Artists Group had been founded in 1936, Jackson Pollock's first one-man show would not appear at Peggy Guggenheim's gallery until 1943. In the meantime, with the entry of the US into the Second World War, attention shifted to art that expressed the national mood and the experience of the time. Eventually in 1951 the legendary curator Leo Castelli, having left war-torn Europe for the US, would mount a show entitled "The 9th Street Art Exhibition" that would announce the arrival of the New York School, including painters such as Robert Motherwell, Robert Rauschenberg, and Jackson Pollock.

Williams' sights were fixed on the American British Art Center (ABAC), where he was at home among other British artists with sensibilities similar to his own. Offering a large exhibition space at 44 West 56th Street, the ABAC was originally founded in London in 1939 with the mission to operate a gallery featuring works by British and American artists. Paintings were to be sold by the gallery, with net proceeds going to "charitable purposes connected with British art." Profits would be used to purchase art works produced by British artists, and the works would then be donated to American museums and galleries. In addition, proceeds could be used to "grant relief to British artists and their families who have suffered hardship throughout the war." For example, an exhibition in 1941 titled "England's Honorable Scars" featured unpublished pictures of blitzed London; the proceeds from an exhibition of paintings by William Yarrow benefited British prisoners of war. The inaugural show in New York, held in January and February of 1941, featured paintings by a number of notable contemporary English painters, including Stanley Spencer, Augustus John, Roger Fry, E. B. Lintott, and Christopher Wood, as well as work by the South African painter Terrence McCaw. Walter Sickert, of the Camden Town group, a pioneer of British avant-garde art, appeared in the show, as did Duncan Grant, Adrian Beach (associated with the Bembridge School on the Isle of Wight), and the Anglo-Irish painter Meraud Guevara.[90] Exhibiting his work at the ABAC among such illustrious and important British artists as these was surely an important goal for Williams as he pursued his artistic aspirations.

In the spring of 1942 he accomplished this goal. First, in February, Williams participated in a show of poster sketches, prepared especially for the ABAC to aid the National Defense Program. An art critic for the *New York Times* offered this ambivalent opinion about the show: "often the ideas submitted are fresh and potentially effective. Sometimes these are tellingly presented, also. But the poster field is a very special one and involves difficulties and problems unlike those encountered elsewhere."[91] But Williams' next appearance at the ABAC was more notable. In an "Exhibition of Paintings by Members of the American British Art Center and Sculpture by Jacob Epstein, held from March 17th to April 4," he presented four of his ink-wash drawings—"East Anglia," "Moyers," "Place de la Concorde," and "Greek Woman of Mistra." These works were displayed alongside Augustus John's noteworthy portrait of James Joyce, a Maine landscape by the modernist painter Carl Sprinchorn, paintings by the colorist Milton Avery, several works by the Ukrainian born Simkha Simkhovitch and two early representational works by Mark Rothko, whose style had not yet emerged into his signature abstract expressionism.[92] In its enthusiastic review of this show of more than eighty works, the *New York Times* noted, "This is a lively and highly diverse show."[93]

By the time of the exhibition, Williams was living at the edge of Greenwich Village. He had taken an apartment at 145 West 14th Street in March 1942, establishing himself in a place already rich in arts and performance.[94] The Provincetown Players had been there since 1924; the Whitney Museum of American Art, before it moved uptown in 1954, was on West 8th Street: and the Abstract Expressionist painter and teacher Hans Hofmann had moved his art school to West 8th in 1938. Williams' daughter Fiona, who later lived with him during the summer of 1945 while her mother was attending social work school in Toronto, remembers their bohemian life-style well: there was a convent next door, and from the fire escape of their building she could watch the nuns hanging out their laundry.[95] The Italian artist and sculptor Rosario (Saro) Murabito (1907-72) lived nearby—and sometimes served as a babysitter when Williams was working or had casting to do. Williams also opened a studio of his own on West 16th Street. Yet he was struggling economically.

In November of that year, Gunda weighed Williams' ongoing problems: "Garth is having a hard time in New York right now, and even in England he had not been able to find work. He is highly qualified, an RA graduate who earned the Prix de Rome. He's doing commercial photographs at present." Even while Williams and other people she knew flocked there, Gunda herself was skeptical of the viability of living in New York: "Frank [Hines, a friend of hers] wants to live there. What do Toronto people see in New York that so captures their imagination? The dynamic twenties of Edmund Wilson? Isn't its vitality due, at least in part, to the influx of artists and writers from Vienna, Berlin, and now Paris? According to Frank, the place is so fully alive, he wants to be part of that scene."[96]

By April of 1943 Gunda told a friend that Williams was beginning to make headway: "Now in New York he's finally managed to get some small commissions for the *New Yorker*. His father was illustrator for the paper preceding that magazine. So perhaps he can help a little."[97] Williams was also able to get similar commissions from the *New York Times*—amusing little drawings used as fillers for blank spaces in the paper. Since the drawings were not always signed, it remains a difficult task to trace Williams' productivity during this period. Similarly, little evidence of Williams' work for the *New Yorker* exists, though others— most notably the humorist James Thurber, who worked at the *New Yorker*—have provided vivid accounts of what Williams might have encountered in the editorial offices and beyond.

Thurber describes the intimidating atmosphere that Williams would have encountered as he tried to make his mark at the prestigious publication: "In the center of a long table in the art meeting room a drawing board was set up to display the week's contributions from scores of artists, both sacred cows and unknowns. It wasn't easy, and still isn't, for a new artist to break into the *New Yorker*."[98] In an interview with Leonard Marcus in 1990, Williams recalled that, although he did manage to sell some drawings to the magazine, he was told that his cartooning style was "too wild," "too finished" and "too European" for the magazine.[99] Still, in his autobiography he recalled with pride what was probably a modest contribution. He wrote that when he asked the *New Yorker* if he could call himself one of their artists, "they showed me the conference room with the lists of artists on the wall and my name was on it."[100]

All through this period, Williams struggled to make enough money to support himself, let alone to send money to Gunda and his daughters. But an earlier friendship paid off, as it turned out that John Sebastian, a classical harmonica player whom Williams had met during his earlier time in Rome, was also in New York trying to make his career. Eventually Sebastian would achieve the ultimate New York success by playing at Carnegie Hall. During Williams' early days in New York, Sebastian's friendship was crucial to him, especially since Sebastian could afford to be generous with him: "he lent me money every week until I found a job and settled down as a peaceful citizen in New York," Williams recalled.[101] When Sebastian's son was born in 1944, he named him John, Jr. and asked Williams to be his godfather. Half a century later John Sebastian, Jr.—whom Williams had photographed as a baby and who had in the meantime founded the '60s rock band, *The Lovin' Spoonful*—wrote a children's book, *J.B.'s Harmonica*, about a musical bear who played at Bearnegie Hall and taught his son to play as well. Williams did the illustrations, representing his old friend, John Senior, in fur. Strong connections between the two families persisted, as Williams' daughter Bettina remembers that she and her sister Fiona owned tiny harmonicas with the name "John Sebastian" engraved on them.[102]

Yet somehow, by December of 1942, Williams was doing well enough to send Christmas presents to his daughters. Gunda remembers receiving two dresses, which were much appreciated and worn proudly on special occasions. However, the issue of child support would continue to plague him. In her diary for nearly one year later, December 11, 1943, Gunda noted receiving a "disagreeable letter" from Williams, who had been contacted by the Canadian Children's Aid Society concerning the conditions at the house where she and the girls were then living: "They also wrote to Garth, the children's father, to remind him of his responsibility. Social workers do this automatically." Yet Williams blamed Gunda for the circumstances, reminding his wife that she and the girls would have been well taken care of had Gunda remained as the "war guests" of family friends in Barrie, Ontario. Gunda defended herself by writing that she had been compelled to leave Barrie for Toronto—most likely because she felt her welcome had been worn out and because she was eager to strike out on her own.[103]

A few weeks later Williams wrote to Gunda with devastating news: his mother Dé had been killed in London while riding her bicycle home from her Red Cross work. With the streetlights kept purposefully dim as a protection against the night bombings, a driver had been unable to see her. Gunda, who admired her mother-in-law as an artist and a free spirit, felt her loss very deeply, and she recorded her feelings in her diary. For her, Dé had been a role model, and there were similarities in the lives of the two women. Like Gunda, Dé had been an artist who married another artist and emigrated to North America; also like Gunda, Dé had left her husband and started again in Canada. Later, when Dé returned to Sutton, then a suburb of London, she had continued her independent life. When the war began, like so many other Londoners, she had devoted herself to helping however she could. One month before Christmas she had mailed a handmade doll to Canada as a gift for Fiona. As Fiona sat cradling the doll, Gunda recalled Dé's house in England, with its untidy piles of newspapers and magazines, and everything covered with hair from Dé's shaggy little dog. "Oh, for such a helpful grandmother, here and now," Gunda lamented.[104] Williams' own immediate response to his mother's tragic death is not known. However, upon his departure for North America, he had recorded his mother's prescient fear that they would never see each other again.[105] More evidence of Dé's impact on her son lies in the fact that, in Gunda, he had chosen a mate possessing many of his mother's strengths and capabilities, even if that marriage ultimately proved untenable.

1944 brought a gradual improvement in Williams' financial situation, so that by May he was ready to approach Gunda about a divorce— "a fearfully expensive and endless business," she wrote. Though the two had previously discussed the possibility of officially ending their marriage, one major obstacle presented itself: the only grounds for granting a divorce, either in New York or Ontario, was adultery, and how was this to be handled? Williams and Gunda agreed to meet that June in Barrie, where they both could visit with Mary Elgood, Dé's old friend. Once there they slept in separate rooms—a tacit announcement to their friends that the marriage was over. They agreed on a strategy: Williams would get friends from New York to testify that they had witnessed Gunda committing adultery. Williams took Fiona with him to spend the summer in New York. Though Gunda's friends warned her about the possibility of the children becoming hostages to maneuvering over the divorce, she wasn't concerned: "Garth is very good with small children. . . Fiona, who was three when she last saw him, has never forgotten, and I don't see how I can deprive her of her father," she wrote at the time.[106]

In fact, Gunda seemed not only resigned to the inevitability of a divorce, but oddly positive about it. She told one of her friends that it would be better to have things clear-cut, and she added that if Williams could afford it he should bring over Dorothea, with whom he had started his affair before leaving for New York. She added, "She's young and beautiful and tougher than I am. She's Jewish and she probably lost her entire family. At least one Jewish person will be made happy."[107] Gunda continued to consider the possibility of her husband remarrying, and Dorothea's special circumstances brought still more reflection: she confided in her friend Margot that, as a German, she believed she was "racked with guilt over all that's been done to the Jews. I'll not stand in their way. He—I mean Garth—should marry her, don't you think?"[108] Still later she would compare the sadness she felt over the plight of Native Americans to the sadness she felt over the German treatment of the Jews, and she would explain her feelings about the break-up of her marriage this way:

> I know perfectly well that my inability to condemn Garth's affair with our teenaged Jewish refugee; my insistence that he must marry her and give her, who lost her own family, one secure relationship—all this is rooted in absurd and ineffective guilt feelings… I was a greenhorn when I followed him to Italy and still absurdly ignorant when I married him there. He represented all I wanted—art, freedom, wit, and wisdom—as I saw it then. It took me a long time to discover that this dynamic personality did not represent other values I couldn't give up: decency, the ability to put yourself in someone else's place, an idealism I'd absorbed early in life from reading Schiller. . . I always assumed that it was I who was at fault, who was naïve, who lacked the sophistication of his—to me, aimless and cynical—bohemian world.

Until we were separated by the physical barriers of distance and war, until I found others who had the same ideals I had and who actually lived for them, I had not known what was wrong.[109]

What Williams would have thought about such a sentiment is unknown: how would he have responded to Gunda's veiled charges that he lacked "decency" and "the ability to put yourself in someone else's place"? However, the comment does suggest that Gunda was in a peculiar mood of self-sacrifice as the plans for divorce went forward. That mood continued into late July, when she went to Montreal to meet Williams and finalize the details for the divorce. He brought with him the two friends, a husband and wife, who were to act as witnesses in the proceedings. They all met at a nightclub on Sherbrooke, where they listened to jazz and the couple met Gunda for the first time. She noted that they genuinely liked Williams—"They think his work as an illustrator original, perhaps even slightly kinky (much as I had thought when seeing his drawings for the first time)"—but they also learned what they had not been told before: that they would have to swear under oath that they had witnessed Gunda committing adultery. Each of them took her aside separately to ask whether she really wanted to go through with it—whether they would be doing her any harm: "I assured them, with a sigh, that it was the only way." She asked them to sign Williams' statement and do whatever else was needed.[110] A lawyer to whom she talked a few days later was far less yielding, warning her that she must keep her children with her during divorce proceedings if she didn't want them taken from her later by social services. When she tried to explain that it wasn't a hostile divorce but merely a mutual parting of ways, he scolded her for that, too: collusion between divorcing parties was illegal.[111]

Though the marriage was officially ended in 1944, Williams and Gunda remained in frequent correspondence about matters pertaining to their two daughters. The tone was most often amicable, but disagreements did arise: in December Gunda decided to have the children's tonsils removed in the hopes of ending frequent bouts of tonsillitis, Williams wrote back to object. He subscribed to the theory that tonsils protected more important organs like bronchial tubes and kidneys and that removing them would lead to worse diseases. But Gunda herself had had her own tonsils removed a couple of years before and had suffered no infections of any kind since, so she overrode Williams' objections: "It's easy to have a theory when you don't struggle with day-to-day problems and it doesn't cost you anything. But there's a point when one has to make a choice." She arranged for tonsillectomies for both Fiona and Bettina the following March.[112]

All of this domestic turmoil was in the background as Williams continued with the pressing need to establish himself, both professionally and financially, as an artist in New York. In 1945, things were to turn for the better, as Williams would be given a crucial opportunity—the chance to illustrate a forthcoming children's book written by the poet and writer E. B. White. In the earlier part of 1945, Williams must have been working on the pictures for *Tux 'n Tales*, a fictionalized version of the exploits of a waiter named Raymond Andrieux. That work would later be published in November, when Williams received special notice in the *New York Times* for his "delightful illustrations."[113] He was probably also working on the illustrations for two other books, *The Great White Hills of New Hampshire* by Ernest Poole and *In Our Town* by Damon Runyon, both of which would be published in 1946. He also illustrated a children's book based on an old English rhyme called *The Chicken Book*, published by Howell Soskin in 1946.

In the meantime, it is not clear when Williams first met E. B. White, familiarly known as "Andy." According to Williams' family, the two men were never intimately acquainted, though Ursula Nordstrom, under whose supervision *Stuart Little* would eventually appear, reminisced in 1974 that the two men "worked closely together on the sketches when they were both in New York, and when Mr. White went to Maine in the spring, the collaboration continued by mail. Garth would bring his work in to me and I would airmail it to Mr. White for approval. The author's comments were always encouraging and helpful."[114] Thus White and Williams enjoyed a cordial relationship well into the 1960s, when White was to speak of the debt of gratitude that the author felt towards his illustrator. "Without your contribution," he later wrote, "I don't think Stuart would have traveled very far."[115]

What is clear is that Williams had come to the attention of Ursula Nordstrom, the powerful and visionary editor of children's literature at Harper's, in March of 1945. Sending the contract for the manuscript of *Stuart Little* to Katherine White (then the head of fiction at the *New Yorker* and the wife of Andy White), Nordstrom wrote of the ongoing search for an illustrator for the book. Later she would remember that she considered eight different illustrators.[116] She had just received a set of rough sketches from Don Freeman, who was then known for capturing the New York theater scene but who would later become famous as the illustrator of *Corduroy*, the story of a toy brown bear in green overalls. Freeman envisioned Stuart as a "rather zoot suited character," and Nordstrom knew Katherine would be disappointed. Other artists also vied for the commission: Aldren Watson, who later illustrated *The Jungle Book*, was dismissed by Nordstrom as not being right. Another unnamed artist, whom Nordstrom acknowledged as being "well known in the art world," was also a long shot. She expressed a slight preference for Robert Lawson, best known for illustrating *The Story of Ferdinand*, but he was bound by contract not to work for anyone other than Little, Brown, and Viking.[117]

In his autobiography, Williams omitted any mention of the prestigious artists with whom he was competing and simply recorded that Nordstrom had given him the manuscript, and that he took it home to his apartment on 14th Street, where his older daughter Fiona was visiting with him from Canada. He wrote that "On my pillow was a mouse. I said to my daughter Fiona, 'There's Stuart Little. You must be his friend. Feed him and I hope he stays.' I made three sample illustrations: one of him taking a shower and two others. I got the job, and Stuart the mouse stayed with us until the book was finished."[118] Even as an adult, Fiona remembers that there was indeed a mouse on the premises—and she recalls him "twitching a sharp little nose" as they sat eating at a round table. Fiona also recalls that her father's attention was divided between the illustrations and other employments designed to earn income, such as making busts and taking and printing photographs, including some of John Sebastian's baby.[119]

Williams' memory of Stuart's first appearance in his life contrasts with E. B. White's, who in 1966 was to recount for his inquiring readers in the *New York Times* the genesis of Stuart. He recalled that Stuart Little "came into being as the result of a journey" he once made in the late twenties on a train to Virginia. "While asleep in an upper berth, I dreamed a small character who had the features of a mouse, was nicely dressed, courageous, and questing. When I woke up, being a journalist and thankful of small favors, I made a few notes about this mouse-child—the only fictional figure ever to have honored and disturbed my sleep."[120] White further recalled that he thought it prudent to arm himself "with a yarn or two" about the mouse-child in case he was asked to entertain his eighteen nephews and nieces: "I named him Stuart and wrote a couple of episodes about his life. I kept these stories in a desk drawer and would pull them out and read them on demand." Then, in 1938, he carried them to an unnamed publisher, who did not encourage White to expand them.

Frequently suffering from bouts of depression, White nonetheless displayed an ironic sense of humor about his own mental state, tracing the completion of the *Stuart Little* manuscript to a moment in the winter of 1944-45, when he was "sure I was about to die, my head felt so queer. With death at hand, I cast about to discover what I could do to ease the lot of my poor widow, and again my thoughts strayed to Stuart Little."[121] He finished the book some time that winter, and it went to press in 1945. Yet the story is not complete without a mention of the role of Anne Carroll Moore. As director of the New York Public Library's Office of Work with Children since 1906, Moore exercised the ultimate right to decide which children's books were to be purchased for the library's collections. She famously possessed a rubber stamp with the words "Not recommended for purchase by expert," and once she made her decision, the fate of a book was fixed. According to White's biographer, Moore was initially excited by the prospect of White writing a children's book after he published a comment in *Harper's* that "it must be a lot of fun to write for children—reasonably easy work, perhaps even important work."[122] She urged White to write a book "that would make the lions roar" The formidable Moore sent no fewer than five letters to White, offering him both writing tips and copies of her reviews of other children's books.[123]

Yet, once she had set the book in motion, Moore was horrified with the final product. After receiving a set of proofs of the upcoming publication, she responded in a highly critical fourteen-page, handwritten letter that the Whites would later destroy. According to White's recollection in 1966, Moore had opined that the book was "non-affirmative, inconclusive, unfit for children, and would harm its author if published." She wrote as well that the story was "out of hand" and that Stuart was always "staggering out of scale." She charged that White had mixed up reality and fantasy—"The two worlds were all mixed up" and she feared that "children wouldn't be able to tell them apart."[124] Moore recommended that the book be withdrawn from publication.

If White was surprised and disappointed by Moore's letter, he was also unprepared for the response of Harold Ross, his "boss" at the *New Yorker*, as he also recounted in 1966: a few days after the book was published, Ross appeared in White's office:

> His briefcase was slung over his shoulder on a walking stick and he looked unhappy. "Saw your book, White," he growled. "You made one serious mistake."
>
> "What was that," I asked?
>
> "Why the mouse," he shouted. "You said he was born. God damn it, White, you should have had him adopted." The word "adopted" boomed forth loud enough to be heard all down the corridor. I had great respect for Ross's ability to spot trouble in a piece of writing, and I began to feel uneasy. After he left I sat for a long time wondering

whether Miss Moore had not been right after all. Finally I remembered that Harold Ross was not at home in the world of make-believe, he was strictly for the world of 43rd Street, and this cheered me and revived my spirits.[125]

While Moore and Ross were both disturbed by a story that allowed a human to give birth to a mouse, Edmund Wilson's response was quite the opposite: confronting White in the halls of the New Yorker, he told him he wished that he had developed the theme "more in the manner of Kafka."[126] It seems he would have enjoyed a story where the treatment was more surreal, and where Stuart's physicality might have come across as more weird.

Yet the enduring success of *Stuart Little* lies in the way that White handles the issue of a hybrid subject who is neither animal nor human but a curious combination of the two. Perhaps in a prickly mood about the criticisms concerning Stuart's birth, White once insisted to Ursula Nordstrom that he had never actually described Stuart as a mouse in the book: "he is small guy who looks very much like a mouse, but obviously he is not a mouse. He is a second son." (He subsequently corrected himself, finding one explicit reference to Stuart's status as a mouse in the book, but he added "He should not have been.")[127] This story would contradict White's earlier recollection that the story found its origin in a dream about a mouse.

But for Williams there was never any question about Stuart's rodent origins—as we've seen, he based his drawings on a life model who had become his roommate. More likely, he began with some sense of the actual animal, only to significantly enhance its appearance. He later explained his approach to drawing animals: "I start with the real animal, working over and over until I get the effect of human qualities and expressions and poses. I redesign the animal, as it were."[128] The result of this redesigning was a hero who is, in the words of one critic, a "neat, thoughtful, spare, [and] adult-looking mouse."[129]

No doubt Ursula Nordstrom knew she was taking a chance by choosing to work with an unknown illustrator. In a letter to Katherine

White, Nordstrom explained why she felt Williams was the right choice: "for instance, in the picture of the doctor examining Stuart, Stuart is standing up. Mr. Williams had him lying down in the first sketch but changed it because he was afraid he might look like a dead mouse if he were lying down. (That is probably a silly detail to pass on to you, but somehow it is encouraging to us.)"[130] Clearly anxious to please Nordstrom, Williams told her that he hadn't had enough time to prepare the sketches, but it seems that he spent considerable time pondering the issue of Stuart's scale in particular. Nordstrom recounts that the two discussed Katherine's suggestion that Stuart's size be treated in a manner similar to the animals in *The Wind in the Willows*, as illustrated by Ernest Shepard, where scale is handled with a flexible realism. In one illustration, for example, Toad wears evening clothes with a white bowtie and boutonniere and waves a cigar—all scaled to his size. In another, Rat and Mole row a boat of appropriate dimensions down the river, but a hovering dragonfly signals how small they really are.

For Williams, getting the scale right entailed paying attention to small details in order to create a realistic impression, as Nordstrom further explained to Katherine White: "But when he got down to work he found [it] difficult, because Stuart's size is mentioned so often. Mr. Williams felt that since, for instance, a dime can come up to Stuart's waist he (Mr. Williams) should be pretty consistent in the proportions in most of the pictures. (This sounds very dull and literal, I'm afraid, but Mr. Williams didn't mean it that way and, in fact, said it much better than I'm saying it.)"[131] In the finished illustrations, Williams often integrates real life objects into the scene to establish proportion and to anchor the scene. For example, Stuart's bed is made of a cigarette pack, with four clothespins as the bedposts. To further suggest the scale of Stuart's mouse-size bedroom, Williams places an airmail stamp on the wall above the bed as his poster-decoration.

In another scene, Stuart lounges comfortably with his back up against a candy bar that is, to him, the size of a bolster. When the little bird Margalo takes her temperature, Williams draws the thermometer

Illustration from *Stuart Little*.

outstretched on the floor before her, longer in length than she is.

But Williams' more powerful technique for conveying a sense of scale entails putting Stuart in poses that paradoxically announce how he becomes large in his very smallness. That is, although Stuart is incontrovertibly a miniature creature, he is also a hero of nearly epic proportions. In one scene, mimicking Atlas, Stuart pushes a ping-pong ball, going at it with all his might, a drop of sweat hanging from his brow.

Illustration from *Stuart Little*.

To climb up to the washbasin, Stuart, wearing a dapper dressing gown, pulls himself up a rope (described in the text as a "tiny rope ladder"), arms outstretched, left knee bent at a perfect ninety degree angle, head thrown back—with the grace and elegance of a yogi perfecting a pose. The image speaks volumes about Stuart's enormous determination while also affording him tremendous style and dignity. In another scene, Stuart takes up a bow and arrow to ward off Snowball the cat's imminent attack on Margalo. That Stuart is smaller than Snowball and in truth relatively defenseless against his menacing opponent (for surely Snowball could simply swat him away) is belied by his noble stance, his keen focus, and his arms upraised in anticipation of the shot—which he will make, hitting the cat on the ear.

Later in the story, the reader easily believes that Stuart has the capabilities to rule over the students in School Number Seven when Williams draws him (exactly as described by White) wearing "pepper and salt jacket, old striped trousers, a Windsor tie, and spectacles" on his way to the school.[132] The grass parts around the mouse instructor, while his confident, upright posture, purposeful stride, and focused, bespectacled gaze assure the reader of Stuart's supreme confidence. The illustration is the perfect rendering of a character who, when asked by the superintendent, "Do you think you can maintain discipline?" replies "Of course, I will make the work interesting and the discipline will take care of itself. Don't you worry about me."[133] On the following pages, his small size is once again signaled by a pile of books that is equal in height to him. But his body language—his wide-legged stance and his

Illustration from *Stuart Little*.

arms akimbo—suggest that he rules his classroom. Indeed the facing page shows a girl eagerly raising her hand to gain Stuart's attention and, most likely, his approbation.

Most memorably of all, perhaps, Williams' illustration of Stuart on the very first page of the story portrays him in his dapper suit, with his fedora and walking stick, and with a self-assured expression as he turns back to glance at the reader. Without any other clues in the drawing to indicate scale or size, Williams somehow manages to create the perfect expression of how smallness becomes noble and self-assured through qualities that emanate from within. He convinces the reader that Stuart is both an animal specimen and yet a believably diminutive gentleman. Though Stuart will be challenged by the physical size of the human world, we know that he will also be capable of deep ratiocination.

Illustration from *Stuart Little*.

This is not to say that Williams always got everything right. Vetting the early drawings, White asked for two minor changes in the art: that a schoolhouse be made "plainer-looking" and that a dentist friend of Stuart's also be made to look "more ordinary"—more, that is, White told Williams, "like Harry Truman."[134] In May of 1945, when *Stuart Little* was already in production at Harper & Brothers, White wrote to Ursula Nordstrom, to protest the way that Williams had drawn Harriet, Stuart's tiny human companion: "I'm returning the picture under separate cover. I like Stuart's crawl stroke very much, but I agree with you that Harriet isn't right. Her hair should be smoother and neater, also her legs should look more attractive (Harriet has beautiful legs), and her skirt should be fuller. I am enclosing a clipping from a Sears Roebuck catalogue showing a girl that looks like Harriet. Also Montgomery Ward's No. 21, which I suspect is the same girl. I hope Mr. Williams can save the Stuart part of this drawing and insert a new Harriet without having to redraw the whole thing. . ."[135] In fact, White may have had a point: arguably Williams' illustration for Chapter XIV, "An Evening on the River," disappoints by depicting Harriet as relatively inert as she sits on the shore, while an animated Stuart swims freestyle around her. Williams would continue to struggle with the representation of human figures, which, as we will see, he would later come to capture fully only by recognizing the animal-like qualities within them.

In the end, critics and readers alike judged Williams' illustrations for *Stuart Little* a terrific success. Katherine White, for one, offered this assessment: "I think I can, without bias, speak in praise of Garth Williams' beautiful and humorous pen-and-ink illustrations for E. B. White's fantasy because, by any standard, they are outstanding examples of imaginative illustration. Williams has visualized the hero perfectly, added original detail, and has greatly enriched the text."[136] Writing in the *New York Times* just after its publication, Charles Poore praised Williams' "meticulously appropriate drawings."[137] Other critics have also responded favorably to the way Williams perfectly captured Stuart's fundamental nature, for example the way in which Stuart was a "Lilliputian in whom we see ourselves reflected."[138] Despite Malcolm Cowley's dour assessment at the time that E. B White had failed to write an American classic, the book now belongs to the canon of children's literature, and it continues to be enjoyed by readers of all ages.[139] Serious critics continue to engage as well with the book for its expression of abiding human themes.

In one of the more interesting scholarly readings of the book, Marah Gubar argues that, in the figure of Stuart, White created not a child, but someone who is caught between childhood and adolescence and whose many adventures evoke deep psychoanalytic themes. She judges the book to be a quintessentially adolescent narrative that "celebrates the glory of independence and autonomy and underscores the woe of powerlessness and vulnerability."[140] As Gubar develops her reading, it is not difficult to imagine how Stuart's story might have deeply reverberated with its illustrator as well, despite the fact that Williams was obviously a fully-grown man by this time. Having ended his first marriage to Gunda, and having come to New York with the hope of starting a life all over again, Williams' position was not unlike that of Stuart who, according to Gubar, is "poised at the outer limit of the family, almost ready to make the leap into the outside world."[141] Still awaiting Dorothea, uncertain of what lay ahead, in 1945 Williams himself remained on the threshold of a new and unseen life.

There is further relevance in Gubar's reading of the final section of the book, which she describes as expressing "the fantasy of not needing a home, of transcending the trouble of relating to one's immediate family," a fantasy that proves more problematic than Stuart—or Williams—anticipated.[142] Though Williams would continue to play an active and loving role as the father of his daughters Fiona and Bettina, evidence suggests, as we have seen, that there were times when the burden of paternity weighed heavily. While some readers have expressed puzzlement or even dissatisfaction with White's last chapter, Stuart's status as "a creature at the crossroads" might well figure Williams' own predicament.[143] In Williams' final illustration for the book, the landscape looms large over a tiny, indistinct car whose inhabitant is undetectable. Still, despite the shadow etched in the foreground, the drawing exudes hope and optimism through its symmetry and balance—and in the fact of the welcoming town that lies in the distance.

In an interview with Leonard Marcus, Williams remembered feeling a sense of pride in his contribution to the success of *Stuart Little*. He reminisced that "I'd get into a bus and see three people reading *Stuart Little*. People everywhere were reading it, which made me feel very good. So I thought, Well, here's my profession."[144] But it is not clear that he easily embraced his new vocation as children's book illustrator then, or even later in life. Instead, he seems to have thought of this work as a means to support himself and dependents until he could, some day, return to the business of making "real"

Illustration from *Stuart Little*.

art. As late as 1991, he was still expressing this sentiment, as when he wrote, in a comment for *Something about the Author*: "I am busy illustrating books until I strike a gold mine. I hope to retire and to be able to go back to some serious art, painting and/or sculpting some day soon."[145] Though up-to-date sales numbers are not available, *Stuart Little* had sold 3,182,566 copies in paperback by 2004: in the first month of publication alone, as E. B. White noted, the hardcover sold 42,000 copies.[146] It is difficult to say precisely how much the illustrations contributed to the extraordinary success of the book. But there is little question that Williams' drawings brought Stuart's character to full fruition and created the indelible images that endure in the minds of readers to this day. Surely this was an art worth creating.

Wedding Announcement of Garth Williams and Dorothea Dessauer.

Chapter Three

ILLUSTRATING THE LITTLE HOUSE BOOKS (1945-1951)

"Thought-kin is closer sometimes than blood-kin"

With his divorce from Gunda finalized, Williams spent much of 1945 eagerly awaiting Dorothea's arrival in the US. His daughter Fiona remembers a game that she and her father would play as they walked home from the playground in Greenwich Village: "maybe Dorothea will be waiting on the doorstep with her suitcase when we return," he would say.[147] Dorothea embarked from Liverpool, bound for the port of San Francisco, on the 29th of October—though she appears to have disembarked in New York. On the passenger list, her nationality was listed as "stateless."[148] It could not have been easy for Dorothea to immigrate to America: since the Immigration Act of 1924, quotas had been created for those seeking to enter the country. During the depression, President Hoover had further tightened rules for immigration, though these were relaxed somewhat under President Roosevelt. After the bombing of Pearl Harbor, refugees like Dorothea who had been born in enemy countries were classified as "alien enemies." They would have had to pass through three levels of security screening. In 1943, the required application for a visa was four feet long, to be filled out on both sides and submitted in six copies.[149]

By 1944, the visa procedures had been simplified, and on December 22nd, 1945, the "Truman Directive," a document issued by President Truman himself, urged a policy of more lenient treatment of displaced persons from Europe.[150] Though this directive came after Dorothea and Williams had arranged her passage, it may have facilitated the process of her immigration. In any case, Dorothea would have required sponsorship to come to the US, a responsibility that Williams readily undertook. In his autobiography, Williams remembers that Dorothea arrived in the US on her twenty-first birthday, but in fact she had already turned twenty-one on October 28th, the day before she embarked for the United States. With a four-year separation now behind them, Williams and Dorothea were married at the home of their friend Henry Simon in Harrison, New York on the 7th of December, 1945. In their wedding announcement, Williams drew himself and his bride astride a glorious steed making its way through a magical landscape populated by an assortment of characters, including a rotund, laughing ogre balancing a bowl of coins on his head, a naked nymph peering out from behind the trees, and a dragon with its tongue unfurled. Williams depicted himself, accoutered in armor and brandishing a huge sword as the couple makes their way to a castle in the clouds. In 1945, Williams clearly saw himself as Dorothea's protector, and the whimsical, richly detailed drawing exudes a sense of promise, despite the obstacles that appear along the way. "Semper Fideles" reads the motto on the inscription, indicating just how much hope Williams had for this second marriage.

When Williams' daughters came to live with them in the summer of 1946, the couple left the cramped quarters of their small apartment in Greenwich Village and relocated to a farm near Watertown, New

York. In 1953, Williams remembered the place as very primitive, as they lived without telephone or electricity:

> The house had five barns and a smokehouse. Our water came down from a crystal-clear spring in the woods, and our only mechanical contrivance was a hand-pump in the kitchen, located in a lean-to with a very leaky roof. We were situated on a high hill surrounded by two hundred acres. The house was almost two hundred years old and the main barn was a giant, built when farmers vied with one another to build the largest. Three years earlier, the farm was still being run by the old couple who had lived there for 80 years exactly in the manner of the Wilders of Malone, as described in *Farmer Boy*.[151]

To be sure, this description was written after he had undertaken the illustrations for the Little House series, and Williams sounds eager to convince his readers that he himself had experienced a life much like the one Wilder described in her books. He even paints a picture of himself cleaning and trimming the wicks of an oil lamp, just as Caroline Ingalls is described as doing in the stories. Family photographs from the period, taken by Williams, provide documentary evidence that the Williams family was enjoying aspects of the existence that Wilder described. Williams' photographs of Dorothea, Fiona, and Bettina suggest a relaxed, bucolic

Dorothea Williams with Bettina and friend.

lifestyle, with the girls, now seven and five, looking tanned and fit as they romp with the family dog.

Dorothea must have bonded easily with the children, as Gunda remembers that Dorothea declared her intention to keep the girls. Gunda had to insist that they be returned to her in Canada.[152]

It was during this time that Williams began what would be a long and successful collaboration with Margaret Wise Brown. In 1946 he drew the illustrations for *Little Fur Family*, a children's book that was originally bound in actual rabbit's fur. In the meantime, Ursula Nordstrom, the editor at Harper & Brothers who had commissioned Williams for *Stuart Little,* had a project in mind for him—the illustrations for a new, uniform edition of the Little House books, originally published in the 1930s, with illustrations by Helen Sewell and her co-illustrator Mildred Boyle. Though Sewell's reputation had been distinguished, by the 1940s Nordstrom felt that her illustrations, done in an "extremely decorative and stylized" manner, were "less and less suited to these forthright realistic frontier stories."[153] This time, having worked so successfully with Williams on *Stuart Little*, she immediately turned to him as her first choice of illustrator. In the end, the project of illustrating the original eight-book series would not be completed until 1953. Williams would return to the project again, providing the illustrations for a ninth volume that was discovered in 1971 and printed under the title of *The First Four Years*.

Williams later remembered that the prospect of illustrating the Little House books did not immediately appeal to him. In an interview with Leonard Marcus, he recalled telling Nordstrom that the project was "not about animals," only to be adamantly told by Nordstrom that he "'must not have read the books properly.' She 'shooed me out of the office!'"[154] But Nordstrom was undeterred in her desire to obtain Williams for the job. In a letter written to Doris Stotz in 1967, Nordstrom recounted her choice of an illustrator, remembering that, as she came to know Williams and Dorothea and the girls, she "became convinced that he could do the perfect pictures for a revised format. He is British and certainly had no roots in any part of the Wilder Country. But as we know, thought-kin is closer sometimes than blood-kin, and Garth certainly had all the emotional equipment, as well as the technical, to illustrate these wonderful family books."[155]

In coining the phrase "thought-kin," Nordstrom was intuiting something about Williams. Though he had been brought up far from the American prairie, and though most of his formative experiences took place in Canada and England, nonetheless she had faith in him as an interpreter of American pioneer life. With *Stuart Little*, he had demonstrated his ability to distill the essence of a story and to capture its deepest meanings. Now, with his family near him, he would encapsulate the domestic values reflected in Wilder's series. He would do so in part by becoming "Pa," with his young wife and his two little girls tumbling around him. From Nordstrom's perspective, the Williams family appeared to be living an idyllic domestic existence. In September of 1947, she wrote to Williams from New York City: "I like to think of you and Dorothea in the country now; the weather is so wonderful. Take a deep breath of fresh air for me, will you? I am chained to this cement island and hate it."[156] Nordstrom often fondly remembered Dorothea and the girls, on one occasion sending books, including *Herself Surprised* and *The Horse's Mouth*, by Joyce Carey, for Dorothea to read.[157]

Her dismissal of Williams' comment that the books were not "about animals" is certainly curious, as of course human characters do dominate the Little House series. Yet perhaps she understood that, in order to bring the Wilder family saga into relief, what was needed was a facility with the animal existence, or an understanding of how the human is animated by the animal within. If, in *Stuart Little*, Williams had brilliantly captured how the mouse becomes person-like through his desires and aspirations, in the Little House illustrations he would successfully express how the person draws energy and life from her animal spirits. The very first illustration of Laura in *Little House in the Big Woods* depicts a small girl arrested in mid motion as she skips across the ground, swinging her hat by its ribbons above her head. Scarcely earth bound,

Illustration from *Little House in the Big Woods*.

she seems to spring off the page for the reader's consideration.

This compelling sense of Laura's energy is echoed throughout the series. An illustration for *By the Shores of Silver Lake* (which appears both on the cover and at the beginning of Chapter Six) captures the now-adolescent Laura clinging to a horse's mane as she gallops bareback across the prairie. Horse and rider appear in close affinity, powerfully conveying the motion and vigor of both.

After accepting the commission for the Little House series, Williams visited Rose Wilder Lane, Wilder's daughter, who was then living in a farmhouse in Danbury, Connecticut. She encouraged Williams to visit the Wilders in Missouri, assuring him that her mother was sharp-minded and likely to be responsive to him.[158] In November of 1947, Williams and Dorothea, along with five-year-old Bettina, started on a car trip to meet Laura Ingalls Wilder and to research the people, landscape, buildings, and artifacts that he would later need to draw. Though as a young man Williams had set out to be a "serious artist," and not an illustrator, his work on *Stuart Little* and other children's books had already brought him critical acclaim and financial rewards. These must have made the transition to a career as an illustrator more palatable. It now became apparent how his extensive training in life-drawing, sculpture, photography, and even architecture, gained during his apprenticeship at the Royal Academy, could serve him well as he set off on the monumental task of recreating Laura Ingalls's world from scratch. Williams approached the research for the series with energy and enthusiasm.

As Williams himself recorded in 1953 in *Horn Book Magazine*, the ten-day drive to meet Mrs. Wilder, following a route suggested by Rose Wilder Lane, took the family south from New York State, through the Great Smokey Mountains, and then west to Mansfield, Missouri. Williams found Mrs. Wilder weeding her garden. Later, in 1986, when Williams made a return trip to revisit the places that he had originally researched, he reminisced that he had found Wilder "to be frisky, a person who seemed to be willing to try anything and go anywhere. She was a very cheerful character, very sprightly, very much alive with a good sense of humor."[159] At the time of his visit, Williams and Mrs. Wilder discussed details from the books, including the location of her father's fiddle, kept at that time in a museum in Pierre, South Dakota. (It is now housed in the Laura Ingalls Wilder Museum in Mansfield, Missouri.) She shared photographs and other memorabilia. Williams was especially impressed to see that Almanzo, Wilder's husband, was still doing chores at the age of 90.[160]

Sometime after his trip, he sent a full report to Wilder, most likely intended to further convince her that he was the right person to illustrate her childhood experiences. For example, about his time in De Smet he wrote, "I drove south to the shores of Lake Henry and on beyond where your first school must have been. I almost saw Almanzo driving out to fetch you home across the endless snow. For a long time I peered into the windows of a house just south of the big slough; and I have never seen or known such an enormous sky. Although the country must feel settled to you today, I completely felt the minuteness of the people & carts & houses—out in a prairie." About his visit to Plum Creek, he wrote, "It was most exciting to sit on the bank and imagine the footbridge and you and Nellie Olsen splashing in the water."[161] But beyond these letters suggesting that Williams was happy to communicate with Wilder, little record exists of the tenor of the relationship between the two. What did Mrs. Wilder think of her visitor, a man known for his ability to put people at their ease and to make friends easily? How much might she even have known of his reputation, which in 1947 still depended largely upon his success with *Stuart Little?* Unlike E. B. White, Wilder apparently had no interest in weighing in on the illustrations for her books. Williams later recalled asking her whether she wanted him to draw portraits of the real life family who inspired the stories, or whether he should draw some "pleasant-looking people."[162] When she said it didn't matter, he offered to send her the illustrations—as he had done with his illustrations for both White and Margaret Wise Brown—so that she could ask for changes.

In a letter to Ursula Nordstrom dated November 7, 1947, Wilder wrote that she thought that Nordstrom would like to know that Williams, his wife, and daughter had arrived safely and had visited her and her husband: "They are very charming and I think I helped a little in his work. He made drawings of old family pictures I have of the same dates as my stories and seemed very pleased to have found them. I feel sure his illustrations of my stories will be beautiful." Then she asked for one correction:

> One thing I should have told him is that "Jack" the bulldog was not
> as pictured in the published books [as illustrated by Sewell and Boyd].
> I think that strain was developed later. Jack's legs were straight and
> he stood tall on them. His face was not wrinkled all out of shape but
> was smooth with powerful jaws. He was tall enough that I rode on
> his back without touching ground.
>
> Mr. Williams will know that kind of English bulldog and if he is
> told will make no mistake if he should picture Jack.[163]

However, beyond this reference to Jack, there is no evidence that Wilder asked for further changes.

Continuing his journey in search of material for the illustrations, Williams and his family next drove to Kansas, where he met an elderly man driving a two-horse wagon. Though the man knew nothing of the Ingalls family, he did remember the people who had lived in the house after Laura's time there, so that Williams was able to locate the spot the little house on the prairie had most likely stood. The next stop was Independence, Kansas, and in particular, the banks of the Verdigris River, where Williams had access to the real-life setting of scenes that take place in the third book in the series, *Little House on the Prairie*. [164] As the Williams family traveled onward to Walnut Grove, Minnesota, Williams claimed that he could "imagine [himself] as Pa Ingalls in a covered wagon creeping slowly across the vast prairie." In Walnut Grove, he met with the editor of the town paper, *The Walnut Grove Tribune*, who was surprised to hear that his town was the setting for a Wilder book, so that Williams was the first person to identify the actual site of the story. Documentary evidence published in the paper in 1916 established that Charles Ingalls, Laura's father, had once been successful in a town election there.[165]

After receiving valuable photographs of the town and its people from the editor, Williams went to the site of the sod house described in *On The Banks of Plum Creek*. A younger couple living in a farmhouse gave him directions, and he set off about a quarter of a mile. He records:

> I left the car in their yard and followed the stream, taking my camera with me. I did not expect to find the house, but felt certain it would have left an indentation in the bank. A light rain did not help my search and I was just about to give up when I saw what I was looking for, a hollow in the East Bank of Plum Creek. I felt very well rewarded, for the scene fitted Mrs. Wilder's description perfectly.[166]

Later in the same essay, Williams explained the process by which the real-life experience of being on-site amid the actual ruins of the house became an illustration. Noting that "illustrating books is not just making pictures of the houses, the people and the articles mentioned by the artist," Williams wrote, "the artist has to see everything with the same eyes." Illustration, he further explained, is a process of transforming the real until it presents itself as it would to the eyes of the young protagonist:

> For example, an architect would have described the sod house on the bank of Plum Creek as extremely primitive, unhealthy and undesirable—nothing to seal the walls from dampness, no ventilation, no light. But to Laura's fresh young eyes it was a pleasant house, surrounded by flowers and with the music of a running stream and rustling leaves. She understood the meaning of hardship and struggle, of joy and work, of shyness and bravery. She was never overcome by drabness or squalor. She never glamorized anything; yet she saw the loveliness in everything. This was the way the illustrator had to follow—no glamorizing for him either; no giving everyone a permanent wave.[167]

In this way, Williams wrote with insight about tensions that permeate the story and must have made his job as illustrator more difficult, as we'll see later. Having been given the task of providing a set of "realistic" illustrations, Williams felt compelled not to embellish or distort—he had to try to stay with the "truth," even when the story turned to darker or more oppressive themes. His primary mission was a task that he had never before been given: to convey faithfully a particular time and a particular place as it "really existed." That time and place were remembered and filtered through a very distinct and individual narrative presence. To make matters more challenging, that narrative presence changed as it aged over the length of the series—so that the world as it appears through the eyes of young Laura is quite different, in both tone and subject, from the world seen through the eyes of the older protagonist. The illustrations would need to capture this change and to reflect an evolving narrative perspective.

After Plum Creek, the Williams family drove on to De Smet, South Dakota, where the publisher of *The De Smet News* gave Williams a tour of the relevant places and sites, as well as a fiftieth-anniversary edition of the town newspaper in which references to the beginning of the long winter of 1880 (the subject of the sixth book in the Little House series) appeared. Williams wrote that he could "imagine the children playing in the buffalo grass out on that vast prairie."[168] He visited other sites from the later books, including the place where Laura taught school and was courted by her husband. He rounded out the visit with some conversations with elderly people who had known the Ingalls girls as children. Outdriving a snowstorm, the Williams family sheltered with friends in Sherburn, Minnesota.[169]

As for the research for *Farmer Boy*—the one book in the series depicting not the Ingalls family, but the childhood of Wilder's husband, Almanzo—Williams maintained that he gathered much of his information in upstate New York, near his farm. The Farmer's Museum in Cooperstown furnished examples of pioneer artifacts and equipment. He was clearly eager to convey the extraordinary care and effort that went into his preparations for the illustrations for the books. He also added, "Yet even with the data I collected it must not be assumed that every character is a portrait or that every detail is accurate. With the limited space of illustrations I could only dip into the large amount of illustration available and use what seemed most important."[170]

One crucial aspect contributing to the success of Williams' illustrations was his ability to select exactly the right detail or set of details from a myriad of possibilities. Once chosen, such representation would have to convey a wider set of ideas, circumstances, or even geographic location. Having never been west of the Hudson before his car trip, Williams was setting out to illustrate a world he did not know—and a world that no longer existed as it once had. A mound of dirt may provide evidence that a sod house once existed, but it is not the sod house itself. Williams would have to recreate from his own imagination the Ingalls' primitive prairie home, and he would do so by very carefully presenting evocative images anchoring a "realistic" scene within a carefully composed illustration.

The full-color book jacket for *On the Banks of Plum Creek*, for example, is "realistic" in its depiction of a carefree Laura Ingalls, skipping with abandon, blue dress held out over her bare legs, on the roof of her sod home, while her mother, appearing in a window below her, bends at her ironing. The carefully drawn features of Laura's and her mother's faces, the individual strands of their hair, the delicate details on the collar of Laura's dress, the variegated prairie wildflowers, the captivated face of

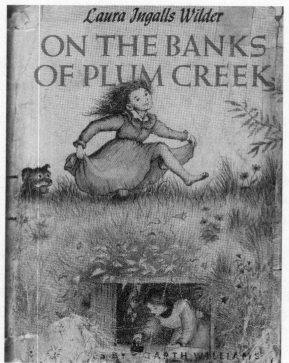

Cover illustration for *On the Banks of Plum Creek*.

Jack the brindled dog as he watches Laura dance, and even the old-fashioned iron in Ma's hand, all provide authentic evidence of a "real" scene. Yet, in a sense, "place" is most present in the scene because it is not there: nothing in the drawing insists that the scene is nineteenth-century Minnesota. Only the flatness of the landscape, limned out to cover both the front and the back of the book jacket, suggests a wide-open space, and the blank, undrawn sky does the work of suggesting the expansive prairie. In this way, the illustration presents the singularly sensuous experience of the young child who processes that life in her unique way.

The 80-year-old Mrs. Wilder was a well-beloved author with a long successful career behind her by the time Williams met her in 1947.

The outline of her life was already well known to her readers. Born on February 7, 1867, Laura Ingalls experienced a nomadic girlhood, as her restless father moved the family often, with stays in Wisconsin, Kansas, Minnesota, and Iowa before finally establishing roots in De Smet, South Dakota. In South Dakota, Ingalls taught school at age 16, and then married Almanzo Wilder at age 18. He familiarly called her "Bessie" or later "Mama Bess" to distinguish her from his sister, who had the same name, Laura. Early in their marriage, the couple was beset by tragedies of biblical scope, including the death of a newborn son, fire, drought, and a bout of diphtheria that left Almanzo debilitated. The couple made an attempt to live in Florida, but eventually migrated, with their daughter, Rose, to Missouri, where they bought land near Mansfield. There they grew an apple orchard, though the profits from that venture would be a long time coming. Eventually Laura succeeded as a purveyor of superior eggs and butter. Her first experience as a published writer consisted of a bi-weekly column, written for the *Missouri Ruralist*. She later became the editor of the publication.

By all accounts, the roots of the Little House series lie in an early autobiographical piece called "Pioneer Girl" (first printed in 2014)[171] and then a children's story entitled "When Grandma was a Little Girl," later rewritten as *Little House in the Big Woods* (1932). All the books describe the experiences of the Ingalls family, except one, *Farmer Boy* (1933), the second book in the series, which tells the story of the Wilder family in Malone, New York. The other seven books: *Little House in the Big Woods*, *Little House on the Prairie* (1935), *On the Banks of Plum Creek* (1937), *By the Shores of Silver Lake* (1939), *The Long Winter* (1940), *Little Town on the Prairie* (1940), and *These Happy Golden Years* (1943)—are largely faithful to many of the circumstances experienced by the Ingalls family. But there two notable exceptions: no mention is made of a son who died as an infant in 1876, and Wilder chose to omit an account of how the family worked in a hotel in Burr Oak, Iowa in 1877.[172]

Having been published largely during the Great Depression, the books that Nordstrom set out to reissue had already enjoyed critical and popular success. With the support and encouragement of her daughter, Wilder had first aimed to publish *Little House in the Woods* (the original title for her rewritten story) with Knopf, under the editorship of Marion Fiery. But Knopf closed its children's department just before the book went into production. Wilder then sent the manuscript to Harper & Brothers Children's Department (a company which was subsequently known as Harper and Row and is now HarperCollins), where it came to the attention of Virginia Kirkus, a powerful editor who created the prestigious review service that still bears her name. Kirkus immediately recognized the value of the story, writing that "the real magic was in the telling. One felt that one was listening and not reading." She then sent it to Helen Sewell to be illustrated.[173]

Appearing in 1932, the book, now entitled *Little House in the Big Woods*, garnered very positive reviews in notable publications, including *The New York Times Book Review*, where Anne T. Eaton praised its "refreshingly genuine and lifelike quality." Details of farm life were described "with zest and humor," and the characters were "very much alive" and drawn with "loving care and reality."[174] Similarly positive reviews followed for the publication of each subsequent volume. In 1935, Eaton reviewed *Little House on the Prairie* with praise, again, for its life and realism: "Mrs. Wilder has caught the very essence of pioneer life, the satisfaction of hard work, the thrill of accomplishment, safety and comfort made possible through resourcefulness and exertion. She draws, too, with humor and with understanding, the picture of a fine and courageous family, who are loyal and imaginative in their relationships to one another."[175] In 1939 a notice in *The New Yorker* called *By the Shores of Silver Lake* "Touching, unsentimental, and real Americana."[176]

The enthusiasm and affection of ordinary readers were as important as the positive reviews. Some encountered the books for the first time through book clubs like the Junior Literary Guild (still active today), which selected *Little House in the Big Woods* for its list in April of 1932. Others learned of the series from trusted librarians or from teachers who embraced the books as part of their school curriculum.

At the age of sixty-five, Mrs. Wilder suddenly found herself a most celebrated and popular author, someone to whom children often wrote heartfelt letters and who was courted for public appearances, including a speech at a local book fair in Detroit in 1937.[177] Though some of Wilder's experiences as a homesteader had also been experienced by other midwesterners of her generation, her children's books filled a literary void by carefully conveying that experience through the unique perspective of a child.

Willa Cather, for example, had similarly written about the tribulations of settlers on the Nebraska plains in *O Pioneers* (1913) and *My Ántonia* (1918). But Cather was not speaking to the youngest readers, especially those who could pick up *Little House in the Big Woods* at the age of seven or eight and read it to themselves. Where regional writers like Hamlin Garland or Sinclair Lewis wrote for adults, Wilder's target audience was a rapidly expanding population of juvenile readers. In addition, the ambitious scope of her eight-volume series distinguished her from a writer like Carol Ryrie Brink, whose popular story *Caddie Woodlawn* (1936) described the life of a young girl growing up in Wisconsin, but who produced only one sequel, *Magical Melons* (1939). Wilder's stories uniquely offer a narrative style that matures as the protagonist ages, allowing young readers who read all eight books to "grow up" along with Laura Ingalls.

Nordstrom understood that in order for the series to have continuing commercial success it would a need to evolve in relation to changing demographics: an earlier group of readers who had grown during the Depression—some of whose own grandparents might have been Wilder's contemporaries—were beginning to have families of their own. As this generation matured and aged, often moving further away from the rural settings of the stories, it must have made sense to revisit the question of what the series meant and how it would speak to an upcoming generation. Nordstrom also comprehended that a new set of illustrations could engage that generation and provide evidence of what was no longer accessible on a daily level as America transitioned into its next, more suburban phase. In an expanding book market, where books would sell better than they had during the Depression, it would clearly be advantageous to issue an attractive uniform edition, a series that would appeal to libraries that were rapidly expanding their juvenile collections. Though a new edition of the Wilder books would remain pricier than the popular Nancy Drew and Hardy Boys series, it fit into a broader trend towards a rapidly expanding consumer market for children's books that had been set in motion in part with the creation of Golden Books in 1942. (The Little House books would not be published in paperback, however, until 1971.)[178]

Nordstrom's plan for the new series was ambitious. She originally envisioned that Williams would produce oil paintings depicting seasonal scenes from the series, but this would have made the books too expensive.[179] Williams tried pen and ink sketches, but eventually he and Nordstrom decided that he would draw the illustrations with carbon pencil, which the press would reproduce by means of an offset printing technique that would transfer inked images from the original to a rubber surface and then the page. Each illustration was drawn on semi-transparent tracing paper in pencil, with fine pen used for intricate detail. In the end, to keep publishing costs down, Williams drew the pictures in exactly the same size that they would appear on the page. The publisher used a "direct contact process," a method of printing that breaks up the light and dark lines into little dots, so that the drawing appears to have been done in lithographic crayon (that is, a crayon containing ink or grease).[180] As Williams himself commented, though drawing at this scale kept the costs down, it placed an added burden on the artist who had to stay within the careful confines of the predetermined space.

Though they had been meticulously researched in the States, the illustrations for the first three Little House books were not produced on American soil. Instead, Williams, Dorothea, and their daughter Estyn (born March 16, 1948) took passage on March 15, 1949 on the S. S. *de Grasse*, eventually arriving in Italy and celebrating Esytn's first birthday en route.[181] For the journey they took along their new car, packed full of luggage and jars of baby food.[182] A friend, the writer and journalist Bruce Bliven, took up residence in their New York apartment in their absence. In his autobiography, Williams does not explain how he decided to go to Rome in 1949, nor does he discuss the impact it may have had on his work. It remains, then, a matter of speculation why, after working so hard to establish himself in New York, he would have decided to return to Europe for what was meant to be a lengthy period of residence.

Several possibilities arise: in the postwar years, first and foremost, Italy was far less expensive than New York. That money continued to be a concern is suggested by a letter Nordstrom wrote in March of 1950, offering to return to a system of paying Williams $500 a month "if all your recent troubles make that necessary." She proposed reissuing *The Little Fur Family*—likely to be a lucrative proposition—and asked Bliven to locate the originals stored in the Williams' apartment. Bliven claimed the task would take him a lifetime, a complaint that suggests the apartment was crammed with art stockpiled in inaccessible places. [183] A few months later, Nordstrom began the process of arranging with E. B. White for Williams to do the illustrations for *Charlotte's Web*. It seems that plenty of work was available for Williams to do in the US. But perhaps Italy appealed as a residence for the Williams family because of its very positive pre-war associations. Clearly he had enjoyed his time there under the Prix de Rome, and living once again in Rome meant returning to a place where he had felt such promise as a young man.

According to Williams, the family stayed with friends in a monastery near Tivoli, Rome during 1949-50. Though no one is alive who can remember the exact location of the Williams' Italian residence, Williams mentions the property as once having belonged to an English professor; he also mentions that the rent was ten dollars a month, the same amount they had paid for their farmhouse in upstate New York.[184] It is not difficult to imagine postwar Tivoli as it must have been when Williams and his family arrived. The town and its surroundings have changed very little over the past sixty years—except in some arguably better ways.

The massive paper mill that once loomed in the distance, for instance, now lies dormant. Surrounded by the stunning, picturesque, green hills that ring its medieval streets, Tivoli is a town of superb prospects and lovely sights, including the famed sixteen-century gardens of the Villa d'Este. But it cannot be said to resemble the American Midwest in any way. How, then, did Williams manage to capture the landscape of Laura Ingalls' girlhood with the Roman countryside in his sight daily?

He had two resources at his disposal. The first was photographs. Williams was a skilled and avid photographer. That he had extensively photographed his travels through Wilder country is evident from the pictures that accompanied a later publication entitled *Laura Ingalls Wilder Country*. It is probable that at least some of the earliest illustrations were drawn with photographs as a point of reference. Second, Williams appears to have had a keen visual memory, as well as the uncanny ability to distill complex visual impressions, gathered from first-hand experience, into singularly clear representations. Using his mind's eye, Williams created powerfully evocative settings that would come to stand in for a quintessentially American pioneer experience.

Williams and Dorothea were not entirely cut off from their American friends and acquaintances during their stay in Italy. They were visited in 1950, for example, by Margaret Wise Brown, with whom he continued to collaborate throughout this period. On a train en route to visit the Williamses, she had an adventure when a man entered her compartment at Turin, took out a cigarette and began to smoke most nervously. As Williams retold the story, "She awoke in Rome, to find two Police officers shaking her, in an empty train. She had been robbed—and was not sure about what else had happened, but she invited us to a birthday party for her son, whom she would call ESPRESSO, nine months hence."[185] Fortunately, her manuscripts were not stolen, and so Williams chose one called *Three Little Animals*, which proved to be the first draft of *Little Fur Family*. In any case, Brown found the Williams family to be flourishing. In photographs from the period, Williams and Dorothea appear happy and fulfilled, posing playfully in sunlight and shadow with their young daughter against the backdrop of impressive Roman sites. It seems that the family had settled in and planned to stay for a while in Rome, until circumstances dictated otherwise.

In recent years, the reputation of the Little House series has been dogged by the issue of Wilder's authorship: the publication of William Holtz's book *The Ghost and the Little House: A Life of Rose Wilder Lane* in 1995 raised a suspicion that the role of Lane, Wilder's daughter, in the creation of the Little House Series was extensive enough

Dorothea Williams and Estyn in Italy.

to cast doubts about Wilder as an author. In effect, Holtz argued, Lane did not merely edit her mother's manuscripts, but ghostwrote the books, making significant decisions about both form and content. Holtz's controversial position sent scholars back to the archive to examine both the original manuscripts and the correspondence between mother and daughter. The current consensus is that Holtz may have overstated the case somewhat. The correspondence of Wilder and Lane, archived in the Herbert Hoover Presidential Library in West Branch, Iowa, suggests a more nuanced, if oftentimes touchy, relationship between the two.[186] Yet throughout this debate, rarely have scholars asked about the role of the illustrator in the text, even though the question of how a book is illustrated can weigh as heavily on a reader's interpretation of a story as can a series of edits.[187] As Williams himself reflected later in his life, "the author produces the most important part…an illustrator can give different meaning to the words."[188] Illustrations provide visual clues as to what is important in a story and what demands the reader's special attention. In addition, they can establish a mood that in turn affects the tone of the book. To offer one extreme example, the illustrator Susan Jeffers alters the dark and brooding tone of Robert Frost's well-known poem "Stopping by Woods on a Snowy Evening" by depicting the narrator of the poem as a Santa Claus-like figure. (He has "miles to go" before he sleeps.) In the case of the Little House books, the two very different set of drawings, the first done by Helen Sewell, later with the assistance of Mildred Boyle, and the second done by Garth Williams, make clear just how much illustration matters and why it makes sense to consider the illustrator as another kind of "ghostwriter."

THEY LOOKED LIKE SHAGGY DOGS

Helen Sewell, illustration for *Little House in the Big Woods*.

Born in California, Helen Sewell (1896-1957) traveled as a girl around the world with her father, a navy officer who was appointed governor of Guam in 1902. At the precocious age of 12, she attended the Pratt Institute in New York, where she met Mildred Boyle. Sewell's first published illustrations appeared in a book called *The Cruise of the Little Dipper* in 1923. Having come to the attention of Louise

Seaman Bechtel, a highly influential children's book editor, she began to do illustrations for Macmillan. She also spent some time illustrating greeting cards. Eventually she illustrated over fifty books for both children and adults, for titles ranging from *Cinderella* (1934) to Jane Austen's *Sense and Sensibility* (1957). *The Thanksgiving Story*, by Alice Dalgliesh, which Sewell illustrated in 1955, took a Newbery Honor Award. When Kirkus chose her for the original Little House series, she did so in part because she believed that Sewell's skills would enhance the marketability of the books.

Two notable influences shaped Sewell's illustrations. The first—which she herself mentioned—is the time she spent in tropical climates.[189] This experience resulted in her drawing a lush, highly stylized version of nature. Her rendering of vegetation, often drawn to suggest symmetrical and even spiky plants, does not realistically imitate the verdure of the American Midwest, though it can be evocative in its own way.

Helen Sewell, cover illustration for *Little House in the Big Woods*.

Similarly, her representation of the woods, often drawn as if to suggest the thickness of banyan trees, aims not to capture geographic specificity but to imply the weighty presence of nature. This interpretation is apparent on one version of the cover of the 1932 *Little House in the Big Woods,* where the tiny cabin is overshadowed by the ornamental trees that surround it.

In another version of the original cover the cabin is larger, yet a leafy, vaguely tropical tree still fans around the front of the house.

The second influence on Sewell's illustration was her teacher at Pratt, Alexander Archipenko (1887-1964), a Ukrainian graphic artist and sculptor, who had been involved with cubist and other avant-garde movements of the early twentieth century. Known especially for his rejection of the classical representation of the human body, Archipenko taught Sewell to view the human figure not in realist but in sculptural, nearly geometrical terms, and in fact her drawings of the Ingalls family are, for the most part, generic, with very simply done faces. The features of the children are indicated with a simple dot or line. When Mary and Laura appear side by side, they are distinguished only by the

Mary and Laura clung tight to their rag dolls

Helen Sewell, illustration for *Little House on the Prairie*.

fact that Mary is taller.

Sewell often gives the grown-up figures a rotund appearance, as if they are weighed by their heavy clothing and, as a result, static. Pa remains the exception, as he is shown in motion—pretending to be a mad dog, in one illustration, for example. Depicted as hatless and with a big beard, he bears resemblance to a 1930s version of Abraham Lincoln. In the first edition of the Little House books, captions taken directly from the text indicate exactly what is being illustrated. The pictures tend to come after the text, sometimes not even on the same page or overleaf, so

Mildred Boyle, illustration for *Little Town on the Prairie.*

that they supplement what the reader has already read and processed. Several of the illustrations for *Little House in the Big Woods* are set at night, with a dark background created through heavily etched lines. These contribute to a somber, even reverent mood, especially as the book draws to a close with a full-page illustration of Ma and Pa by the fireside, he with his fiddle and she with her knitting.

Though it is not documented exactly which illustrations belong to Sewell and which belong to Mildred Boyle, it appears that Boyle came in to assist Sewell when illness made it difficult for her to complete the illustrations for *On the Banks of Plum Creek*, the third book in the series. From then on, the two seem to have shared the work, with Sewell drawing the faces and bodies and Boyle providing the book jackets, frontispieces, and background.[190] The faces show more expression, and more attention is paid to dress and furnishings. However the dress often shows the influence of 1940s style—in much the same way that a period film will contain tell-tale traces of the age in which it is made, no matter how carefully the director tries to be faithful to history. The girls' hats, for instance, belong more to the 1940s than the 1870s.

During the Depression, financial considerations dictated production costs for most books. Wilder's original series consisted of smaller books than the current versions. *Little House in the Big Woods,* for instance, was seven by eight and three-eighths inches. It had one color plate, three full-page illustrations, and only fourteen black and white drawings in all. After the publication of *On the Banks of Plum Creek* in 1937, the books became smaller in size—first only five and three-quarters by eight and one-quarter inches and then five and one-quarter by seven and three-fourths inches. This smaller size, as well as other cutbacks in design, may have had something to do with government regulations for saving paper, once the US had entered the Second World War.[191] Williams clearly had the advantage, then, in doing his illustrations in the postwar period when production budgets could be more generous and when fewer limits were placed on the production costs. Though he had to deal with some stipulations from the printer, he was able to illustrate the series much more extensively than did Sewell and Boyle. Where they provided drawings to suggest in a general way what the characters might have looked like, his drawings are more thoroughly integrated into the text and more directional in the way they focus the reader's attention on specific aspects of the story.

In Williams' version of the Little House series, the use of art is lavish. It not only illustrates, but also ornaments the book. There are no full-page illustrations. Instead, book designer Helen Gentry placed the illustrations in the middle of the text, so that text and image flow into one another. Williams also frequently draws in little miniature scenes, or sometimes just a small animal, a miniature person, or an object—like

Ma's china shepherdess—to embellish a chapter heading or a break in the text. Possibly he first learned to use ornamental illustration in this way during his time at the *New Yorker*. But here, these small additions are important because they ensure that the illustrations and the story flow in close proximity to one another: while reading the story, the reader never loses track of the consistent vision of the artist who is interpreting the story alongside the author. Williams achieved his apotheosis as an illustrator in the Little House series. In his astonishing use of detail, in his extraordinarily meticulous drawing, and in the simple scope and magnitude of the multi-volume series, he demonstrated a kind of artistic mastery and expertise that has rarely been duplicated in the history of children's literature. His drawings accomplish four major purposes, each of which deserves to be discussed in turn.

First, Williams realistically reproduces an uncommonly wide range of objects from the nineteenth century, thereby providing juvenile readers with a visual encyclopedia of the things of everyday life. He duplicates the work of a historian, or perhaps more accurately a museum curator, by providing evidence of a long-gone world, including how people worked the land, raised their animals, prepared their food, furnished and lived in their dwellings, traveled, and even how they groomed themselves. *Little House in the Big Woods* is especially rich in this kind of visual detail that augments the text by showing exactly what things looked like. On the overleaf for the first chapter of *Little House in the Big Woods*, severed tree trunks, hewn at rough angles, surround the little cabin, documenting the labor that went into making the shelter and suggesting how recently the cabin has sprung into existence. Small illustrations, precisely rendered, show young readers exactly what Pa's rifle, accompanied by its powder horn and pouch of gunpowder, looked like as it hung on the wall. Another, drawn to accompany the description of how Pa loads the rifle, lays out the full range of accouterments necessary for making bullets from lead. To illustrate the story of how Pa built the girls a sled, Williams draws the sled in the middle of its construction, allowing the reader to see both what the sled looked like and how it was put together.

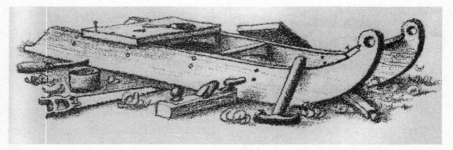

Ilustration for *Little House in the Big Woods.*

From Williams' pictures, readers—many of whom lived far from a rural setting—could see exactly what a bear trap looked like. They could see the equipment necessary for extracting sap from maple trees and turning it into syrup—the pegs and buckets and caldrons, the wooden yokes to carry the buckets, and the long handled wooden ladle made of basswood. They could see the size of a butter churn relative to a small child and how she placed her hands on the handle. Wilder's depiction of how the family pig was slaughtered and turned into meat is often praised for its realism, but Williams takes the realism further by showing exactly how Laura and Mary played with the pig's bladder once it had been inflated and tied with a string. When Williams depicts interiors, no detail appears too small or insignificant to capture; his drawing of a country store echoes Wilder's text, with its marvelous catalogue of items for sale, but also gives a sense of physical space, how so many objects jumbled together vie for the consumer's attention and how they provided a rich sensual experience.

In a book that gives careful attention to nineteenth-century clothing and grooming, Williams provides an illustration of how Laura's aunts carefully coiled their hair in braids on the back of their heads. Readers are told how nineteenth-century decorum required that women cover their ears, and indeed, Williams never depicts Ma with her ears exposed.

Though the setting and the tone of Wilder's writing shift over the course of the series, and as it embraces the psychologically more complex and sometimes darker themes of Laura's growth, Williams continues

Illustration for *Little House in the Big Woods*.

to shape the reader's visual understanding. His drawings demonstrate a genuine, life-long curiosity in how things are put together—from the primitive agricultural machinery in *Little House in the Big Woods*, with its literal eight-horse power drive, to the construction of a frontier town in *By the Shores of Silver Lake*. Sometimes, as in the illustration to accompany a chapter called "The Building Boom," the sense that Williams is working off period photographs is clear, as he captures the men at their labor. Other times he appears to piece together an interior setting from notes or sketches—as when he draws the nineteenth-century telegraph office in which Laura celebrates a friend's birthday in *Little Town on the Prairie*.

Certainly, observant critics have found mistakes or limitations: one critic, for example, takes exception to way that Williams draws Mary's carefully tailored dress in *Little Town on the Prairie,* charging that "It is as if the prevailing illustrative vocabulary of 1950s U.S. children's books could not accommodate the elaborate, proliferating detail that the print text lavishes on this crucial Victorian object."[192] But it must be said that realism is always selective; art rarely attempts any copy that includes everything of the original. Wilder herself sometimes omitted crucial details from her realistic chronicle when she thought readers might misconstrue her meaning. For example, she changed a muddy river into a spring in *On the Banks of Plum Creek.* As she later told her daughter Rose, "I have an awful suspicion that we drank plain creek water, in the raw, without boiling it or whatever. But that would make the reader think we were dirty, which we were not. So I said a spring. There could have been a spring where Pa watered the oxen or there could be one near the plank footbridge."[193] In this way, "realism" incorporates the truth of what was, yet filters details to shape an audience's interpretation of what seems most important. While Williams' drawing of Mary's dress leaves some sartorial details to the imagination, he captures Mary's stunning and elegant Victorian silhouette, the way the dress transforms her from being simply Laura's sister into the independent college girl she is about to become.

The second notable accomplishment of Williams' illustrations for the Little House series is his representation of the American landscape. Where, in the earlier version of the series, Sewell aimed for a broad, evocative setting with a faintly tropical flavor, Williams aims to establish a very specific sense of geography. Like Sewell, he had not been brought up on the American prairie, yet unlike Sewell, he successfully captured a key theme conveyed in the Wilder text—namely the psychological impact of living, as the Ingalls did, in the highly volatile natural environment of the American frontier. Wilder's texts often portray how nature offered moments of deep loveliness and spiritual contentment. Here is a selection from Chapter Eight of *By the Shores of Silver Lake*:

Illustration for *By the Shores of Silver Lake*.

Ducks quacked among the thick grasses to the southwest, where the Big Slough began. Screaming gulls flew over the lake, beating against the dawn wind. A wild goose rose from the water with a ringing call, and one after another of the birds in his flock answered him as they rose and followed. The great triangle of wild geese flew with a beating of strong wings into the glory of the sunrise.

Shafts of golden light shot higher and higher in the eastern sky, until their brightness touched the water and was reflected there.

Then the sun, a golden ball, rolled over the eastern edge of the world.[194]

Williams' illustration for the scene captures the adolescent heroine, her face turned away from the reader and towards the distant view, where the wild fowl fly at a distance.

In the middle ground, between Laura and the endless horizon, lies the town itself, where tiny human figures appear to be at work not far from an even more distant settlement, which Williams sketches as a small semi-circle of primitive buildings. The reader gets a very distinct sense of expansive space; we are looking down at Laura, who is looking down at the scene below her. He doesn't draw the sun rising. Instead, the illustration encourages the reader to process what Laura feels and experiences as she takes in the scene. At the same time, the illustration is true to the tension in the text. When Laura returns home and tries to explain her lovely moment, she will be gently chided by her mother for taking too long at her task. A love of nature's beauty must be balanced by discipline and hard work. Williams' illustration, by choosing to include the tiny figures of the men already at their labor, as well as the primitive settlement beyond, encompasses the complexity of Wilder's textual message.

If, on the one hand, Wilder's text suggests the often arresting power of the frontier landscape, on the other hand it also reflects the cruelty of nature, and in particular its capacity to vex, torment, and threaten human life. Storms brew, locusts swarm, crops fail, and epidemics rage. Where Sewell and Boyle tend to omit this darker side to nature, Williams often chooses to foreground it, thereby highlighting this aspect of the stories. His drawings often show the ways in which nature sets itself up as an obstacle to humans—in the dangerous roiling of a river, for instance, or in a wind that menaces the construction of a roof, or a prairie fire that threatens to consume all in its path. Never condescending to his young readers, he is willing to depict realistically the way injury swells Ma's foot to an enormous size, or the way malarial fever enfeebles Laura as she struggles to reach for a dipper of water.

As might be expected of an artist known for his talent at representing animals, Williams' illustrations for the series afford lots of space for all sorts of creatures—horses, to be sure, but also bears, dogs, wolves, rabbits, and birds. Some, like the wolves, are magnificent in their wildness; others are more threatening. For a chapter called "Blackbirds" in *Little Town on the Prairie*, Williams draws the birds' ruthless attack on the corn and the humans with a chilling intensity that competes with scene of the avian attackers in Alfred Hitchcock's *The Birds* (a movie that would not appear until 1963).

That he is willing to represent such dark scenes alongside more bucolic prospects is a crucial contribution to a narrative that often swings from one extreme to another, from a moment of serenity and comfort to a state of menace and discomfort.

Williams' third major contribution to the Little House books is the way he shapes

Illustration for *Little Town on the Prairie*.

the readers' interpretation by alerting them to specific concepts, themes, and ideas. As we've already seen, Nordstrom might have been thinking of this possibility when she urged Williams to reconsider the series. Across the nine books, one of the most important motifs is that of motion or animation. Though Sewell and Boyle also show some predilection for representing surprise or unexpected events, Williams' illustrations often feature Laura's dynamic corporeal movements. This is especially true in the earliest books where she is youngest and most lively. She skips, dances, climbs, and jumps. She rides ponies bareback. Even when she's meant to be well behaved and still, Williams manages to capture a sense of her energy. Later, in the series, as Laura becomes more decorous and refined, he often moves the energy and motion into the background, where it now surrounds the main character. In *Little Town on the Prairie*, Laura has had to become a disciplined young lady. Yet activity occurs all around her—boisterous men crowd

Illustration for *Little Town on the Prairie*.

the counter behind her seated figure hunched over her sewing, or small boys run pell-mell in the streets in front of her.

Though Laura's movements as a "lady" are more limited, Wilder describes her as using her physicality to develop her skills as a rider and later as a driver of Almanzo's spirited horses. Williams captures this idea with an image of Laura, leaning forward and holding onto the reins for dear life, as the horses race across the prairie.

Where Sewell and Boyle drew expression with simple, suggestive lines, Williams individuates his character's expressions. His fourth contribution to the series is the way his drawings facilitate the reader's identification with the characters and their situation. In an illustration for a chapter entitled "Sent Home from School," he perfectly catches the look on Laura's face as she rocks the heavy bench for her younger sister Carrie, who has been given the task as a perverse punishment by an odious teacher. Outraged at the unfair treatment of her sister and determined to make a point, Laura leans forward in mid-motion while the smaller children pull back in terror of what is to come.

Illustration for *Little Town on the Prairie*.

The illustration heightens the tension in the text and adds immediacy to the verbal description of the scene, ensuring the reader's identification with Laura's rebellious emotions. Though the series offers no real villains, it does describe a range of badly behaving characters—entitled mean girls who flaunt their advantage, or characters who are desperate and driven by their extreme situation. Once again, Williams' illustrations embrace the darker moments of human psychology. In *These Happy Golden Years*, he depicts Mrs. Brewster threatening her husband with a butcher knife while a terrified Laura peeks from behind the curtain separator.

In the absence of comments from Wilder on the nature of Williams' illustrations, unfortunately we cannot know whether she was pleased with the way he responded to her narratives. Certainly, she would have been glad of the commercial success of the new edition, and she may have been gratified to know that the reputation of the books would endure after her death. A few years before she died, she sent a telegram to Harpers with the following comment to be used for advertising purposes: "Laura and Mary and their folks live again in these illustrations."[195] For a generation of postwar readers, Williams' illustrations became the "reality" of the Little House series. His drawings made sure that Wilder's nineteenth-century world remained accessible, and they provided an enduring portrait of the Ingalls family.

1962 saw the publication of *On the Way Home: A Diary of a Trip from South Dakota to Mansfield, Missouri in 1894*.[196] Designed to address the readers' deep curiosity about Laura Ingalls Wilder's life, this book provided documentary evidence, in the form of photographs of Laura and Almanzo, of the places they had lived, and of the objects they had owned. Yet despite their status as the "actual" representation of the real people, places, and things, the photographs could prove disappointing to readers who already carried Williams' images in their memories. It wasn't hard to feel that the photographs were less real than his drawings. From 1974 to 1982, NBC aired a television version of the Little House series, with Michael Landon as Pa and Melissa Gilbert as Laura.[197] Though the show was successful with an audience who enjoyed family dramas like *Bonanza* or *The Waltons*, it had little to do with the themes of Wilder's books. It never aimed to capture the nuances of frontier life, and it took license with the small details—described by Wilder and meticulously illustrated by Williams—that gave the series its depth and its unique appeal. Most of Wilder's commentary concerning daily life, dress, diet, and comportment were ignored in favor of broad, sentimental themes of family life.

Finally, in 2006, HarperCollins reprinted the Little House series without Williams' art. They issued a statement claiming that the illustrations made the series seem "old-fashioned" and that they hoped to keep the books "vibrant and relevant for today." As editor Kate Jackson explained, "A childhood book is an emotional, tactile object, and you want it to be as it was. But Laura Ingalls was a real girl, not a made up character. Using photographs [on the cover of the book] highlights that these are not history but adventure books."[198] In part, this version of the books may have been designed to compete with the stories written to accompany the highly popular American Girls Dolls. For example, the story of one doll, the fictional Kirsten Larson (who could be purchased with her numerous clothing changes and accessories), was set in 1854, among the immigrant population settled in Minnesota. Perhaps marketing directors at HarperCollins hoped to capitalize on the fact that the Little House series would prove to be engaging with a new generation of readers expecting a high level of action. Over the years, the press has continued to issue a nine-book box set of the series (including *The First Four Years*) with Williams' illustrations, now colorized. It remains to be seen whether the future success of the series rests on its appeal as "adventure stories" that endure because of their contemporary themes, or whether their very success lies in their appeal to a young imagination craving historical specificity. Perhaps it is true that, in an age of technology, where the flick of a finger across a tiny screen can call up a butter churn or maybe even show what an "eight horse power" machine really looked like, Williams' illustrations are superfluous. But perhaps too something significant is lost when a second eye no longer advances the story, enhancing its themes and visualizing its characters in precise and clear terms.

If Williams once planned to do all the illustrations for the Little House books in Italy, this did not happen. The family returned to the U.S., arriving in New York from Le Havre, France, aboard the S. S. *Nieuw Amsterdam* on September 2nd, 1951.[199] Williams' fourth daughter, Jessica, was born in New York on October 6th. The circumstances surrounding the family's return remain unclear. Williams' third daughter, Estyn, who would have been an infant at the time, recalls being later told by her mother Dorothea of a car accident in which Williams was involved. Dorothea, who had been pregnant with Jessica at the time, told her daughters that she sustained injuries in the crash, as did passengers in another car. According to Estyn, the car crash precipitated the family's return to New York—perhaps out of concern for Dorothea's pregnancy. Yet it is equally possible that Williams had other reasons for wanting to return to New York. Certainly his ongoing collaboration with Margaret Wise Brown would have been facilitated by residence in New York, as would his other professional commitments. Perhaps postwar Europe no longer offered him the stimulation it once had. In any case, it is clear that by the fall of 1951, the family was back in the states, where Williams finished the illustrations for the Little House books. Soon the family would relocate to Aspen.

Chapter Four

"SOME PIG": ILLUSTRATING *CHARLOTTE'S WEB*
(1952-1962)

Drawing of the Jerome Hotel, Aspen, by Garth Williams. Courtesy of the Aspen Historical Society.

On August 18, 1955, *The New York Times* featured an article under the headline "A Mountain Shack Becomes a Mountain Retreat." The piece described the transformation of what had been an old mine, and then a boarding house, into a summer home just outside Aspen for owners Garth Williams—whom the reporter identified as a "cartoonist"–and his wife Dorothea. The building had once been a dormitory for miners, built on the site of the old Hope mine. The reporter from New York, a well-known interior designer by the name of Betty Pepis, was especially impressed with major design choices, including a diamond-patterned pink, mauve, yellow, and white wallpaper in the master bedroom and the display of the couple's tin and paper maché objects collected on their travels to Mexico and Central America.[200] This house served as the Williams family's summer retreat, and it testifies to both their sophisticated taste and their intention to make Aspen their home. During the winter when the road would have been impassable—and when his young daughters would have been attending the local school—the family lived in town, at a small, bright, late nineteenth-century cottage on the corner of West Main and 3rd Streets. Later, a neighbor would recall seeing Williams sitting at the window in the front, sketching.

This house sat right on the main road into Aspen, which was still unpaved in those days. From there, Williams could easily walk the short, nine block distance to a studio that he rented in town—first in a space in the Elks Building (which then housed the post office) and afterwards in a railway station that no longer served passengers. Years later, in his autobiography, Williams reminisced that:

> All found Aspen great fun; it was then just developing, and everybody knew everybody in town. There was one ski lift, and one T-bar for beginners. We had an old miner's hotel, seven miles up the Castle Creek Valley, that we rebuilt and redecorated. We bought two horses; one for twenty-five and the other for thirty dollars. Mine was the expensive one. The children had Shorty, a small, fat one. We learned to ride.[201]

While his comments on Aspen focus on family memories, there is a great deal more to be said about the ten years he lived there.

This was the most prolific period of his life. Since his return from Rome in 1951, commissions had been pouring in, and Williams had become a highly regarded and eagerly sought after children's book illustrator. Working quickly and efficiently, he had finished the pictures for all eight of the Little House Books, which were published in 1953 and which garnered broad critical acclaim for the illustrations. He had also continued his collaboration with Margaret Wise Brown, who is perhaps best remembered as the author of *Goodnight Moon* (1947) and *The Runaway Bunny* (1942) (both illustrated by Clement Hurd). After Williams illustrated Brown's *Little Fur Family* (1946), *Wait Till the Moon is Full* and *The Golden Sleepy Book* (both 1948), he also did the pictures for a number of her stories, including *The Sailor Dog* (1953), *The Friendly Book* (1954), *Mister Dog: The Dog Who Belonged to Himself* (1954), *Home for a Bunny* (1956) *Three Little Animals* (1956), and *The Whispering Rabbit and Other Stories* (1965). Yet all of the books appearing after 1952 were posthumous publications for Brown, who had died on November 13th of that year after complications from surgery for an ovarian cyst. Though she should have made a full recovery after the surgery, she was killed by an embolism that travelled from her leg to her brain as she playfully kicked up her leg to show how well she was.[202]

Williams learned of her death in a telephone conversation with his friend Bruce Bliven. He went her to funeral in New York, and then, one year later, attended an event on the anniversary of her death. He recalled many years later, "She wanted us to have a gay party and drink champagne [though she would only] attend in spirit. It was not gay, but we all noted that none of us could really accept the fact that this was not another of her practical jokes—her worst."[203] He also continued to remember her fondly as a wonderful friend "who would banish worry and make the world shine with fun." Citing his relationship with her as "the closest and happiest type of collaboration," he reminisced that their working relationship "was like a competition to outdo the other in bettering the book. I made no hesitation in criticizing her words or ideas and she would tear into any pictures that she wished to. We both fought back, but there are many changes we each made for the best, due to each other's criticisms."[204]

Several of the books done for Brown were the result of a contract that Williams had recently signed with the Little Golden Books, which—as we will see in the next chapter—not only provided much work, but also positioned him as a significant illustrator in the world of postwar children's literature. During the decade that Aspen was his home, his domestic situation also underwent yet another drastic transition, as his second marriage gradually disintegrated and his family situation was once again reconfigured. It was also during this time that he began his peregrinations to Mexico, where he would eventually begin a new chapter in his life.

Both before and after their sojourn in Rome (1949-51), Williams and Dorothea had cultivated a broad circle of cosmopolitan friends and acquaintances in New York. Dorothea was, after all, an attractive and spirited woman who got along well with Williams' friends from before she arrived—people like the sculptor Rosario ("Saro") Murabito and his wife. But she also made new friends easily. Among them, one woman in particular became one of her best friends—Katherine ("Kay") Leach, wife of Richard Leach. This connection would lead Dorothea and Williams right to the heart of the burgeoning art scene in Aspen. In 1951, Leach— who founded the Saratoga Arts Center, among his other accomplishments—had been tapped by wealthy philanthropist Walter Paepcke to run the Aspen Institute and the Aspen Music Festival, which were both in their fledgling days. Keeping an office in New York during the winter, Leach quickly won the respect and affection of the Aspen musicians. But he and Paepcke clashed over a number of management issues, and Leach was eventually fired as director.[205] Well before that, however, Kay urged Dorothea to bring her husband and family out to Aspen for a visit. After spending the summers of 1952 and 1953 there, Williams and Dorothea decided to stay. According to Williams, at that time, he had with him only two pairs of nylon shorts and a pair of sneakers.[206]

In choosing Aspen, Williams may have had several things in mind. Certainly the spectacular beauty of the mountains would have been attractive to a well-traveled couple familiar with dramatic landscapes. In addition, beginning in the 1940s, Aspen was gradually becoming a cultural mecca. Most notably, in 1949, Walter Paepcke urged the University of Chicago to use Aspen as the site for its Goethe Bicentennial Convocation and Music Festival. The idea behind this festival was that "music, combined with athletics, intellect, love of nature, and integration with the other arts, can forge what the Greeks had referred to as the Whole Man."[207] Among the participants that first year were the playwright Thornton Wilder, the philosopher José Ortega y Gasset, pianist Arthur Rubenstein, poet Stephen Spender, and conductor Dimitri Mitropoulos and the Minneapolis Symphony Orchestra. The world-famous humanitarian Albert Schweitzer gave two speeches, one in French and the other in German, both of which were simultaneously translated by Thornton Wilder.

After 1949, Aspen continued to attract a wide range of talented individuals, with the Aspen Music Festival and the Aspen Institute serving as the main draws during the summer months. Aspen's notable residents included Herbert Beyer, a Bauhaus designer, painter, photographer, and architect who had been brought out to Aspen by Paepcke; Fritz Benedict, also an architect; photographers Ferenc Berko (originally from Hungary) and Patrick Henry; and champion skier Dick Durrance. Thornton Wilder and Gary Cooper were also in residence. Other luminaries visiting Aspen included Igor Stravinsky, Aaron Copland, Elliott Carter, the violinist Roman Totenberg and his daughter Nina, who would later win fame of her own as the legal affairs correspondent for National Public Radio.[208] At the end of one summer, Fiona and Bettina, who had been spending the summer season with their father in Aspen, rode back to New York with the family of the great pianist Claudio Arrau.

To be sure, like Durrance, several of these people had first come to Aspen for the opportunity to ski, but many stayed on for the vibrant cultural life. As Williams remembered, in 1952 only Lift IA took skiers up the mountain, but other lifts—most notably at Buttermilk and Snowmass—soon followed. Beginning in January 1951, the town hosted "Winterskol," a winter carnival designed to fill the time during the three weeks after Christmas when the ski lifts were closed. For Williams and Dorothea, Aspen must have held out the promise of a small but energetic international community of like-minded souls. And the town embraced them in return.

We can see this in a satirical drawing Williams did in 1955, possibly as a placemat. (See the illustration above, p. 97.) He depicted a lively scene on the slopes, as Lift IA carries an assortment of comic characters up to the mountaintop. One skier is chased by what seems to be a bear on skis, while another whizzes through a slalom course. At the base of the mountain, evidence of the town's mining roots can be seen in the two old-time miners operating the lift and in the two ghosts with pick axes in their hands. The drawing clearly spans the seasons, as scenes of fishing, swimming, and the summer music festival—sketched to offer just a peek inside its tent—also make their appearance. Among other buildings, the Opera House stands out for its representation of the oversized musician and singer. But pride of place is given to the Jerome Hotel—qstill an Aspen landmark to this day—with its inhabitants, as glimpsed through

the hotel's windows, pursuing their various, crazy activities. In short, this is a lively and whimsical drawing that conveys the artist's affection for his adopted home. Further evidence of Williams' social life in Aspen appears in a photograph from 1955, depicting Edgar Stanton, chairman of that year's Winterskol festival, Dorothea, and a very photogenic dog (unnamed). They sit on the floor while a gigantic papier-mâché

Dorothea Williams and Edgar Stanton. Courtesy of the Aspen Historical Society.

snowman looms over them. These decorations were designed by Williams.

In 1955 Williams also designed a poster celebrating National Children's Book Week (November 13-19). An article for the *Rocky Mountain News* noted this accomplishment and credited Williams as "one of the celebrities who have contributed to Aspen's growing reputation as a cultural capital." The reporter, Robert L. Perkin, found Williams to be "a quiet, almost painfully modest man." He continued, "Williams would be the last person to endorse that statement [lauding his celebrity], but he's strictly bullish on Aspen's future." In response to the reporter's questions, Williams cited the mixture of artists, writers, musicians, and thinkers who were moving to Aspen, and he joked, "So many of them are moving out from the East that it looks like New York will become a ghost city." The reporter went on to give a verbal portrait of Williams' physical appearance at mid-life:

> Williams is a stocky, rounded, muscular man. The roundness of his face is heightened by a high forehead which is steadily working its way backward at the expense of a blonde mane. The top is liberally freckled by Aspen's sun.[209]

Though Aspen's culture was certainly appealing, Williams also appreciated that, before its transformation into an elite resort town, Aspen was a cheap place to live. Williams was always seeking less expensive places to work and raise his family, which would vary in size: in the summer, he, Dorothea, Estyn, and Jessica would sometimes be joined by Fiona and Bettina, who would visit from Canada. In addition, the family once accommodated Williams' half-sister Denise, who came over from France for a year to help manage the household. It wasn't easy to support so many people, and Williams was always on the look out for bargains. When he later moved to Mexico, he often marveled at the inexpensive price of a good steak.[210]

Throughout the early 1950s Williams worked at a terrific pace. While much of this work will be the subject of Chapter Five, one work warrants its own extended discussion: *Charlotte's Web*, written by E. B.

White and published by Harper & Brothers in 1952. Though the book has gathered innumerable accolades, perhaps Peter Neumeyer's assessment is most apt: "*Charlotte's Web*, an American pastoral, is a hymn of praise, a glorious prose poem, a human and animal comedy in the old sense of the word 'comedy,' a celebration of life—and it is one of the first children's books to deal seriously, without sentimentality or condescension, with death."[211] Or, as the novelist Eudora Welty once succinctly wrote, White's volume—the story of a pig named Wilbur and a spider named Charlotte—is "just about perfect, and just about magical in the way it is done."[212] As late as 1996, it was the all-time best selling paperback for children, recorded as selling 7,894,103 copies.[213] Well into the twenty-first century, its reputation remains secure, as does that of Williams' illustrations. Today it is possible to buy a t-shirt adorned with his illustration for the cover. Though the book did not win the Newbery Medal in 1953, in 1970 E. B. White was to be awarded a special Laura Ingalls Wilder Award for both *Stuart Little* and *Charlotte's Web*. (Coincidently, Williams designed the medal for that Award.)

The origins of the story can be traced back to 1947 when White—who had had some experience as a farmer in upstate New York—was meditating upon what it meant to raise a pig only to butcher it. Remembering a pig that had once died despite his best efforts to keep it alive, he recorded in *The Atlantic Monthly*, "the loss we felt was not the loss of ham but the loss of pig."[214] Then, in 1948, White found himself closely observing a spider in his barn in Maine. He watched as she spun an egg sac and then disappeared. Carefully placing the egg sac in an empty candy box, he transported it to New York City, where the baby spiders hatched on his bureau.[215] By 1949, White had begun sketching the layout of Zuckerman's farm—the setting for his emerging story. He also did further research into spiders. Consulting Henry McCook's *American Spiders and Their Spinningwork* led him to the insight that Charlotte, the sapient spider at the heart of the story, would have to be nearsighted.[216] Further consultation of John Henry Comstock's *The Spider Book* led White to identify her species: *Aranea cavatica*. White then visited Willis Gertsch, a curator in the Department of Insects and Spiders at the American Museum of Natural History, who was able to show him photographic images, including one of the courtship and mating of black widow spiders.[217] By March 1951, the manuscript of *Charlotte's Web* was well under way, though it would not be delivered to Ursula Nordstrom until March 1952. White brought only one copy with him to the Harper office. This meant not only that Nordstrom was being entrusted with a valuable commodity (this being in the days long before photocopying was possible) but that she had no copy to rush off to Williams.[218]

Yet despite the supreme importance of *Charlotte's Web* for Williams' reputation as an illustrator, it does not seem to have been his favorite project. Moreover, his drawings, superlative though they are, convey his occasional struggles with this project. As Williams later wrote in a letter to Peter Neumeyer, he initially found it less interesting to illustrate this book than *Stuart Little*—in part because it did not offer the same challenges in figuring out a sense of scale: "Stuart was more interesting to illustrate as it was crazier. A little girl the size of Stuart. An invisible car racing around the dentist's office. Stuart driving his car through the country and talking to people." He continued, "Charlotte required me to make the people—with the exception of Fern—very ordinary indeed. The animals had to be very real, with the sole peculiarity that they talked to themselves and to some people." Echoing Eudora Welty's review, he added, "But the story was just perfect."[219]

For all Williams' initial lack of enthusiasm, Nordstrom had wanted him to do the illustrations from the very beginning. As early as March 1951, she wrote to White,

> Thanks for your letter telling me that you've recently finished another children's book. That's the best news I've had in a long long time.
>
> We assume that you will want Garth Williams to illustrate it and I'm warning him to keep his schedule as flexible as possible... I'll just keep hoping that Garth won't be in the middle of anything with an urgent deadline for Simon & Schuster [the publisher of the Little

Golden Books]. Any Harper book he ever does is given to him with the understanding that he can stop work on it the minute the E. B. White manuscript arrives. I wish I could speak as firmly for S & S![220]

Once again, Nordstrom's preference to commission Williams was inspired, for reasons that can be gleaned from a comment by White's biographer. Describing *Charlotte's Web* as "a fabric of memories," Scott Elledge emphasizes the retrospective nature of White's accomplishment. White's experience, he writes, "was sharpened by his having seen many things come to an end." Williams had already proven in his illustration of the Little House series that he was especially responsive to projects requiring research and that he had a talent for historical reconstruction. Elledge continues:

> But for White, the most important things that had passed were the sensations and images of infancy, childhood, and youth; and if he could remember them clearly, he could remember the self that had experienced them. If he could evoke that self and keep in touch with it, he could imagine a fiction, write a story, create a world that children would believe in and love.[221]

Similarly, in the illustrations for the Wilder books, as well as those done for Margaret Wise Brown and other children's authors, Williams had successfully captured (in Elledge's words) the "sensations and images of infancy, childhood, and youth." But this is not to say that the collaboration with White was without its tensions.

Drawing Charlotte, the story's protagonist, necessitated the first set of negotiations. To get her image just right, White recommended that Williams consult the same sources that he had. On April 2nd, 1952 Nordstrom wrote to assure White that "the copy of *American Spiders* came and we sent it right down to Garth. We also sent him the New York Public Library slip on the McCook books. As you have probably heard from him, he loves *Charlotte's Web* as much as I do and is at work on the illustrations."[222] A few days later, in a letter to Katherine White on April 10, 1952, she reported on Williams' progress, indicating that he was doing research for the book: "Garth and I had a talk over the 'phone this morning. He says he is starting slowly and is making many sketches now. He was on his way to the Natural History Museum when I telephoned."[223] Later, Williams would remember that White had given him

> Two enormous tomes on spiders about 30,000 different kinds, all with different faces, all gruesome. I struggled to invent a loveable spider-face. They all have 8 eyes. Mouth like pincers. So I used the wooly spider-type, placing 6 eyes in the hair, leaving two as we are accustomed to finding them. Finally I gave her a Mona Lisa face, as she is, after all, the heroine of the story.

White rejected Mona Lisa and insisted that Williams draw Charlotte as a "real" spider. Williams remembered that "White accepted the accurate rendition of the *Aranea Cavatica* and suggested we skip a full-face. He put two dots on the edge of her face looking down and put 3 strokes to suggest hair on top of her head—and the problem was solved. But I contend he cheated."[224] Williams' last comment speaks to an apparently

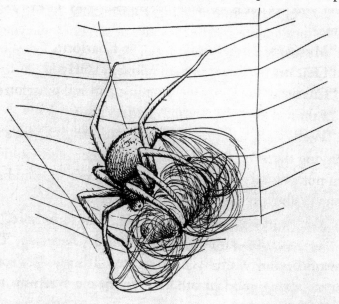

Illustration for *Charlotte's Web*.

on-going struggle between the two men. While White resisted Williams' tendency to anthropomorphize the animal characters, he nonetheless had created speaking creatures who inevitably seemed to warrant human characteristics in their representation. He does seem to have "cheated," then, in asking his illustrator to remove Charlotte's human markings, only to replace some of them himself.

Williams' retrospective glance at the creative process of illustrating *Charlotte's Web* also leaves out Ursula Nordstrom's active—and tactful— role as she brokered the negotiations between the two men. For instance, on April 28th, she sent a few rough sketches and finished drawings to White. She wrote that she was "worried" about a number of drawings of Charlotte, which she marked with an A—but encouraged White to let her know if she was wrong in her assessment. "Garth wants to meet the challenge of doing a close-up of a spider, he says. But when he comes right up to it he doesn't meet it by giving her a *face*."[225] Nordstrom was clearly walking a delicate line between the two men, wanting to satisfy White's sense of what Charlotte should look like without offending Williams. To White she wrote of telling Williams that "he had managed to make Charlotte a more *spider-y* attractive figure. But I said you might like Charlotte and if so she would be all right with us, of course."[226] This letter indicates the extent of her interest in Williams' illustrations, right down to suggestions for small improvements. For example, she thought that if Williams made her nose dots larger, Charlotte would be more attractive—and more of a spider. Removing her mouth line, she thought, would make her less like a person.

In a letter to White detailing how Williams had made some of the revisions on the sketches that morning in her office, Nordstrom suggests how eager he was to oblige her. In the days before the internet and the fax machine, the editor and illustrator were at the mercy of hand couriers, who had to rush the drawings between Williams' studio and Nordstrom's and White's offices, with Williams awaiting further instructions: "Will you telephone me this afternoon if you possibly can?" wrote Nordstrom to White. "Garth agreed with me and said that if *you* wanted less of an actual face he'd do some more samples. He and I would like to get Charlotte and Fern settled before you go to Maine, and I'm sure you would too."[227] But in the end, Nordstrom put White's interests first. Once, as one of White's letters was being retyped at Harper & Brothers to be circulated to Williams, she instructed the typist to omit a sentence from White indicating that he was "quite willing to be overruled on any or all." This was apparently a sentiment she did not think it wise for Williams to see.[228] Moreover, she may have recognized the extent to which White would not be flexible over artistic matters.

Years later, White would remember his collaborations with Williams with deep ambivalence. In a letter to Nordstrom in 1969, he expressed gratitude to Williams especially for his "superb" representation of Stuart Little. But he also wrote, "His Charlotte (until we abandoned everything and just drew a spider) was horrible and would have wrecked the book."[229] A letter he had written Louis de Rochement in 1961 provides more context for this later, harsh assessment. White had explained that:

> When Garth Williams tried to dream up a spider that had human characteristics, the results were awful. He tried and tried, but we ended up with a Charlotte that was practically right out of a natural history book, or, more precisely, out of my own brain. And I pulled no punches in the story: the spider in the book is not prettified in any way, she is merely endowed with more talent than usual.[230]

This letter intimates that White had been frustrated with Williams at times, though they had ultimately been able to come to agreement.

Nordstrom also brokered further negotiations over the drawings of the human protagonists in the story. Apparently, Williams initially struggled with how to draw Fern, and in particular how to establish the scale of her human proportion. In the end, he solved the problem by working off earlier sketches, drawings, and photographs of Fiona, his own daughter, who was by then an adolescent. Later he would send her a signed copy of the book, with the endearing note, "Hope you recognize yourself on page 6."[231]

Illustration for *Charlotte's Web*.

In the meantime, Nordstrom wrote to reassure the Whites that "I gathered that Fern will appear in many drawings, and I think you will both like her. I think [Williams] meant he didn't want to show Fern in *all* the drawings simply because if he does Charlotte and the other creatures will have to be so small. At any rate, you will both see sketches and I know you will find Garth still open to suggestions."[232] Later Nordstrom wrote to ask what White thought: "How do you like Fern? Please be absolutely frank about Fern because Garth can make her any sort of a little girl you want."[233] Always more comfortable drawing animals than people, Williams also struggled with the question of how to represent Mr. and Mrs. Arable, Fern's parents. In a later letter to Peter Neumeyer, he claimed he had drawn them to resemble E. B. and Katherine White. But—as Neumeyer points out—it is the Littles, not the Arables, who resemble the Whites, and Williams, who was 71 when he wrote the letter, was probably misremembering.[234]

Illustrating *Charlotte's Web* was a very different kind of project from the work Williams had done on the Little House series. Though with White he also retained the choice of which scenes to illustrate, he had less artistic independence than he had had with Laura Ingalls Wilder. With White and Nordstrom, he frequently had to respond to suggestions, or, on occasion, even mild complaints. For example, White fussed over Fern's hairstyles, writing to Nordstrom about one illustration that he wished "Garth would give Fern the horsetail [sic] hairdo again instead of the pigtails." He thought Williams had drawn her with too much hair, given the time that had passed since an earlier illustration.[235] He also wrote to Nordstrom that he was unhappy with the way Williams drew the barn: "Garth has drawn a set of double barn doors on a track, but they are at least twelve feet off the ground. Anybody coming through those doors would fall and break his neck. They (the doors) ought to be on ground level—on the side of the barn, not the end of the barn."[236] On another occasion, Nordstrom called Williams out on a British expression that popped up in an illustration. He had to change to word "Ices" to read "Ice" (as in "ice cold") on the awning of an ice-cream stand at the county fair.[237]

Yet Williams found his stride in the representation of Wilbur, the book's animal protagonist. White may have been keen to resist any tendency to "disney-ize" Wilbur—a desire that was, ironically, to be

Illustration for *Charlotte's Web*.

ignored much later in a Hanna-Barbera animated cartoon version of the book.[238] But in Wilbur, he gave his illustrator a deep and empathetic character to draw. Williams took full advantage of the situation to animate him, giving him a wide spectrum of lively facial expressions, ranging from utter despondency brought on by loneliness,

to deep contentment as he experiences his first buttermilk bath.

Illustration for *Charlotte's Web*.

As Neumeyer writes, Wilbur is a "creature of mercurial emotions, mood swings, hysteria."[239] Williams drew facial expressions that facilitated the reader's identification with the character's deep feelings, a capacity he had developed in his illustrations for the Little House books. For example, what child reader would not sympathize with Wilbur's tearful countenance as he ponders the possibility of his own death?

Williams gave the book's audience a young pig, someone perhaps not unlike them in his carefree and joyful physicality, his capacity to live in

Illustration for *Charlotte's Web*.

the moment and to experience the simple pleasures of a sensual existence, as well as his tendency to feel the deep pain brought on by a temporary sense of helplessness and despair.

Also, as in the Little House series, Williams privileged a sense of dynamism, often capturing both animal and human protagonists in mid-motion, and this served White's narration well.

Perry Nodelman sees *Charlotte's Web* as a static novel in which action is retarded by poetic descriptions. He suggests that Williams' "energetic" drawings balance "the often dreamy music of the text."[240] As he further explains, "They ensure that there is not a surfeit of inactive exposition."[241] Similarly, Neumeyer appreciates how Williams' illustrations imbue the story with energy and enthusiasm.

Williams occasionally took license with White's text. For example, as Charlotte spells out the word "terrific" in her web to describe Wilbur, White writes nothing about Wilbur's expression. Yet in his illustration, Williams provided a broad, almost goofy grin—offering what Neumeyer calls "testimonial to Williams' own creative bent."[242] Neumeyer refers

to this collaboration between writer and illustrator as a "duet"— a term that captures well the two-part harmony emanating from every great children's book.[243] Pictures "do not merely reproduce what the words say," writes Neumeyer, they enrich, enliven, deepen, broaden; they create a denser and

Illustration for *Charlotte's Web*.

more comprehensive reading experience.[244] Williams' contributions to the texture of *Charlotte's Web* are decisive.

For example, as Neumeyer notes, Williams drew Fern among the animals gathered in the barnyard to discuss Wilbur's problem in Chapter XII: "White says nothing about her being there for that amusing barnyard planning session, and it is solely because Williams put her in the illustration that we know she was there."[245] It is not exactly an oversight on White's part, but Williams saw what a perfect note it

Illustration for *Charlotte's Web*.

Illustration for *Charlotte's Web*.

was for Fern to participate, silently, in the scene and placed her there on his own accord. In still other ways, Williams seems to have kept track of Fern's role in the story and to have been especially attentive to her abiding presence in the narrative. After all, her profile on the cover illustration announces her importance to the story, as her gaze directly fixes on Charlotte.

A now famous illustration from the first chapter of the book, in which Fern cradles the infant Wilbur while bottle-feeding him, beatific expression on her face, directly alludes to innumerable iconic representations of the Madonna and Child from the western artistic tradition (see page 110 above). Though the narration describes Fern as sitting "with her infant between her knees," Williams depicts her as seated cross-legged. This detail reminds the reader of Fern's girlishness. The quasi-spiritual tone, coupled with the representation of pure girlhood evoked by this representation, belongs to the illustrator, and not the author, who only writes, "The pig, though tiny, had a good appetite and caught on quickly."[246] Beginning with the girlish energy of his own daughter, Williams produced an exquisite drawing.

Certainly the "duet" between author and illustrator can have its moments of dissonance as well. Based on archival material, Neumeyer surmises that Williams drew a frontispiece for the book depicting Templeton the rat, which White may have rejected—possibly because such placement of another rodent character might suggest that *Charlotte's Web* was a sequel to *Stuart Little*.[247] Williams does seem to have been drawn to certain transgressive qualities in Templeton. In any case, it is clear from elsewhere in his work that Williams greatly enjoyed drawing not just mice and rats (think Miss Bianca or Tucker Mouse) but also other rodent-like creatures.

The effectiveness of Williams' illustrations for *Charlotte's Web* has never been in question, though critics have had differing opinions about the nature of that effectiveness. The powerfully influential librarian Ann Carroll Moore, who had already attempted to scuttle *Stuart Little*, read White's new novel in manuscript and wrote to Ursula Nordstrom with mixed praise and criticism. But she added, "I've no doubt Garth Williams will make a fascinating book out of it," as if she expected the illustrations to overcome her misgivings about the text.[248] In her subsequent review of the book, she further emphasized her disapproval of White's story while referring elliptically to "Garth Williams' fine pictorial interpretation . . . Fern, the real center of the book, is never developed. The animals never talk. They speculate. As to Charlotte, her magic and mystery require a different technique to create that lasting interest in spiders which controls a childish impulse to do away with them."[249] That Williams paid special attention to Fern, giving her nearly mythical status in some illustrations, may have soothed the qualms of this cantankerous critic and made, in her opinion, for a better book.

The illustrations also caught the attention of the Harper sales force. When Ursula Nordstrom presented *Charlotte's Web* to them, she noted an uncommon reaction. As Michael Sims records, "Usually the salesmen didn't have patience for much synopsis of a book, but Nordstrom found to her surprise, as she distributed copies of some of Garth Williams' illustrations, that the men were examining the pictures closely and asking for more and more details. They seemed to find the premise of the book touching—and they quickly became enthusiastic about its sales potential."[250] Yet despite this evidence of Williams' important contribution, most early reviews—and many subsequent reflections—praised Williams' drawings as pure manifestations of White's imagination. This assumption that the drawings function as little more than representations of the author's idea resulted from Williams' own conscious decision to serve the text. As we have already seen in connection with the Little House books, Williams considered the artist's responsibility to be to "see everything with the same eyes" as the author.[251]

This is not, by any means, to underestimate Williams' powerful artistic techniques. Perry Nodelman has argued that in the best illustrations for black and white children's books, the artist emphasizes line over shape. Artists, and particularly skilled draftsmen like Williams, "have numerous complexities of line that either imply activity in the environment or else force the eye into activity in its act of perception."[252] Nodelman helps us to see how, in Williams' art, the picture doesn't present itself in blocks of space, but rather develops in the movement of line across the page. The viewer's eye follows and engages the speed and energy of the line's movement. A dynamic, skillful line contributes to the liveliness of the text. In other words, like other artists of the early twentieth century—the Synthetic Cubists, for example—Williams deftly opts for line over shape or form, thereby creating drawings that display vigor and an economy of means.[253]

Was *Charlotte's Web* Williams' best work? Critics remain divided on this topic.

Michael Sims, for one, considered the illustrations for George Selden's *The Cricket in Times Square* to be his finest achievement.[254] To be sure, the work for *Charlotte's Web* was accomplished during a period of terrific artistic production and experimentation. Williams had recently finished illustrations for three books by Margaret Wise Brown and a fourth, *Mister Dog*, was published the same year as *Charlotte's Web*; and he had tried his hand at a youth novel of his own, *Benjamin Pink* (1951). Later in the decade came work with Charlotte Zolotow, Margery Sharp, Natalie Savage Carlson, Russell Hoban, and many others, vastly expanding his repertoire of animals, children, scenes, and actions and expanding his techniques and media to ink wash and oil painting. Yet in this collaboration with E. B. White the combination of words and pictures—the duet spun by writer and artist—is supremely effective. *Charlotte's Web* is firmly established as one of the small handful of masterpieces of children's literature.

Cover Illustration for *Mister Dog*.

Chapter Five

GOLDEN YEARS, GOLDEN BOOKS (1952-1962)

*A*s Williams explained to an interviewer for *Rocky Mountain News* in 1955, though Aspen was "a little isolated from the main currents of art," it also gave him the time and solitude to create. Moreover, he continued, "the airplane and modern periodicals do much to overcome geographical isolation," so he had little trouble staying in touch with collaborators and publishers. The magnetism of Aspen's developing cultural scene was helpful, too: "Most creative people can get away from major art centers for long periods before they have to go back to get in touch with things. The International Design Conference and the people who come to Aspen keep us well in touch with developments in the world of art." Every morning between 9:00 and 10:00, Williams walked to his studio over the Post Office in the Elks

Building and set to work. He regarded his art as a matter of discipline and application and told his interviewer, "Actually, of course, art is a very straight-forward business. You don't have to wait for inspiration."[255] The result of his focus is evident in the extraordinary productivity of his Aspen years—a dozen Little Golden books, three volumes in Natalie Savage Carlson's "Happy Orpheline" series, two volumes in Margery Sharp's "Rescuers" series, and the beginnings of two other series, George Selden's *A Cricket in Times Square*, and Russell Hoban's *Bedtime for Frances* all date from this period.

And yet Williams was neither satisfied with nor ever completely fulfilled by his work as an illustrator. Sculpture, the focus of his early training, was still his first love, and his ongoing ambition was to bring sculpture to the forefront of the American art scene. In the interview, Williams had a bold and, in retrospect, rather wistful prediction about the role that sculpture would eventually play: "We've been rather unconscious toward it . . . but we're growing in consciousness. I think as time goes on architecture and sculpture will get back together again. More and more sculpture will be incorporated in modern architecture—to the benefit of both."[256] In the meantime, with the burden of supporting a family upon him, Williams turned to illustration as his main employment. It remained his way of making a living while he harbored his loftier ambitions.

Still, in the interview Williams also admitted that, whatever its limitations, illustration had real rewards as well. He remembered overhearing two children talking about books. When the younger one asked what all the words in the book were for, the older answered, "Oh, they're for the people who can't read the pictures."[257] Making the pictures for children to "read" was his specialty and his gift, and Williams loved knowing that he had succeeded. As a survey of his major drawings from this period reveals, Williams' most significant contribution to children's literature lay in the unique fashion in which he was able to create animals. Though they possess human traits, and often engage in human activities, these animals remain unmistakably animalistic. Avoiding the trap of projecting the human onto the animal at the expense of the beast, Williams created creatures who remind us of our affinity to the natural world. At the same time, Williams' creatures are most endearing for what they reveal about their animal origins, their separate inclinations, and their mysterious, un-human motivations.

Yet most of Williams' earliest attempts at illustration entailed the human, not animal, world. Even then, he had labored to make the pictures tell a story the words weren't revealing. In the process, he honed his skills at drawing a range of possible expressions, as well as a range of movement. These skills would later be useful when he turned to drawing animals. His earliest commissions, aside from *Stuart Little*, were for books aimed at adults—Ernest Poole's *The Great White Hills of New Hampshire*, Raymond Andrieux's *Tux 'n Tails*, Damon Runyon's *In Our Town*. In these initial projects he experimented with different styles, creating different effects. *The Great White Hills of New Hampshire* (1946) is illustrated with woodcuts in a densely crosshatched style, rather heavy and dark, and many of the pictures are boilerplate

Illustration for *The Great White Hills of New Hampshire*.

mountain views: in one picture, the full moon shining over a mountain lake; in another, thick forest, deep snow, a listening deer. But even here Williams took every opportunity to humanize and animate scenes. For a short chapter titled "Hill Village Stores," Williams put a cheerful group around a pot-bellied stove.

"Only here and there in villages may one still find some friendly place of gossip and trade, like the Aldrich store in Franconia, to give still some idea of the place which the country store once held as a center of mountain life," wrote Poole. Williams captured the spirit of that place with the cracker barrels and burlap bags, the lounging men in full winter gear, and the "Post Office" sign reminding us that the store really was the focus of village life.[258] For Damon Runyon's *In Our Town* (1946) Williams used the line-drawing style that would be so effective in *Charlotte's Web*, and already the drawings are suffused with antic energy, though here that style is notably influenced by the James Thurber school of *New Yorker* cartooning.

Illustration for *In Our Town*.

Even in what nearly amounts to apprentice work, the deft strength of Williams' mature art is evident. For a scene depicting Runyon's gamblers at their cards, Williams gave each man a specific character and specific emotion, generating a rich psychology:

Runyon's anecdote illustrates the general gambler's rule, "NEVER BLAME THE BOOSTER FOR WHAT THE SUCKER DOES." Williams' picture shows the booster, the sucker, the tension of the game, and the clash and blending of a roomful of personalities.[259]

So far, we have discussed Williams' considerable success as an illustrator of many notable children's classics, including *Stuart Little* and *Charlotte's Web*. In this chapter, we return to 1946 in order to trace the development of Williams' special talent for drawing animals. This chapter surveys his other notable accomplishments as an illustrator of animals, including his contribution to the Little Golden Books.

Illustration for *In Our Town*.

As he wrote in his autobiography, around the time he was doing drawings for *The New Yorker* and before he got the commission for *Stuart Little*, he "worked for a new magazine published by Howell Soskin, illustrating stories. Mr. Soskin thought I could make a children's book out of an old English rhyme. I did."[260] The result was *The Chicken Book*, a new departure for Williams in a number of ways. It was his first attempt to illustrate for an audience of children rather than adults, and it gave a new and different turn to Williams' gift for whimsy. The ink and wash technique marked his first published exploration of color, and the palette of yellows, browns, and greens supplied an inviting warmth to the story. *The Chicken Book* also marked the beginning of his long engagement with animal subjects, a decisive shift in the direction of Williams' career. The story of *The Chicken Book* is based on a traditional children's poem and it is very simple. Each of five chicks wishes for something:

Said the first little chicken,

With a queer little squirm,

"I wish I could find

A fat little worm."

Illustration for *The Chicken Book*.

And so on through a fat slug, yellow meal, a green leaf, and a gravel stone. These are no doubt birds, yet each chick is gently humanized; the beaks are pulled down into a frown, and a few strokes above the eyes hint at very un-avian eyebrows, giving them distinctive emotions.

There is a touch of humor, as well, in the fact that each chick fails to see the thing he or she wants lying near at hand—just around a stalk of grass or behind a stick. In the end the mother hen scolds her brood and tells them how to get the things they want:

"Now see here," said the mother,

From the green garden patch,

"If you want any breakfast,

Just come here and SCRATCH!"

In the final picture the chicks have found what they wanted to eat and look pleased.

With the completion of *The Chicken Book*, Williams joined the company of a long line of those who have used animals to divert children. At least since the time of Aesop's fables, animal stories have instructed and entertained. Such stories were intended for both adults and children alike, with little sense that pre-adults warranted their own version of moral instruction. However, beginning in the eighteenth century with the recognition of childhood as a discrete period of human development, authors began to exploit an assumed affinity between the child and the animal to create a distinct brand of children's literature. One of the earliest examples is Thomas Boreman's *Description of Three Hundred Animals* (1730), in which animals serve as moral emblems to "engage the attention" of children.[261] Later in the eighteenth century, animals were given life and the ability to speak in Dorothy Kilner's *Life and Perambulations of a Mouse* (1784). Here the author's intent shifts from instruction to identification; the child is not presented with a lesson to be learned but encouraged to sympathize with the mouse's life, to share the mouse's emotions, and to draw her own conclusions about how she should treat animals.

A decisive shift in the depth, sophistication, and artistry of children's literature in English came with Lewis Carroll's *Alice's Adventures in Wonderland* (1865). Alice, to be sure, was human, but most of the other characters, from the White Rabbit to Bill the Lizard and the Mock Turtle, were animals cunningly characterized by Carroll and brilliantly illustrated by John Tenniel. The fretful anxiety of the white rabbit, the hapless subjection of Bill the lizard, and the lazy menace of the blue

Caterpillar were rendered by Carroll with a deft and subtle touch, and Tenniel's illustrations captured perfectly their individual personalities.

Alice was the first of a parade of distinguished successors' stories marked by complexity of character and psychological insight. In Britain there were Beatrix Potter's Lake District realism and luminous watercolors beginning with *The Tale of Peter Rabbit* (1902); Kenneth Grahame's full-fledged animal novel, *The Wind in the Willows* (1908), best known in the 1933 edition illustrated by Ernest Shepard; A. A. Milne's *Winnie the Pooh* (1926), also illustrated by Shepard. In the United States, the quasi-folk "Uncle Remus" tales of Joel Chandler Harris, begun in a newspaper column in 1876, with their Southern setting and dialect, preceded local-color animal realists like Cape Cod's Thornton W. Burgess (*Old Mother West Wind,* 1910). All these works, with their relatively complex plots, sophisticated psychology, lyrical language, robust humor, and gentle irony, expanded the resources of children's literature and created a body of work that appealed not only to children but to the adults who, more often than not, had to read the stories aloud to their sons and daughters.

In the second quarter of the twentieth century this evolving literary tradition was confronted, challenged, and modified by a new techno-logical development: animated cartoons. Most notably, Walt Disney's Mickey Mouse made his first appearance in 1928 and rapidly became an inescapable American icon. Shrewd, artistically gifted, superbly organized, and ruthlessly commercial, Disney pushed the boundaries of animation and created an empire that was designed to lodge the image of Mickey everywhere in the United States and around the world. Disney anthropomorphized his mouse far beyond any previous literary animal. Mickey wears white gloves, red shorts, and puffy yellow shoes. His face and ears, three conjoined circles, look nothing like a real mouse's; he is only a mouse by a cartoon convention. He drives a car and plays golf. He has a house in the suburbs, a girlfriend, and a pet dog. He is in fact a sort of American Everyman, with Everyman's problems and aspirations, filtered through a child's sensibility.

The astonishing popular and commercial success of Mickey Mouse has of course created backlash against the "disneyfication" of American cultural life, which was widely regarded as sheer sentimentality, particularly among those who consider themselves serious artists. E. B. White, for one, stoutly resisted any attempt to give the animals about whom he wrote any anthropomorphized features. That's why he gave Williams such a hard time about representing Charlotte the spider and why he later remarked that Williams had nearly ruined the book by giving Charlotte a Mona Lisa face in his earliest sketches. White wanted the spider and all the farm animals to look like animals, with no trace of sentimentality.

But Disney's characters went beyond mere anthropomorphizing. The huge eyes, the round heads, the perky ears, and winning expressions are all characteristics of a process called "neoteny"—a term for the persistence of infantile features in an adult. Infant animals and humans have a different ratio of bodily relations than will occur in adult forms. Heads are much larger in relation to bodies, and the heads tend to be much rounder than in adult forms, which elongate. Eyes are larger in the face and rounder than adult eyes; hands and feet are larger in proportion to the rest of the body. Moreover, human beings seem to find these characteristics broadly appealing. Study after study has found that men find neotenized female faces more attractive than adult ones. Small dogs, of the lapdog varieties—Chihuahuas, Boston Terriers, Pekinese, and so on—with their round heads and eyes have been bred to neotenized standards. So have cartoon characters. Mickey Mouse, Betty Boop, Woody Woodpecker—whether consciously or not, Disney and the flood of animators who followed in his wake were drawing on a nearly universal response to neoteny—the "cute" factor.[262]

That cuteness is, of course, exactly what E. B. White despised and tried to stamp out wherever he found it, including in Garth Williams' illustrations. But Williams, while never going to Disney's lengths, was quite willing to use neotenized characters when it served his purpose. The chicks of *The Chicken Book*, with their round heads and eyes, demonstrate the point. No doubt they are first and foremost birds. Yet beneath their yellow down, they are also easily recognized as infants, pouting and mewling when they can't have their way, excited and happy when they can. They contrast sharply with the mother hen, whose adult features look coarse, awkward, and vaguely threatening by comparison. *The Chicken Book* adopts the perspective of a child in a grown-up's world and invites the reader to share that perspective. Though the chicks are not nearly so anthropomorphic as Stuart Little, they share with Stuart a range of human ambitions and emotions, and Williams' illustrations successfully combine the animal and the human with rare subtlety, humor and empathy. To be sure, his later work didn't always achieve this standard of excellence; one could certainly find *Baby Animals* (1952) maudlin and superficial. But in his early work for children, Williams already displayed the touch of genius that would put his work in the very first rank of picture book artists.

The same year that *The Chicken Book* was published, 1946, also marked Williams' first collaboration with Margaret Wise Brown on *Little Fur Family*. Ursula Nordstrom, Brown's editor at Harper Brothers, was so pleased with the success of *Stuart Little* that she decided Williams would be the perfect illustrator for Brown's new manuscript and introduced the two. According to Brown's biographer, they proved to be a perfect match, not only artistically but personally as well. They shared a lightly subversive attitude toward the serious business of the world and bandied jokes at a dizzying rate: "When he and Margaret got together, new book ideas flew back and forth so freely that they soon adopted the joking precaution of 'copyrighting' their more promising utterances in mid-sentence."[263] Brown's story gave Williams plenty of leeway for his illustrations as well. "Miss Ursula Nordstrom sent me the MSS. [sic] soon after I had finished Stuart Little," Williams wrote later, "and assumed I would illustrate it in pen-and-ink. It became my first children's book in full color. I used oil-color on illustration board and painted the size of the library edition."[264] Though the title of the book is *Little Fur Family*, the species of the family is unspecified. They aren't named as cats or dogs or bears or monkeys, and Williams' pictures not only keep the ambiguity of species but seem to make each member of the family a slightly different indeterminate furry specimen—a sort-of ursine father, a rather feline mother, a canine grandfather.

Illustration for *Little Fur Family*.

But the indeterminacy of the animals is only the beginning of the strangeness of *Little Fur Family*. The language of the story itself has a rhythm and cadence that can only be Margaret Wise Brown's.

There was a little fur family

warm as toast

smaller than most

in little fur coats

and they lived in a warm wooden tree.[265]

The setting, with its images of softness, warmth, coziness, and perfect safety, is recognizably the same as in Brown's most famous book, *Goodnight Moon* (published a year later, 1947, with illustrations by Clement Hurd). But where the coziness of *Goodnight Moon* leads to the perfect interiority of sleep, the little fur child goes out from his home—somehow losing his clothing in the process—into a vertiginous wood.

A "wild wild wood," and yet hardly frightening—wild flowers, wild nuts, wild grass, with nothing more threatening than a sneeze. There the fur child catches "a little tiny tiny fur animal / The littlest fur animal in the world." Brown's text doesn't say so, but Williams' picture makes the tiny animal a double of the little fur child.

Illustration for *Little Fur Family*.

The fur child is the one who might be a threat here, but he behaves with the gentlest of intentions, kissing it on its nose and putting it "gently back in the grass." Then, as evening comes on and "the sky grew wild and red," the fur child runs home (clothing mysteriously restored) and is carried off to bed by his father. His parents sing him to sleep. So an ancient classic pattern of exile and return ends in safety and sleep—"warm as toast" indeed.

The comforting familiarity of the narrative pattern, however, barely contains something strange and dangerous about *Little Fur Family*. At least one critic, in fact, has compared Brown's book with surrealist art, as a work that is "reflective of . . . the 'irrational' aspects of the surreal art form, like the fantastical and the strange. . ."[266] The first and most obvious element of the surreal was the original cover of the book. As a marketing

Original edition of *Little Fur Family* bound in rabbit's fur.

gimmick, Simon & Schuster made the cover of actual rabbit fur.

The idea was to compete with Dorothy Kunhardt's *Pat the Bunny*, the hugely successful Golden Book published in 1940, with its various objects a child could stroke and scratch. *Little Fur Family*, similarly, could be stroked and patted by a child as if the book itself were a member of the family, and in at least some cases it worked that way. Ursula Nordstrom passed on to Williams and Brown "a report from a mother whose little boy had held open his fur-bound copy of *Little Fur Family* at dinnertime and tried to feed the book his supper."[267] But if the cover evoked furry animals for some children, for at least some of their parents it evoked quite a different thing: the surrealist art-object,

Le Déjeuner en fourrurer.

"Breakfast in Fur" (Le Déjeuner en fourrure) by Méret Oppenheim, a tea cup, spoon, and saucer covered entirely in fur.

Comparing the visual impact of furry book and furry cup, Anna Panszczyk has written, "both these works appear to thrust the audience into an immediate surreal experience through the recognition of a familiar object (the picture-book narrative and form, the tea cup with its saucer and spoon) that is physically and visually swathed in the irrational and fantastic (fur)."[268] Though this kind of analysis may seem overwrought when applied to a children's book, Brown herself might well have fully agreed with it. Williams noted that in the wake of the success of *Little Fur Family* she surrounded herself with fur objects:

> In her little house in Cobble Court, she had fur cushions, a fur-covered pipe, fur hats, and I seem to remember fur pajamas; along with many other things covered in fur. The fur used in the FUR FAMILY was rabbit fur, but she had a Mink edition or two for herself she told me. In Italy and (Sweden?) a different fur was used; and the Italian proved not only better fur, but perhaps the words were even funnier than they could be in english [sic].[269]

Illustration for *Little Fur Family*.

Other uncanny and dreamlike effects in Williams' illustrations add to the surreal atmosphere of *Little Fur Family*. In the early pages of the story, the fur child has a red ball that is so important to him that he takes it into his morning bath, and he is holding it as he runs out to play. Later the ball disappears, but it is echoed in the red balls on the mother's slippers and the red interior of the father's mouth as the fur child is sung to sleep at the end.

Moreover, the doubling of the fur child and the "little tiny tiny fur animal" that he finds—a doubling created by Williams' picture, not by Brown's text—is a regular device of the uncanny in narrative, as in Edward Albee's play *Tiny Alice* (1964), where a tiny version of the protagonist herself apparently exists in a dollhouse on the stage. It's evident that Williams responded enthusiastically to the strange tone and playful freedom of Margaret Wise Brown's prose, and that he added to and intensified its surreal dimension. *Little Fur Family* established a working relationship that would be reflected in all the collaborations between the two artists.

Brown was so pleased with *Little Fur Family* that when she was approached by an editor at *Good Housekeeping* to do a monthly page for young children, she expressed her eagerness to have Williams as her collaborator. Their first story, titled "One Eye Open," appeared in the April 1948 issue. They were more than just collaborators, too; in July of 1948, Williams and Dorothea were among Brown's houseguests at Vinalhaven, off the coast of Maine. Meanwhile, Brown made a more serious and far-reaching decision about their future work together. For several years Brown had worked with Clement Hurd, who had illustrated two of her most successful books, *The Runaway Bunny* (1942) and *Goodnight Moon* (1947). Brown had sent the manuscript for her next book, *Wait Till the Moon is Full*, to Hurd and asked him to illustrate a specific scene as a sample. Hurd complied, producing what he later claimed was the finest single piece of work he had ever done. After receiving the sample, however, Brown told Hurd she was dissatisfied and wanted Williams to illustrate the book. As Leonard Marcus reveals in his biography of Brown, there was probably more to this decision than her admiration of Williams' artistry. Brown was at that time engaged in a passionate relationship with another woman, Michael Strange (born Blanche Oelrichs), and while Hurd and his wife disapproved of the liaison, Williams did not. "Williams had gotten on well with Michael from their first meeting, when he mentioned being distantly related to the Barrymores; he came to believe that Michael had helped Margaret break out of the conventional

mold of her family upbringing."[270] This element of acceptance and encouragement reinforced the playful imaginative compatibility of the two artists and cemented their friendship.

Wait Till the Moon is Full is another of the dreamy, wistful nighttime books that Brown loved to make. "Once upon a time in the dark of the moon there was a little raccoon."[271] The little raccoon wants to know

Illustration for *Wait Till the Moon Is Full*.

about the things he hears in the night—the wind blowing through branches, the flight of night birds, the hooting of an owl—but his mother tells him to be patient, to wait until the moon is full. While he waits (for two weeks, as we know), she goes about her household chores and sings him songs about the moon. Williams illustrated the story with simple brown and black drawings, capturing both the *nachtmusik* mood of the cozy setting and the warm relationship between mother and son.

When the little raccoon's patience is finally rewarded and he gets to go out into the moonlit night, the illustration bursts into full color.

Under the full moon, the mothers knit and gossip while their children swing, skip rope, play ball. The reader shares the little raccoon's sense

Illustration for *Wait Till the Moon Is Full*.

of release and pleasure into the full-moon world of sociability and play.

The year 1948 saw a further collaboration between Williams and Margaret Wise Brown, one that introduced still another dimension to his work. Shortly after Williams had agreed to illustrate *Little Fur*

Family, he had met Brown for the first time in the offices of the Artists and Writers Guild.[272] In 1942, despite war-time rationing of paper and the loss of artists and other workers to the military draft, Simon & Schuster, in cooperation with the Artists and Writers Guild, had begun publication of the Little Golden Books with twelve titles, including *The Poky Little Puppy*. Brown had been recruited for Little Golden Books a few years later; her first book for Simon & Schuster, *The Golden Egg Book*, with illustrations by Leonard Weisgard, had appeared in 1947. Little Golden Books, stocked in grocery stores rather than book shops and selling for twenty-five cents per copy, enjoyed an instantaneous and huge success; five million books were sold in 1947.[273] There are several reasons for the astonishing ascent of Little Golden Books. One, of course, is the sheer number of children needing amusement; a jump in the number of American births after 1942 exploded with the return of soldiers after World War II. Another factor was Simon & Schuster's merchandising method. Many families did weekly shopping at a grocery store, and a cheap and attractive children's book was an easy purchase alongside the milk and eggs. Moreover, the Little Golden Books featured a modern aesthetic rather different from the hushed piety of much of the librarian-approved children's literature of the time. In the words of one historian of children's literature:

> Deftly straddling the line between traditional representation and modernist abstraction, each of these inventive artists strove for an airy lightness and brightness of being-on-the-page that belonged to the new streamlined age of glass-box skyscrapers, ribbon highways, and casual middle-class suburban living. Festive colors applied in bold, surprising combinations made simply opening one of their books a challenging as well as playful visual adventure.[274]

All these qualities meant that the Little Golden Books were anathema—hardly better than comic books—to the self-appointed gate-keepers of genteel culture, a fact that could hardly have been lost on Williams after his experience with Anne Carroll Moore's attempts to keep *Stuart Little* and *Charlotte's Web* off library shelves.

There was another and still more compelling inducement for authors to work for the Artists and Writers Guild, however: money. Little Golden Books paid its authors very well. Established writers like Brown and Dorothy Kunhardt could choose either a flat-fee payment or an advance against royalties. With her fee for *The Golden Egg Book*, for example, Brown had purchased a Chrysler Town and Country convertible "just to prove to herself that the check was real."[275] The competition for artists meant that other editors—like Ursula Nordstrom at Harpers—had to sweeten contracts in order to get the work they wanted. For Williams, who was always in need of more money to support his growing family and lavish spending habits, the promise of Little Golden Books was irresistible.

Unfortunately, it proved to be an empty promise as far as Williams was concerned. Illustrators, it turned out, were paid much less than writers. Years later, at a low point in his career and life, Williams wrote a long, bitter screed to Ursula Nordstrom, his old friend and editor, detailing the many outrages he felt that publishers had committed against him in the course of his twenty-five years as an illustrator. Among the worst was his experience with Golden Books. Georges Duplaix, then the head of the Artists and Writers Guild, had promised Williams and Dorothea that "we would earn $20,000. Then much more later. . . ."[276] He showed them what he said were the royalty reports of two other Little Golden contributors, Gustaf Tenggren (author of *The Pokey Little Puppy*) and Feodor Rojankovsky (*Frog Went A-Courtin'*) amounting to $40,000 and more in 1948-49. "Do a good job Garth, and we'll all make a lot of money," Duplaix told him. But the actual result was far less rewarding, as his experience illustrating Dorothy Kunhardt's *Tiny Library* showed. Years later, Williams would feel that promises had been unmet—that Kunhardt should have split her royalties with him and that Duplaix had misled him in his estimations of the money that he would make. Williams' letter to Ursula is not altogether coherent at this point, but his sense of betrayal and rage are very clear:

When Georges Duplaix said that I had been paid in full—$1000. for the Tiny Library; and Mrs Kunhardt had split her royalty with me; and she had [sic] received $11,000. already in royalties from the great sales within three months. Mr. and Mrs Kunhardt dined with me at the Harvard Club. They were shocked and frightened. How did Georges Duplaix reason that by [sic] throwing out an artist who's [sic] first book was a great success was good business?[277]

The facts in the case were explained much more clearly in a letter Williams wrote to Lee Lurie, his attorney, in January, 1958. When Georges Duplaix had first approached him, he had proposed that Williams work for Simon & Schuster Children's Books for a year and do one large and three little Golden Books for $5000. When Williams countered that he worked only on a royalty basis, Duplaix had said that "they did not call them royalties, but they paid large bonuses if books were successful. These were literally his words:—'We are all one big happy family and we trust each other.' I said that if he wanted to call royalties a 'bonus' it was allright with me, providing I received them." In lieu of a contract, Duplaix wrote Williams a short letter confirming the arrangement. After Williams had completed illustrations for Margaret Wise Brown's *The Golden Sleepy Book* (a Little Golden Book) and Kunhardt's *Tiny Library* (a Big Golden Book), Duplaix asked him to do a second *Tiny Library*—the first had been an enormous success—for another $5,000. Williams agreed. But those were all the payments he ever received for *The Tiny Library*. There were no bonuses and no royalties, an omission that rankled for years. As he wrote to Lurie, "I understand that the author made $20,000 on the first edition of the first Tiny Library. I visited her and during discussions with her and her husband it came to light that Georges Duplaix told her that I was a very expensive artist and that she had to share her royalty with me, which she thought she was doing at that time."[278] Although Williams was awarded royalties in contracts for other Golden Books, none had nearly the success of the Tiny Libraries. A royalty statement from 1964 shows that in the five printings from its publication in 1951 (over 180,000 copies),

Elves and Fairies had earned Williams a total of $10,030.56.[279] Five other Golden Books brought him a total of $3,064.28.[280] His relationship with the Golden Books had not made him rich—it made him angry.

However, that rage came later. At the time, the Little Golden Books appeared to be a windfall for a needy artist. The first of the Little Golden Books on which Williams and Margaret Wise Brown collaborated was *The Golden Sleepy Book*, a miscellany of stories, poems, and even a version of the traditional lullaby, "All the Pretty Little Horses," which Brown claimed she had learned from Mammy Ludy Lady Hinton and Sugar Meat Hinton of Halifax, Virginia, with an unusual second verse:

The butterflies and the flies

Are buzzing round your eyes

So go to sleepy little baby

And after you sleep

I'll give you a

Jeep[281]

Williams used a variety of styles in the illustrations, anthropomorphizing rabbits, groundhogs and bears, but rendering horses, birds, and flowers in naturalistic figures. Generally the pictures for *The Golden Sleepy Book* were subdued in color (muted blues, yellows, and green ink and wash or plain black and white drawings) and in activity, as befits pieces meant to lull a child to sleep.

Their next collaboration, *Mister Dog* (1952), was considerably livelier and had particular biographical undertones. For one thing, the dog's name had a special significance: "Once upon a time there was a funny dog named Crispin's Crispian. He was named Crispin's Crispian because he belonged to himself." Crispin's Crispian was in fact the name of Margaret Wise Brown's own dog, "a snappish Kerry blue terrier"[282] whose name came from the famous St. Crispin's Day speech in Shakespeare's *Henry V*, Act IV, Scene III:

This story shall the good man teach his son;

And Crispin Crispian shall ne'er go by,

From this day to the ending of the world,

But we in it shall be remembered—

We few, we happy few, we band of brothers. . .

Williams later remembered that Margaret had been "quite blind to her dog's shortcomings—which were noted by all our friends, such as the number of innocent little dogs he attacked or killed—this dog, Crispin by name, inspired her and me to make the dog [in the story] not unlike him in appearance."[283] The resulting illustrations are brightly

Illustration for *Mister Dog*.

colored and vigorously drawn. Crispin's Crispian is a protean figure who goes through many different phases over his day. Fixing his breakfast, he looks as grumpy and achy as any little old man.

But when he encounters other animals and stops to play, he's all terrier.

When Crispin's Crispian meets a human boy who says he also belongs to himself, he invites the boy to come and live with him and the boy agrees. They buy food for dinner and go home to fix it. Crispin's Crispian's house, as Williams depicts it, is a

Illustration for *Mister Dog*.

rendering of the house Margaret Wise Brown owned in New York. The house in the picture looks ramshackle and hazardous, but it opens into a snug home. In many ways, *Mister Dog* is the opposite of the dreamy, soporific spirit of *The Golden Sleepy Book* or the coziness of *Little Fur Family*. Like its predecessors, however, *Mister Dog* revolves around a fantasy of home, of the safe, welcoming space that holds a self-defining, self-reliant family in perfect comfort. "Crispin's Crispian was a *conservative*. He liked everything at the right time—dinner at dinnertime, lunch at lunchtime, breakfast in time for breakfast, and sunrise at sunrise, and sunset at sunset. And at bedtime—At bedtime he liked everything in its own place—the cup in the saucer, the chair under the table, the stars in the heavens, the moon in the sky, and himself in his own little bed."[284] The reassuring orderliness and security of the dog's life are unmistakable. Dog and boy may each belong to himself, but together they have fashioned a perfect family in a middle-class domestic citadel.

Williams illustrated several more of Margaret Wise Brown's texts in later years—eleven in all—but after her death in 1952 there was no more artistic collaboration, no more creative provocation or playful banter. There were also more Little Golden Books for Williams, some solo productions with pictures and little or no text—*Baby Animals* (1952), *Baby Farm Animals* (1953), *Baby's First Book* (1955)—and some with texts by other writers. The first of the solo books, *Baby Animals*, came about because of Williams' dissatisfaction with a proposed collaboration: "A ms. was sent me with this title. I found it very poor. Mawkish, dreary, often too long on each animal. So I sent suggestions for what

Illustration for "The Fairies."

I thought should be the kind of text. They accepted and printed my suggestions."[285] Of the other books, *The Giant Golden Book of Elves and Fairies with Assorted Pixies, Mermaids, Brownies, Witches, and Leprechauns* (1951) brought together twenty poems and stories from a wide variety of sources, including James Stephens, and inspired a wide variety of pictures in a wide variety of moods. William Allingham's poem "The Fairies," for example, is rather ghoulish; the fairies live a wild life "Up the airy mountain," and have no love for humanity. They steal a little girl and think that she is asleep,

But she was dead with sorrow.

They have kept her ever since

Deep within the lake,

On a bed of flag-leaves,

Watching till she wake.

Williams' picture shows the dead Bridget at the bottom of the lake while the fairies, surprisingly ugly characters (as Williams' humanoid figures often were), carry on with their affairs.

Illustration for "The Cannery Bear."

Much more lighthearted is Ray St. Clair's "The Cannery Bear," the story of a bear who is so hungry for salmon that he gets a job at the local cannery in hope of eating as much of it as he wants. He has to dress as a human in overalls and shoes, but the overalls split and he always puts the shoes on backwards.

While the fairies are illustrated in dark, heavy colors, the bear is drawn in a style much more characteristic of Williams' work, with colored pencil and a much lighter, freer touch.

All these projects of the late 1940s and early 1950s with Margaret Wise Brown and the Little Golden books were illustrations in different colored media for short stories or poems and quite different from the work that had won Williams his early acclaim—the pencil drawings for children's novels by E. B. White and Laura Ingalls Wilder. Moreover, it appears that Williams was sometimes bored by the task of representing animals for the Golden Books. In a letter to Nordstrom, he complained that "I have been struggling with *Over and Over* but must dash off the horrible little golden book for S & S. Three bears, three pigs, three kittens, won't take long at all."[286] This sense of tedium prompted him to try his hand at writing and illustrating his own children's novel.

The Adventures of Benjamin Pink was the story of a rabbit who leaves wife and home to go fishing, gets swept away in a storm and cast away on a desert island, finds a treasure, makes his way back home, and discovers that his greatest treasure was the wife he left behind. It is not, however, a very successful tale. In its bare outlines this plot resembles a Margaret Wise Brown story—*The Sailor Dog*, for example, is very similar—but drawn out to much greater length, so that the energy and surprise of Brown's narratives are completely drained away from *Benjamin Pink*. Williams' prose is serviceable at best and rather drab overall. And the illustrations, too, are rather routine. Brown's stories seemed always to provoke a creative overflow in Williams' drawing. When the sailor dog builds a shelter on his desert island, we see his toolbox and various tools, the crazy pile of brick he's using for a chimney, the roughly nailed boards and makeshift door of his shack, a swinging lantern for light, the wrecked ship on the rocks beyond. In a similar moment, Benjamin Pink digs a hole in a sand dune for his home; there are no witty details to enliven the scene. Williams simply seems not to have inspired himself. He never tried to write a children's novel (a longer, more complex narrative) again.

However, he did illustrate novels by others. In 1957 Natalie Savage Carlson's *The Happy Orpheline* appeared, the first in a series about a girl happily living in an orphanage in a French village. In a reversal of the "Little Orphan Annie" theme, the worst thing Brigitte can imagine happening is that she might be adopted away from the caregivers and other orphans she loves. The theme was so unusual that some of those self-appointed gatekeepers of children's morality found it distressing. Ursula Nordstrom felt obliged to respond to one correspondent who wrote that she was "shocked" by it: "We would be deeply sorry if any book we published offended a child. In your letter you say you understand that the little orphan 'lives in constant apprehension of the possibility of adoption.' I do think, ------- [the name has been withheld], that 'constant apprehension' is too strong a description of the extremely vigorous and humorous approach to this story. We trust that the situation in this book will not offend any moderately well-adjusted child with a normal sense of humor."[287] As was her custom, Nordstrom was much more interested in what a child would think of the story than what a moralist might make of it.

For this and the other two titles Williams illustrated in the series, he returned to the pencil and ink style of *Stuart Little, Charlotte's Web*, and the Little House books. While Carlson's Orpheline stories have never achieved the exalted status of E. B. White's or Laura Ingalls Wilder's, they have become enough of "children's classics" to have the second of those illustrated by Williams, *The Family Under the Bridge*, serve as the source for a musical comedy written by the perky television personality, Kathie Lee Gifford. Retitled *Under the Bridge*, the musical had a brief off-Broadway run but was not a hit with reviewers. Charles Isherwood of the *New York Times*, after briefly summarizing the plot as "the heartwarming story of a spunky group of homeless children who befriend a cranky but lovable old bum," wrote, "If that capsule description does a number on your gag reflex—just typing the words, mine performed the glottal equivalent of a triple toe-loop—it's best to give the Zipper [Theater] a wide berth. But even those more forgiving of spoon-fed sentiment may find it hard to warm to 'Under the Bridge.'"[288] Carlson's book is enough of a classic to have suffered a classic fate: a bad adaptation to the stage.

In 2009, Tim Willoughby, a life-long resident of Aspen, reminisced in the pages of the *Aspen Times Weekly* about being in school with Williams' daughter Estyn and about a visit Williams made to their class. Willoughby was the perfect audience for Williams' art. "I knew nothing about book illustrators and might not have been particularly impressed," he wrote, "had not my favorite book, E. B. White's 'Stuart Little,' included Williams' drawings. As a reading-challenged youth I spent more time scanning the illustrations than stumbling through the text. I had carefully 'read' every pen and ink drawing in 'Stuart Little.'" Predictably, Willoughby could not remember, all those years later, what Williams said to the class, but:

> I do remember his effortlessly drawing large rabbits on the blackboard. With just a few quick chalk strokes, he rendered the rabbits I knew from his books. A review of the sequence of his books during his Aspen years reveals that was his "rabbits" period. He authored two of his own books: "The Adventures of Benjamin Pink," (a lesser known but wonderful third grade level rabbit adventure, still in print) and "The Rabbit's [*sic*] Wedding."[289]

It may be only a slight exaggeration to call the mid-fifties Williams' "rabbits' period"—Willoughby could have cited Margaret Wise Brown's *Home for a Bunny* and the many rabbits in *The Golden Sleepy Book* and *The Friendly Book* as more corroboration—but certainly the most noteworthy book of the period, for many reasons, was *The Rabbits' Wedding*.

On the surface of it, nothing about *The Rabbits' Wedding* courts

Illustration for *The Rabbit's Wedding*

controversy. Williams supplied the text as well as the pictures, and the plot is exceedingly simple; a black rabbit and a white rabbit play rabbit games—Hop Skip and Jump Me, Hide and Seek, Find the Acorn, Race Around The Blackberry Bush, and Jump the Daisies and Run Through the Clover. Conflict, such as it is, enters in those intervals when the black rabbit pauses in his play and looks sad. The white rabbit finally gets him to explain what's bothering him:

"What are you always thinking about?" asked the little white rabbit.

"I'm just thinking about my wish," replied the little black rabbit.

"What is your wish?" asked the little white rabbit.

"I just wish that I could be with you forever and always," replied the little black rabbit.

The white rabbit gives the black her paw, they put dandelions in their ears, the other rabbits of the forest come out and dance a "wedding circle" around the two, and other animals (deer, bear, raccoon and beaver) join in. And the little black rabbit never looks sad again.

Like Williams' other self-generated texts, *The Rabbits' Wedding* lacks the energy, charm, and inventiveness of stories by the likes of Margaret Wise Brown and Dorothy Kunhardt and might well have been forgotten among his "other" works. When the book first appeared in 1958, the *New York Times* reviewer wrote, "Children will hug tightly Garth Williams' THE RABBITS' WEDDING . . . if only for the bold pictures of frisky, fluffy bunnies romping in the forest. The tale of this bashful suitor and his lady fair, however, is too low keyed for many readings."[290] Nevertheless, in November of that year, *The Rabbits' Wedding* was listed at #9 on the *New York Times* "Children's Best Sellers," right behind Dr. Seuss's *The Cat in the Hat Comes Back* (#7) and *How the Grinch Stole Christmas* (#8).[291]

A few months later, though, *The Rabbits' Wedding* leapt into the news pages at the *Times*. "Children's Book Stirs Alabama: White Rabbit Weds Black Rabbit" read the headline. The story noted that Williams' book had been attacked in a front page article by the *Montgomery Home News*, a publication of the Montgomery chapter of the White Citizens Council, "on the ground that it promotes racial integration."[292] In response to that attack, Emily Wheelock Reed, the director of the Alabama Public

Library Service division, had removed the book from the open shelves of the library system and placed it on the reserve shelves. This action was evidently a compromise position; *The Rabbits' Wedding* wasn't banned outright but was made more difficult for readers to access, like other works deemed too controversial for their erotic or political content. But whatever obscurity the dim reaches of the reserve shelves bestowed wasn't safety enough for E. O. Eddins, a Senator in the Alabama Legislature, as the *Times* reported two days later. "This book and many others should be taken off the shelves and burned," Eddins declared. Moreover, "In Florida, a columnist in the Orlando Sentinel assailed the book as 'propaganda' for mixing the races and as a 'most amazing example of brainwashing.'" Miss Reed stood her ground, however, and refused any further move toward censoring *The Rabbits' Wedding*.[293]

Williams' response to the controversy was double-edged. Predictably, he denied that his book had any political significance whatever. "I was completely unaware that animals with white fur, such as white polar bears and white dogs and white rabbits, were considered blood relations of white human beings. . . . I was only aware that a white horse next to a black horse looks very picturesque—and my rabbits were inspired by early Chinese paintings of black and white horses in misty landscapes." He added that *The Rabbits' Wedding* "was not written for adults who will not understand it, because it is only about a soft, furry love and has no hidden messages of hate."[294] Yet one can't help noticing that, although *The Rabbits' Wedding* may not have been written with a political message in mind, this response certainly proclaims one: segregation is a form of hate that distorts the thinking of its true believers. The brainwashing has been the other way around, turning innocent and open-hearted children into the denizens of White Citizens Councils.

Of course the controversy didn't end there; Williams' book became a pawn—though a small one—in the national struggle over Civil Rights. For many Northerners, the controversy represented just how absurd racialist thinking could be. "Rabbits are known to be timid creatures, but there is no reason why the forces in charge of the libraries in

Alabama should be pussyfooting or rabbit-footing," went one heavily ironic Letter to the Editor of the *Times*. "They should remove this book from the shelves altogether, both reserved and unreserved. What is more, they should consider removing all the books which have black ink on white paper."[295]

Equally predictably, the publicity generated by the controversy was a marketing manager's dream. "I stole all the headlines," Williams wrote, "even in Russia and Australia—7000 newspapers . . . headlined it. Walter Winchell read it on the air and it had already been a best-seller, but the publicity let people to buy my other books."[296] Harper & Brothers, the publisher of *The Rabbits' Wedding*, even embraced the Alabama episode as a marketing tool. An advertisement in the *Times* on June 5th quoted the earlier review to the effect that it was "A book small children will cherish" and added, "long after today's ugliness has been forgotten." Among the other positive reviews the advertisement cited was, pointedly, one from the *Montgomery (Ala.) Advertiser*: "Very charming and very appealing."[297]

By 1972 all the kerfuffle over miscegenation had long passed, but *The Rabbits' Wedding* made the *New York Times* again for quite an interestingly different reason. Karla Kuskin, herself an author and illustrator of many children's books, published an article titled "Femalechauvinistmousemaker" in which she reflected on her anxiety about drawing mice: how could she do so without "reinforcing destructive sexist roles," as another unfortunate children's writer was accused of doing? Thinking about the way children's literature is sometimes read for political correctness reminded Kuskin of Williams' earlier run-in with the forces of censorship, and she mused on how things had changed—and not changed—since 1958:

> One rabbit was white and the other black. Esthetically, it was an attractive combination. But a good many angry adults were quick to discern the "true" meaning of such marriage, and the book was hustled out of schools and libraries to spare young eyes the disturbing sight of a black animal and a white animal living happily ever after.

Today *Ms.* [i.e. *Ms. Magazine*] might disapprove "The Rabbits' Wedding" for *its* sexist portrayals of a male and female rabbit. The bunny-fur hues would be laughably irrelevant.[298]

In fact, it would be stretching the point to assert that either the black male or the white female has a sexed "role" in *The Rabbits' Wedding*, except, possibly, for the black rabbit's passivity as the "bashful suitor." Over the decades, however, the whole censorship episode has served as a focus of many writers' anxieties about the cultural taboos they may unconsciously violate and the unexpectedly fierce response they may evoke from testy readers.

More recently, the attack on *The Rabbits' Wedding* and its treatment in the media was revisited by Werner Sollors, Professor of English and African American Studies at Harvard University. In an article amusingly titled "Can Rabbits Have Interracial Sex?" Sollors summarizes the ways Williams and others dismissed segregationist fears: "This episode in the cultural history of racial segregation, reads like a version of 'The Emperor's New Clothes,' in which our 'normal,' commonsense perception of rabbit reality is restored through the voice of an honest child that is still free of adult scheming." And yet, as Sollors goes on to say, there are plenty of reasons to hesitate before we accept the analogy. Williams' rabbits are, after all, "quite explicitly anthropomorphic." None of Williams' other work from the "'rabbits' period" (e. g. *Baby Farm Animals* (1959)) presents the reader with a white and a black couple, although *Home for a Bunny* (1961) pairs a brown-and-white rabbit with a pure white. The whole history of children's literature, from its very beginnings in Aesop's fables, is rich in allegorical tales and allegorical readings. Most tellingly, the two rabbits of Williams' story quite clearly fail to recognize "natural boundaries" (if such things can at all be said to exist): "The text might be said . . . to make readers 'care about' the boundary that the book's context was so strongly bent on upholding."[299] In other words, in a segregationist society, *any* story that suggests that love will overcome apparent divisions and separations is a blow at the foundations of that society. There is no such thing as an innocent child's tale. Williams, Sollors argues, was just as dangerous as Senator Eddins thought he was.

By the beginning of 1960, Williams had grown weary of Aspen: "he decided that the winters there with the perpetual shoveling of snow were killing for a man of his age."[300] In addition, Dorothea's health, which had never been strong, was gradually worsening. In a letter to Ursula Nordstrom from Aspen in 1958, Williams had described migraines that plagued Dorothea for months. On one occasion, doctors tried morphine to ease the pain, and, when that failed to work, they injected Novocain into a vein in her head.[301] Hoping for a change of climate, he and Dorothea, who had been visiting Mexico for some years already, began to contemplate a permanent move there. Before he went, his last years in Colorado were highlighted by the beginning of new collaborations for two series of children's novels: the Miss Bianca stories and the Chester Cricket stories.

No controversy swarmed Williams' illustrations for Margery Sharp's *The Rescuers* (1959). Sharp was already an experienced writer, with eight adult titles to her credit, before her first venture into children's literature, and her tale of a mouse organization, The Prisoners' Aid Society, of Miss Bianca, the pampered white mouse whose impetuous courage wins the day, and of Bernard, her rough but decent side-kick, was expertly crafted. The zest with which Sharp wrote can perhaps be suggested by a brief exchange from the beginning of *The Rescuers*. The Chairwoman of the Prisoners' Aid Society is trying to persuade her membership to go to the rescue of a Norwegian poet who is being held in the dreaded Black Castle.

> "It's rather an unusual case," said Madam Chairwoman blandly.
> "The prisoner is a poet. You will all, I know, cast your minds back
> to the many poets who have written favorably of our race—*Her feet
> beneath her petticoat, like little mice stole in and out*—Suckling, the
> Englishman—what a charming compliment! Thus do not poets
> deserve specially well of us?"

"If he's a poet, why's he in jail?" demanded a suspicious voice.

Madam Chairwoman shrugged velvet shoulders.

"Perhaps he writes free verse," she suggested cunningly.[302]

There was never any question about the quality of Sharp's text, but like other authors, she credited Williams' pictures with giving her work an important boost and paid tribute to his meticulous realism. "I think a great deal of the success has been due to Garth Williams' illustrations. His technique is marvelous, but he shows the most wonderfully sympathetic imagination. For example, in one place I describe the chairman's chair as being made from walnut shells, so Garth Williams carpentered a walnut shell into a chair and then drew it."[303]

Illustration for *The Rescuers*.

The Rescuers was published by Little, Brown in 1959 and has been frequently reprinted, but the fact that it is currently in print as a New York Review of Books Classic (along with Dante's *A New Life*, Honoré de Balzac's *The Human Comedy*, and Jorge Luis Borges' *The Invention of Morel*) may be the surest sign of its exalted status. Williams went on to illustrate three more in Sharp's Miss Bianca series: *Miss Bianca* (1962), *The Turret* (1963), and *Miss Bianca in the Salt Mines* (1966).

George Selden Thompson (who published his children's books under the name George Selden), after a Fulbright year in Italy, set out to become a playwright, but after finding little success, began writing for children instead. The inspiration for *The Cricket in Times Square* came from a real cricket: "One late night Selden was in the Times Square subway station when he heard the unexpected sound of a cricket's chirp, which reminded him of his former home in Connecticut. Immediately, a story rushed into his mind about a cricket who, like him, found himself in the hustle and bustle of New York City and was homesick for the countryside."[304] Old city hands Harry Cat and Tucker Mouse were created as companions to Chester Cricket, and an enduring series was born.

Perhaps Williams was especially inspired by the abiding theme of Selden's fiction, which, as Lesley S. Potts has noted:

> Is the importance of understanding and caring between people of different backgrounds, beliefs, and temperaments. Whether the characters involved in a story are as incongruous as a cat, a mouse, and a cricket or a boy, a dog-turned-man, and an Arabian genie, their differences are minimized and their common bond of humanity is stressed. Selden makes each of his characters unique, a personality possessed of strengths and weaknesses; for him, the individual is important, and individuality is precious, but equally important is how each person relates to others and to the world around him.[305]

Unlikely friendship and the creation of a warm, secure environment: these are themes that echo the stories of Margaret Wise Brown.

Or perhaps Williams was intrigued once again (as in *Stuart Little*) by the problem of point of view and perspective created by having to represent three such different-sized creatures in one pictorial space. Certainly the commission came at a time when he was at the fullest maturity of his powers as an artist. Whatever the reasons, Williams' work for *The Cricket in Times Square* ranks with the finest he ever did; indeed, as we have already noted, at least one scholar, Michael Sims, considers the *Cricket* illustrations to be Williams' masterpiece.[306]

Ironically, however, Selden was an irascible and demanding personality. Stephen Roxburgh, an editor who worked with him, remembers Selden as a "brilliant, volatile, fractious character" who was "liberal with his diatribes."

Here's a memorable and formative incident in our relationship. When I was

Illustration for *The Cricket in Times Square*.

new in the business, young and of an academic mindset, I was editing one of the books in Jerry's Cricket series. I deleted a chunk of text and wrote a note in the margin: "Is this absolutely necessary?" When the manuscript came back, Jerry had reinstated the deletion, and had written me a note: "No, it is not absolutely necessary. NOTHING is absolutely necessary, but texture is everything. Shithead!"

Selden was particularly hard on his illustrator, despite the high quality of the product: "Most of our conversations revolved around his complaints about how slow the illustrator of the books, Garth Williams, was."[307] The outcome was worth the wait, however, and *The Cricket in Times Square* received ecstatic reviews. "This fantasy may well be the charmer of the fall season," wrote Polly Goodwin in the *Chicago Sunday Tribune Magazine of Books*. "And if its reviews sound more like a dust jacket blurb, it's because there is a good deal to praise." She hailed the book as "one which deserves shelf space with such congenial companions as 'Stuart Little' and 'Charlotte's Web.'"[308] It was nine years before Selden decided to write a sequel, but when he did, with *Tucker's Countryside* (1969), Williams was again tapped for the illustrations—and for five more titles in the series, ending with *The Old Meadow* in 1987.

If the middle of the 1950s constituted Williams' "'rabbits' period," as Tim Willoughby had called it, the end of the decade brought him back to where it began—to mouse and insect, to the problems of perspective and movement that had engaged him in *Stuart Little* and *Charlotte's Web*, and to the subtle infusion of animal characters with personality. At a time when Disney's animations weren't quite animals or people, Williams humanized the animal and animalized the human. His Stuart Little was both a convincing animal specimen and a believably diminutive gentleman; he was challenged by the physical size of the human world yet capable of deep ratiocination. Similarly, the endearing protagonists of George Selden's classic *The Cricket in Time's Square*—Tucker Mouse, Harry Cat, and Chester Cricket—straddle the line between human and animal. Dominated by their creature appetites, they nonetheless display the lively, knowing expressions of men about town. Williams' consistent ability to find fresh ways to capture those qualities with pencil and pen was his finest achievement. The decade that began with such brilliant promise ended with an unmistakable body of brilliant accomplishment.

Chapter Six

DISCOVERING THE WORLD OF *AMIGO* (1962-1970)

Illustration from *Amigo* (1963).

*I*n 1962, Garth Williams turned fifty. Having successfully established his professional life, he might have expected his personal life to reach equilibrium. The daughters of his first marriage, Fiona and Bettina, had grown up and were finishing their educations in a way that would make any parent proud. Fiona (once the model for Fern in *Charlotte's Web*) received a degree from the University of Toronto in the Faculty of Household Economics and then a Bachelor of Divinity and Master's of Philosophy in Theology from the University of Edinburg. Bettina received her undergraduate degree in Psychology and Philosophy from Queen's University in Ontario, followed by a Master's degree in Education from McGill. In 1965 she would study social work in Mexico. The two adolescent daughters of Williams' second marriage, Estyn and Jessica, were still in school. However, all was not right in Williams' world. He was beginning to tire of life in Aspen, which was evolving out of its quaint provincialism into a fashionable ski resort, and he was looking for an easier—and cheaper—place to live.

At the same time, Dorothea was plagued by several illnesses, including a severe problem with her circulation. These were likely exacerbated by heavy drinking. Her behaviors had become increasingly difficult and impulsive, and her venture in shop keeping had not been a success. The move to Aspen had once seemed like the beginning of a settled and secure life, but it was coming unraveled as Garth and Dorothea grew increasingly alienated. In 1962, Williams returned to Puerto Vallarta, Mexico. His daughter Bettina remembers a previous trip, involving both Dorothea and all four girls, as early as 1959. But 1962 seems to have marked the next major transition in Williams' life and this year would find him more or less permanently relocated in Mexico, bringing not only new cultural experiences and expressions to his work, but also eventually two more wives, two more families.

In many ways, it is not difficult to imagine what attracted Williams to Mexico. He had long demonstrated an interest in vibrant geographic settings, especially when they were populated by like-minded bohemians or artists. At the start of the 1960s, Puerto Vallarta was still a small, Pacific-coast fishing village, albeit one with a stunning beach and colorful colonial past. John Huston's filming of *The Night of the Iguana* transformed the village into an international destination. Based on the play by Tennessee Williams, the movie starred Richard Burton and Ava Gardner. Huston filmed it over a period of ten weeks in the village of Mismaloya, not far from Puerto Vallarta, where the stars temporarily resided. During that time, Burton was accompanied by Elizabeth Taylor, though both were still married to other people. Huston's enthusiasm for the fishing in Puerto Vallarta, along with the notoriety of his stars' private lives, helped draw attention to the place and kick-started its transition to the resort it is today. The timing of Williams' arrival was, then, fortuitous, especially since in 1963 he was able to buy property and to obtain a building permit on the beach. This location gave him access to parties with Burton and Taylor, though he later told his family that he was not impressed by the famous movie actress, who appeared to him to be drunk and unkempt.

For a few years, Williams traveled back and forth between Aspen and Puerto Vallarta, keeping on eye his daughters. In 1962, Dorothea had decided to sell her shop. Soon afterwards she left Aspen, taking Estyn and Jessica with her to Europe. She announced her impending divorce from Williams to the bewildered girls while sitting with them on a beach in Italy. From there, the girls were first sent to a boarding school in Switzerland, then later to the Lycée Francaise in London, though they often traveled to visit Williams during the summers. Meanwhile, Dorothea herself relocated to Cadogan Square, London, where she would live with her friend Zippa Moore, the wife of a British diplomat. The divorce between Williams and Dorothea was finalized April 2nd, 1962 in Colorado.[309] Yet, Williams never fully relinquished the affection for the woman he had once illustrated himself as bravely rescuing from the ogres and dragons. In his 1986 published autobiography, he wrote wistfully that he had been "sure that she would come back" to him, and that he was "heartbroken" that she never came to see him in Mexico.[310]

During his time in Puerto Vallarta, Williams befriended an Italian architect named Giorgio Belloli, a man who is credited with the discovery and renovation of a series of architecturally significant properties dating from colonial times in Marfil. Marfil is itself a suburb of Guanajuato, a city (and a province of the same name) in central Mexico, 220 miles northwest of Mexico City. Belloli had recently purchased several properties there, and he presented Williams with the option of buying one of several haciendas. Williams was attracted to the largest one—an old silver refinery on the outskirts of the city, inexpensively priced. He also bought the adjoining lands. Though the buildings were dilapidated and ill-suited for a residence, Williams was immediately intrigued by their possibilities and excited by the prospect of tapping his former training in architecture for the renovation. He bought the property and spent the next decade or so transforming it into his studio and home. Eventually, in 1996, he would die there.

The property is currently being renovated once again for another family. However, it still contains strong traces of Williams' ideas and his vision of what his Mexican home would be. The walled, labyrinthine compound of nearly 1,000 square meters consists of a large central structure capped by a tall, imposing tower, as well as a number of smaller structures, courtyards, lawns, and gardens. The main structure still bears the architectural traces of the plant for processing silver that it had once been, with a deep well, now empty, beneath one part of the building. (According to local legend, it still contains buried treasure.) During Williams' time, a clear stream—which once brought water into

Garth Williams in the living room of the Guanajuato home.

the plant—ran along one side of the house, so that a main door was accessed by a stone bridge spanning the stream.

Williams carved the domestic spaces—living room, dining room, kitchen, and a series of bedrooms—out of the rambling main stone structure, stringing them out along the long rectangular shape. He capped the living room with a high cupola made of bricks, which collapsed several times until he got the masonry just right, and he had several large fireplaces built, including an enormous one with a copper chimney in the living room. The master suite was tucked up in the tower, and there was a swimming pool one level above the ground, accessed by a flight of stairs. The interior spaces were cathedral-like in their proportions. With high plaster ceiling and stone floors, they were light, airy, and open. Quirky architectural details, including small sculptural stone figures, were scattered throughout the premises. Williams also had a small studio in a freestanding building, just off an interior courtyard, though it has since been torn down.

The property was eventually staffed by eight people, including a gardener, a cook, and Don Pedro, a man whom Williams had once "purchased" while traveling through Oaxaca. Presented with the opportunity to buy himself a slave, Williams was bemused, but readily offered the small sum required to set Don Pedro free. Yet Don Pedro was appalled by his untimely liberation, explaining that he would have no place to go or no way to make his living. Williams brought him back to Guanajuato and installed him as the residential gatekeeper. Don Pedro remained in his post for many years, even when advancing age had rendered him nearly blind and deaf. The property was also inhabited by many animals over the years—including, at one point, five dogs, six cats, and a number of rabbits, including a large Belgian hare. His daughter Fiona also remembers her father catching an otter in order to study it more closely. For this feral addition, he built a small slide into the swimming pool and bought pieces of meat at the local butcher shop.[311]

The family kept several of the dogs for reasons of security. One was a particularly fierce husky that the family remembers for having nearly torn off the arm of an intruder who had dared to scale the high walls protecting the property. Another dog, a puppy named Ringo, was killed by a piece of poisoned meat that had been thrown over the wall, as Williams took the trouble to certify through a toxicology report. (He blamed the servants of the neighbors, the family De La Harpe, for the dog's demise.) [312] There were also struggles with the neighbors over the property lines, so that Williams had to spend time in court in 1964 proving his ownership of a garden.[313] Williams always kept a pistol— which, as his fourth wife recalls, he once used to scare away would be robbers who had approached him at a gas station.

This was the home that Williams originally built for himself and his third wife, Alicia Rayas, whom he had married on August 20, 1962,

Alicia Rayas Williams and son Dylan.

only four months after his divorce from Dorothea. A nineteen-year-old young woman with a small son named Juan, Alicia had been Williams' housekeeper in Puerto Vallarta. She gave birth to Williams' only son, Dylan, on May 27, 1968.

Williams' comments about his third wife in his autobiography are brief, curious, and perhaps a bit unkind: "Alicia was a girl who couldn't say no! So I waited for one of her boyfriends to carry her off, but finally suggested our marriage wasn't working out."[314] When he wrote his autobiography, Williams downplayed the significance of his third family.

Yet he and Alicia were married for fourteen crucial years that included a number of turbulent events. These included spiraling familial and financial pressures; the deaths of Dorothea's and Williams' fathers; the late adolescence and early adulthood of daughters Esytn and Jessica; a spell of ill health; and a major professional disappointment. In his autobiography, Williams did have one fond memory of traveling to Europe with Alicia in 1965, after Dorothea's death. In his recollection, Alicia (who was, after all, younger than his first two daughters), had been "accepted" by his friends and "was very popular."[315]

Alicia, who still lives in the suburbs of Guanajuato, remembers nine very happy years of marriage, including a number of pleasurable visits with Williams' extended family. In order to communicate with them, she taught herself English and French by listening to LP records. On one occasion, Williams' formidable paternal aunt Greta, or Lady Richmond, came to visit them in Mexico. She and Alicia drove in Alicia's Volkswagen bug from Guanajuato to Oaxaca, stopping at every little village and shopping along the way. They spent so much money that on the return trip they couldn't afford to stop and had to drive the whole 400 miles. Williams and Alicia also took a number of trips abroad to visit family in England and France. In England, Alicia worried that her colorful Mexican dress made her too visible in a world where, to her eye, everything was grey, but she was warmly embraced. In France she met Williams' elderly father, Monty, who also welcomed her, as did the other members of his family.[316]

In the end, however, this was the most contentious of Williams' marriages, leaving bitter feelings on both sides. As with his first two wives, Williams found it difficult to make the compromises necessary to keep the marriage alive, and at some point, as his own comment indicates, he seems to have lost all interest in this family. He was never willing to adopt or even recognize Juan ("Johnny") as his son. And although he was initially very happy to have a son of his own, once Dylan became a teenager their relationship was marked by conflict. He did supply support for his son—on one occasion going to considerable trouble to help Dylan get an American passport—but their relationship was far from ideal.

The divorce settlement for the third marriage was similarly conten-tious. According to Alicia, only under duress did Williams provide her with a small house to live in and $10,000 per year child support for Dylan. In a handwritten account entitled "Settlement 1976" found among Williams' archive, he tallied the values of the assets given to Alicia differently. He saw himself as being very generous in giving her not just the house and child support but also two cars, two lots in Puerto Vallarta, and furniture, bedding, and utensils.[317] Whatever the case, the financial repercussions of the divorce were not easy for Williams.

In the decade between 1960 and 1970, Williams had often been struggling financially. First, renovations on the house had been expen-sive and ongoing. Writing to Lucille Ogle, his editor at The Little Golden Books, in 1963, he calculated that he lacked nearly $9000 to complete the work he envisioned, with $1,000 needed in the immediate future.[318] Second, in the first years after his divorce from Dorothea, Williams was apparently making substantial alimony payments to her. As he explained to Ogle, "my finances are very bad, so I am hoping to get as many books in the near future as possible. Dorothea is still un-married, so gets a wallop (I had not planned on) to live from me, the alimony which I thought would only be for a year or two at most." He also playfully claimed, "On my income-tax I have 13 dependents living wholly on my income; quite staggering. The majority being Mexican, and myself, on about $6000 annually. I am therefore planning to write some best-sellers and to win the lottery as well."[319] The reference to the large number of "Mexican" dependents, though obviously exaggerated, suggests that perhaps Williams was sometimes helping members of Alicia's family. Third, in 1964, he was still struggling to sell his house in Aspen. He and Dorothea, who was now battling increasingly poor health, including the threat of gangrene brought on by her circulation problems, had been hoping that the money realized on the sale of the house might be used to pay her medical bills.[320]

He also desperately wanted to buy a car, a "baby" Volkswagen, as he called it. To Ursula Nordstrom at Harper he wrote, "I support nine (including myself) on $6000. I am beginning to wish I could afford a car. Sometimes I wait at the side of the road a whole hour for a bus. Hours are shorter here, but it is tiring for an old Manhattan boy. While the rich man flies across the continent at 200 mph I have been performing like a Beatle for years, why didn't I grow my hair and collect?"[321] Handling Williams with characteristic good humor and sympathy, Nordstrom had earlier assured him, "It is quite silly that you are not enormously rich."[322]

In the meantime, Dorothea was leading a fast-paced life in London, attending a round of social events and parties, and drinking heavily. Now teenagers, Esytn and Jessica were living with her, attending the Lycée Francaise during the daytime and watching with concern as their mother made her social rounds in the evening. They could do little to convince her to curb what were rapidly becoming self-destructive behaviors, given the already perilous state of her health.[323] For a while, it looked as if Dorothea would remarry, as she had fallen in love with an American diplomat and former Rhodes Scholar. However, he was married to a woman who was suffering from cancer and in the end was unwilling to divorce her in order to wed Dorothea.[324]

Against the background of his unstable domestic circumstances, Williams capitalized on previous contacts while also finding new professional opportunities. Harper continued to reprint illustrations that Williams had done for Margaret Wise Brown, with a new edition of *The Sailor Dog and Other Stories*. Following on the success of *Over and Over* (1957) and *Do You Know What I'll Do* (1958), he also illustrated a third book for Charlotte Zolotow, *The Sky Was Blue* (1963).[325] Nordstrom once again acted as mediator between author and illustrator, as Zolotow expressed her concern about various issues, including the proportions of the figures and the representation of the doll in the story. "I wish he could make the little girl's face and age the same (and a bit younger) from picture to picture with just the costume changing," Zolotow wrote to Ursula. "It would be possible that the ladies all looked alike when they were seven years old except for the period differences. And it would bear out my point of the human constant in the inconstancies of history." She also wrote that she loved "the mother and daughter pictures and all the goodnight ones."[326] On one occasion, Williams wrote back somewhat testily to Nordstrom to explain that the pages were laid out differently than he had assumed.[327] One year before her last collaboration with Williams, Zolotow had published a book entitled *Mr. Rabbit and the Lovely Present* with illustrator Maurice Sendak, who was himself soon to publish *Where the Wild Things Are* in 1963. The two men were to later cross paths, as Williams readily responded to Sendak's undeniable talent.

The paths of Williams and Sendak also converged (though they didn't yet intersect) a short time later on the work of the brilliant American poet, Randall Jarrell. The story of Williams' commission for Jarrell's *The Gingerbread Rabbit* (1964) begins in the early sixties, when Michael di Capua, then a fresh young editor at Macmillan, decided to approach Jarrell, whose poetry he admired, with a proposal that Jarrell translate some of Grimm's fairy tales for his press. Di Capua's letter reached Jarrell in a hospital where he was recovering from hepatitis. Jarrell liked the idea and finished the translations in short order. Pleased with that success and eager to continue the new relationship, di Capua suggested that Jarrell try his hand at writing for children. "It didn't take too much penetrating insight to think of this, since children were a pervasive theme of Jarrell's poetry," wrote di Capua. "He was fascinated with how their minds work and how things looked from a child's point of view."[328] Over the next eighteen months, Jarrell produced three children's books. When the first of them, *The Gingerbread Rabbit*, was complete, Jarrell himself suggested that di Capua secure Williams as the illustrator; after sampling a number of children's books, he had decided that the pen-and-ink drawings for Margery Sharp's *The Rescuers* were just what he wanted. Mary Jarrell, the poet's widow, later wrote, "Turning the matter over to di Capua, Jarrell had no idea of the difficult task he was setting for a very junior assistant editor at a very early stage in his career: to induce the established and much-in-demand illustrator of, among others, E. B. White's *Charlotte's Web* to add a first book by an unknown children's writer to his backlog."[329]

Against all odds, di Capua succeeded, and though the two artists never met, the collaboration went smoothly, with di Capua negotiating between them. "You've chosen the best possible situations," he wrote to Williams in June, 1963, "and the descriptions on your list are very frustrating—trying to visualize the finished illustrations doesn't work out very well, obviously, but judging by the finishes you sent and the subjects you've picked I know that the pictures are going to be very funny and tender, just like the story."[330] Williams' third wife, Alicia, baked a gingerbread rabbit to serve as a model, and he gave Alicia's features to the harried mother who tries to chase the rabbit down.

The result pleased both author and editor: "[Williams] had a lighthearted touch that was perfect for this first book, and Randall was very pleased with his illustrations."[331] Of the ink-and-wash illustration Williams made for the jacket, Jarrell wrote, "The old rabbit in the colored sketch makes me want to be adopted by him."[332] Indeed, Jarrell was so happy with the illustrations for *The Gingerbread Rabbit* that he wanted to ask Williams to do his next two children's books, *The Bat Poet* and *The Animal Family* as well, but di Capua had in the meantime seen some work by another illustrator he thought might be more appropriate for those darker, more provocative stories. So he turned to Maurice Sendak, whose edgier imagination, with its gleefully anarchic action and its probing of unconscious impulse, seemed a better match for the emotional territory that Jarrell was venturing into in the two later books. Anyone who has seen the results would be hard-pressed to argue that Williams could have done a better job than Sendak with those two stories, but he was perfect for *The Gingerbread Rabbit*, which had a whimsy and high good-humor that matched his own.

The ambitious and expensive compound at Guanajuato was one sign of Williams' increasing engagement with Mexico, its culture, and its people. Another was his acceptance, amid his work on the books by George Selden and Margery Sharp and Russell Hoban, of a commission to illustrate Byrd Baylor's *Amigo* (1963). Baylor, born in Texas, had grown up in Arizona and has been a life-long devotee of the desert.

At the time of this writing, she is living in an adobe house without electricity near Arivaca, Arizona, writing in longhand on yellow legal pads and then typing up her manuscripts on one of her three manual typewriters. All her work has reflected her deep connection with the landscape: "She thinks of these books as her own kind of private love songs to the place she calls home," according to the "Author's Biography" posted by one of her publishers.[333]

Model for Francisco.

Of her many children's books (four of which have won Caldecott honors) *Amigo* was the first. The plot concerns a boy named Francisco who wants a dog he will name Amigo. The family is too poor to support another mouth to feed, so Francisco befriends a prairie dog instead. Baylor's editor at Simon & Schuster apparently thought a prairie dog would have limited appeal, but she held firm: "That first one was in rhyme," she told an interviewer years later. "It was about a prairie dog. The publisher asked me if I would make it a squirrel. I said no."[334]

As a model for Francisco, Williams used a photograph he took of a Mexican boy, and he used his encounter with the Mexican landscape for the background. The ink-and-wash illustrations in a muted palette bring a dreamy, fable quality to Francisco's story.

Amigo, as it turned out, was Williams' only full-fledged use of his new Mexican milieu; work kept drawing his imagination back to New York City (for the Chester Cricket series) or the American prairie (for the *Bread-and-Butter Indian* series). But this one sally into the local afforded him the opportunity to capture the people, animals, vistas and spirit of Mexico in a fully realized work of art.

In 1964, Williams' reputation ensured another successful collaboration with a popular author—Anne Colver, well known for her children's biography of Abraham Lincoln. Colver's two volume series entitled *Bread and Butter Indian* and *Bread and Butter Journey* was based on the experiences of an actual early nineteenth-century girl, Barbara Baum, who lived in the Burnt Cabins Community of Pennsylvania. Editors at Holt, Rinehart & Winston wanted to have the illustrator of the Little House Series for their books as well. They were particularly eager to have an artist who had proven himself as an attentive and nuanced depicter of

Illustration from *Amigo*.

Native Americans. Williams' earlier images, such as those of the Osage Indians who appear in the Ingalls' cabin in *Little House on the Prairie*, respond both to Wilder's narrative cues and to research that he did in the museums of upstate New York. For the Colver stories, Williams seems to have reprised earlier efforts and not to have done any additional research. The images in both *Bread-and-Butter Indian* and *Bread-and-Butter Journey* are reminiscent of those he did for the Wilder series, yet arguably they lack the kind of precision and specificity that once made Williams' work remarkable.

In fact, despite the satisfaction of working with authors like Randall Jarrell, Anne Colver, and Byrd Baylor, Williams was not able to work to full capacity during the early sixties. Sometime in 1964, he contracted a form of hepatitis and he struggled for some time to regain his full health. His archive contains several pieces of correspondence on a project that he never completed, though he was under contract with Simon & Shuster to do so—*The Tall Book of Animals.* As early as May 1961, Williams was writing to Lucille Ogle, his editor at The Golden Books, with ideas about the animals he would draw, including "several lovely, neglected and lesser known animals," like the cuddly "POTTO, the LORIS and the BUSH BABY." As he explained, "the potto and slow loris both hang by their feet and catch insects with their very human hands. So I have a potto on a branch, and a loris—hanging—catching a bug. A bush-baby sits on another branch."[335] Ogle does not seem to have been especially enthusiastic about Williams' unorthodox choices.

Once Williams began to experience the effects of his illness, the work on the project bogged down. In February of 1963, he was planning to finish the illustrations in August. But in March of 1964, he was still making lists of animals and struggling with the concept of the book: "I wonder if it would be any advantage to go so far as to call this THE TALL BOOK OF ANIMAL RELATIONS," he wrote to Ogle.[336] Doing her best to remain patient, Ogle was hopeful that Williams would meet his next projected deadline, September of 1964. Yet the book was never finished. Williams clearly regretted disappointing Ogle, but he also wrote to her somewhat defensively that he hoped the press understood that *"but for Lucille Ogle* I never would have worked for Golden Books; Western; Artists and Writers; etc." He also wrote that he was "most distressed that my private life and health interfered with my work schedule during the last three years. However, I did one book for Golden; two for Little Brown; two for Harper (not counting work on Tall Book); two for Macmillan."[337]

In the summer of 1964, Estyn and Jessica came to live with their father for the summer vacation. Estyn, now fourteen, spent her time studying photography, painting in oils, and learning guitar, while Jessica was learning the guitar and Spanish.[338] Then, in January of 1965, Dorothea died. Though the circumstances of her death remain clouded, it appears that she committed suicide. Had the excruciating symptoms of her physical ailments simply become unbearable? Or was the overdose of sleeping medication accidental on her part? What we do know is that, on the evening of her death, Dorothea had visited both of her daughters, assuring them that she would always love them. The pair left for school, believing that their mother was sleeping in, as she often did after a late night. But later that morning they were called to the office of the headmaster, who gave them the cryptic message that "votre mere s´évanouit"—"your mother has fainted." As the truth was slowly revealed, Fiona, who was then living in Edinburg, raced to London to take care of the girls and to help make arrangements.[339]

Williams heard the news in Guanajuato, where, with Bettina in temporary residence, he was still recovering from hepatitis. He did not travel to London for the funeral, but made a trip a few months later, where he was relieved to see his daughters, who were under the care of Fiona and English friends, looking well. He took the pair to the continent for a camping trip and then continued to closely monitor their movements for the next few decades as they sorted out both academic and personal plans. In a letter to his daughter, Estyn, in 1964, he clearly looked forward to the time when the girls would come to Mexico for a visit and he and Esytn could paint together: "I have a light-weight sketching easel you can use," he wrote to her. "I fix a canvas on a flat wall and paint on that, or on the floor OR on a table. Feel sure we can fix you up. Bring brushes and paints."[340] However, family matters also had a way of putting a lot of pressure on him around this time, as his children often needed both financial and psychological support from him.

For instance, writing on January 30th, 1970 to Ursula Nordstrom, he admitted that he "did almost nothing" during the previous year, citing the burden of both the house and his daughters' travails. He fretted over Esytn's "awful predicaments" as she continued to find her own way, and he explained how Jessica, then nineteen, needed a "guiding hand." In his postscript to Nordstrom he wrote:

> Jessica interrupted me when I was addressing the envelope, and I would like to ask a question on her behalf...after listing her training, the highlights of her cv: schooling in Aspen, Switzerland, London, a few years at Simon's Rock, manager and assistant to a photographer. [He was] a young man who does pages in the big fashion magazines. She had no contract but signed bills on his behalf. That ended when I had to pay $2000 worth of bills [apparently mostly for hotels] in my daughter's name. She spends her time experimenting with writing. Becket [sic] is her god this week, Samuel. Can you suggest anything? I have little faith in courses, neither college nor night school. Prison is one of the best places to go, but so far she has been overlooked....I contribute $200 a month to the problem of solving life...[341]

Jessica Williams and Claude Picasso.

Eventually Jessica would find her vocation as a well-regarded jewelry maker, but first there would be a series of adventures, including a time during which she dated Claude Picasso, son of the famous artist. In the meantime, correspondence in Williams' archive makes it clear that he

174

was not only taking care of Jessica but also sending money to Estyn, Fiona, and Bettina. In one handwritten memo to lawyer Richard Ticktin, Williams listed and detailed the amounts, as if he was trying to make sure that each child was receiving his or her fair share.[342]

Driven by the urgency to support his large, unwieldy household, Williams returned to tried and true ventures for much needed cash. With the Little House series more popular than ever, he allowed his original illustrations to be reprinted in other commercial forms, namely *The Laura Ingalls Wilder Songbook* edited by Eugenia Garson, with music for piano and guitar arranged by Herbert Haufrecht (1968), and *A Horn Book Calendar* (1968). The opportunity for new work on the series presented itself when Roger Lea MacBride, the executor of the estate of Rose Wilder Lane, Laura Ingalls Wilder's daughter, discovered the manuscript of a ninth Little House book among Lane's belongings after her death in 1968. Written out on a dime-store tablet, as were all the other books, this story was unique in that it does not appear to have been edited by Lane. It picks up the story with the courtship and early-married years of Laura and Almanzo and includes the birth of their daughter. This slender volume is darker in mood and subject than the previous books. Once again, Williams did not shy away from realistic depiction. For instance, he captured not only the drama of the Wilder's home on fire, but also the troubled, uncomprehending expression of their toddler, who approaches her traumatized parents with a crumpled wildflower in her small hand.

Yet Williams almost did not do the work for this final volume in the series due to his increasing resentment over the state of his contractual negotiations with Harpers. On September 12th, 1970, he wrote to Ursula Nordstrom about his response to first receiving the contract for *The First Four Years.* Closer to a tirade than anything else, the five-page, single-spaced letter ranges over a number of topics about which he had deep and angry feelings. Some of these were long festering issues over contracts which occupied a lot of time and concern in the last decades of his life. Here the first issue was payment, as he notices that

Illustration for *Little House on the Prairie.*

Harper and Row promised him royalties of .011 on the ninth volume, whereas, he had been previously paid .055 for the other eight volumes. Obviously irked and frustrated, he wrote to Nordstrom that his lawyers had instructed him to leave the negotiations to them. Yet he appealed wistfully to Nordstrom as an old friend:

> We used to be able to meet over tea and crumpets in a dark corner of the large hotel on the corner of 34th and Park. We could share our troubles, plan great books for the future, and I only wish I could return to that table, those times. But now that the world of books has grown into very big business—we must be cut-throats. —
>
> I don't mind what happens to the ninth Wilder book. What I mind about is the death of a lovely partnership: Harper Books, with me as the illustrator or author,—you as the editor, and we can include a good other author or two. [343]

Eventually, Williams' lawyer, Jeremy Nussbaum, would soothe Williams' spirits and persuade him to go forward with the project.[344]

Clearly, the late sixties were a difficult time for Williams, with the publishing world rapidly changing in ways that defied his comprehension, and family issues continually in the foreground. Then, on January 28th, 1969, a handwritten letter from Williams' French, half brother Alain announced the burial of their father, Monty, who had died three days earlier. In a missive that carefully avoided recrimination or blame, Alain described the "miserable" state of Monty's last days, as the family struggled with his care. "I paid the expenses of the burial and cemetery..." he wrote. "Monty may not have been a most brilliant man," he also wrote, "but who can pretend being so? He is our father and I think he deserves an affectionate thought. I could explain it all better in French but never mind." What might Williams have thought in response? In many ways, he had surpassed his father's expectations for him, achieving a notable reputation in the publishing world both in the U.S. and, with increasing frequency, internationally. Yet he had never become the "real artist" he had once promised to become, and the messy state of his domestic affairs, including his then deteriorating third marriage, could be said to mimic his father's.

But one of the biggest disappointments of Williams' life struck at his identity as an artist; when E. B. White completed his third book for children, a different illustrator was chosen for it. The story of this omission is a tangled one. On April 1st, 1969, Ursula Nordstrom wrote to Williams with news on two fronts: one, that the inheritor of Laura Ingalls Wilder's estate had found the manuscript for a ninth Little House book among her papers, and the other, that "EBW is almost finished writing his new children's book." She assured Williams that this was no April Fools' joke, and she ended the letter this way: "It would kill us all to have to have someone else illustrate E. B. White's new book!" At the bottom of the letter is Williams' penciled note: "Ursula YES!"[345] On April 29th Nordstrom wrote again, replying to a letter she had received from Williams in the meantime, but saying only "No more news about the E. B. White ms."[346] It appears that Williams' response had been written before he received the April 1st letter and made no mention of the White manuscript (though Williams later claimed that it had), because her next communication, dated November 10th, 1969, shows her uncertainty. She wrote that White would send his new manuscript by Thanksgiving, but "He does not know whether or not you will want to illustrate it." Nordstrom had told White that Williams was very busy, "But I told him I thought you would move heaven and earth to illustrate his new book. . . But he said something about seeing sketches, and he assumed that you were at the stage in life where you did not care to do sketches."[347] On this letter Williams penciled a New York City telephone number—presumably Nordstrom's. If he tried to call, however, he evidently was not able to get through because two weeks later Nordstrom wrote again with devastating news:

> I wrote to you on the 19th about E. B. White's book and cabled you last Friday. No answer. I have talked to EBW on the phone and if we are to make spring publication we realize that we cannot ask you to illustrate it even if you were to be able to read it at once and let us hear

from you. We need the pictures by the middle of January, so it will have to be someone very close to home. The mails from Mexico are so impossible, and besides which I gather your schedule is very heavy and you wouldn't be able to get to it for a while no matter what.[348]

Williams let a few days go by before replying to Nordstrom's last. "In reply to your letter of 11/25/69. in which you say I am too busy and too far away to do TRUMPET OF THE SWAN, may I answer that latter, as it is very much on my mind, and extremely upsetting it was at the time." Williams went over the sequence of the letters that had passed back and forth, and he insisted that Nordstrom's letter of April 29th had confirmed that she knew Williams wanted very much to illustrate *Trumpet*. He summarized the climax of the affair this way:

> On 21st you sent telegram—Sending MSS asking me to phone you when I have read it.
> MSS mailed 21st November, same day as telegram.
> MSS arrived 25th. Nov 1969. I began reading it that afternoon and making illustration notes; queries to ask. I did not finish before 5.0pm on Nov.26th. and continued to plan on thanksgiving day, at midday Of 27th. I received your letter of 25th. on November 28th. I tried to call you; in New York they said you were not listed, and nobody was at Harper & Row on 28th.

Williams clearly didn't believe that communication between New York and Guanajuato was the real reason the commission was being denied him, and he hypothesized that White or Nordstrom was unsatisfied with his work or that someone else had already done the illustrations. "My jet plane from Mexico to New York makes pretty good time," he wrote, and in a dig at the fact that E. B. White had been living in Brooklin, Maine, for several years, "I am told often far quicker than planes from Maine to New York." Finally, he added a bitter note: "Please send me an early copy of TRUMPETER, —I don't want to be the *last* to see it. In other words—kick me out of HARPER & ROW to the sound of taps."[349]

Many years later, in a letter to Peter Neumeyer, Williams recounted what had gone through his mind at the time. "I was shocked and extremely upset. They had not *telephoned* me." He had considered jumping on a plane and flying to New York: "I could even fly to Maine and illustrate the book in Maine in a hotel." But he was stopped by two possibilities: that Harper & Row had discovered a "brilliant new artist"—another Maurice Sendak, say—whom they preferred, or that White had never really liked his work on *Stuart* and *Charlotte* and had asked for someone different for *Trumpet*. "Should either of these two solutions be true, then my visit to New York next day would be a harder blow."[350] Simply losing the commission was less wounding to his self-esteem than learning that some other artist was considered better than he. And so he let it go.

In the last analysis, it appears that E. B. White was afraid that the difficulty of communicating with Williams in Mexico would lead to delays in the production of *Trumpet* and that he had insisted on another artist because of that. White was anxious for *Trumpet* to appear in the spring, rather than waiting for the fall list, as Harpers would in fact have preferred, because he needed the income. His wife, Katharine, was gravely ill and required constant care. "Our house is rigged up now like a hospital," he wrote to Williams, "complete with hospital bed and nurses in white uniforms and off-white shoes." The need for money had overcome all other considerations. Nevertheless, White wanted to assure Williams that he had very much appreciated the contribution the illustrations had made to the success of *Stuart Little* and *Charlotte's Web*: "I had always hoped that Williams and White would be as indestructible as ham and eggs, Scotch and soda, Gilbert and Sullivan."[351]

Years later, Williams was philosophical about the *Trumpet* episode, considering it the concatenation of a series of errors. "But," he concluded, "I received the best book reviews in the N. Y. Times when Trumpet was reviewed by John Updike—He began by noting with no uncertain regret that I had not *illustrated it*."[352] (Updike wrote, "At first glance, one's heart a little falls to see that wash drawing [sic] by

Edward Frascino have replaced Williams' [sic] finely furry pen-and-ink illustrations, which are wedded to White's other children's texts as well as Tenniel's to 'Alice' and Shepard's to the Pooh books."[353]) The last somewhat bitter laugh was Williams'.

Another kind of controversy eddied around Williams' illustrations for *Bedtime for Frances*, a book that had become a contemporary classic since its original publication in 1960. Russell Hoban's original manuscript had been titled "Bedtime for Frances Vole," but Williams hadn't thought a vole made a suitable character. As he later wrote to one of his lawyers, Harriet Pilpel, "A vole is a tiny mouse-like creature, but very small. There was no reason to use a small creature, the text could have been about an elephant; so I suggested a much neglected little animal—the Badger. And the book was a great success." In fact, the book was such a success that Hoban wrote six sequels to it, the last published in 1970. A few years after *Bedtime for Frances*, Williams came across the first of the sequels and was caught completely by surprise. "I was upset that I had never heard about the sequels, I don't remember having refused to do a sequel—but I may have done verbally talking to Ursula." Hoban's wife Lillian had illustrated the sequels, and she had (for obvious reasons) copied Williams' characters and style exactly. His primary concern, however, was less with this mimicry than with his interest in the character of Frances as a badger. Hadn't she been *his* invention? "I feel that copyright should give me at least the right to sell the right to copy my drawing (copy my character to be precise)." He still needed money, to be sure, though Jeffrey Nussbaum had just completed the first in what would be a series of vastly improved contracts from Harper & Row. Moreover, Williams was still smarting from having lost the commission for *The Trumpet of the Swan* and his anger was spilling over to all publishers and editors. Here, he insisted, was a point of artistic integrity:

> What an artist feels so strongly is that to create a successful character
> is the hard thing to do; once the character has been designed, it is a
> simple matter to go on drawing the same; witness Walt Disney studios.

I felt copyright protected me as far as having my invented character used by other artists.[354]

Williams may have had some idea about using the badger character in another children's book—at least he threatened to do so—but in fact he never did. This dispute simmered along for five years without ever coming to any real resolution, but in 1975, when Harper & Row proposed a new edition of *Bedtime for Frances* with generous royalty terms for Williams, it went quietly away.

As the 1970s approached and Williams faced the prospect of turning sixty, he was increasingly finding himself less sought after by publishers. According to William Anderson in a piece about Williams in his later years for *Horn Book Magazine*, "The long sojourns in Mexico gave some publishers and editors the notion that Garth Williams was retired or incommunicado, or both."[355] Indeed, correspondence between the States and Guanajuato was often slow and inefficient due to the state of the Mexican postal service. Letters did sometimes fail to arrive. Moreover, as we have seen, during the 1960s Williams was often distracted by the renovations on his house and property, the state of his family matters— including his now failed third marriage—and his health. At this point, it might have looked as if Williams' career as an illustrator was over. Yet during his lifetime Williams had previously come to apparent dead ends—when his first marriage failed and World War II precipitated his departure from Europe, or when the life he built for himself, Dorothea, and his daughters in Aspen fell apart, for instance. On those occasions Williams had boldly moved on, making the necessary adjustments to new geographical, social, and cultural circumstances. Quite simply, he had recreated himself and refashioned crucial aspects of his identity: the promising young European sculptor necessarily became the renowned children's book illustrator. The Englishman returned to his New York roots, and then reintroduced himself as citizen of the American west. The wartime father of two tiny Canadian girls became the father of two more American daughters—and then father of two Mexican sons, one of whom he would never acknowledge as his. Speaking English, Italian,

French, and Spanish, Williams easily slipped in and out of different national contexts, maintaining an impressive range of friendships and affiliations across the world.

And so in the midst of his long, fulminating letter to Ursula Nordstrom in 1970, he nonetheless had reasons to be optimistic. "It is my hope that I shall see many more years, in spite of the fact that so many notable men of my age are dropping dead from being overly successful, or from barbiturates," he wrote. "Though the time is getting depressingly short I hope to proceed in far better achievements—even in children's books."[356] Indeed, new professional opportunities would arise in the next decades. But first, there would be one more chance for renewal, one more new beginning, one more family. On September 19, 1976, Garth Williams would marry for the fourth time.

Chapter Seven

LIFE CAN BEGIN AT 60 (1970-1996)

Garth Williams with wife Letty and daughter Dilys, Guanajuato, Mexico.

s early as 1970, Garth Williams was clearly excited about new developments in illustration. These developments became especially apparent when someone—he was never sure whether it was the author Maurice Sendak or Ursula Nordstrom—sent him a copy of *In the Night Kitchen*, newly published. Williams wrote a long letter to Sendak, beginning with a summary of his recent "war" with Harpers and Ursula over royalty payments, but then shifted to the book. Williams expressed his appreciation and made a shrewd prediction: "It is certainly a great pleasure to have a quite different kind of book from you. Color, color, color. I predict that you will follow this with many more color books—as opposed to tinted drawings."

He also took note of the most "shocking" element of *Night Kitchen*, the full-frontal nudity of Mickey, which was not only controversial in 1970 but has kept it on the list of the American Library Association's "Most Banned/Challenged Books" ever since.[357] "I told Ursula she and you will be arrested," he joked, "the book will sell like mad while you both sit out a long jail sentence, pronounced by the Agnew of the new puritanism, and that you will die in prison having made millions on the outside—quite legally."[358] Perhaps, Williams wrote, the controversy would work like the one that surrounded *The Rabbits' Wedding*, with the book "spat upon and banned" but also generating record sales. "I wish you this luck. Perhaps the Cock a Doodle Doo will be THE page."[359] And he added, "These good wishes come to you from the communist brain washer of tiny innocent little bastards in Alabama, Louisiana, Florida, and all points south—Me. What else matters, be damned, and thou shalt be blessed in heaven and on earth."[360]

In another, related letter on the same topic, Williams wrote to Nordstrom and Sendak jointly, responding once again to the "censorship" of Sendak's work—this time, when a librarian apparently painted a pair of pants on Mickey: "I had hoped that [Maurice] would have been burned in effigy, and carted off to prison," he joked: "At any rate the book at least should have been banned. With such a small protest how can Maurice have any real claim to fame." Subtly reminding Sendak that he too had once enjoyed some notoriety, he wrote, "And I *did* want to see Night Kitchen alongside Rabbits' Wedding (that communist attack on southern children, defiling their minds with ideas of integration,— worse, miscegenation.)" Then, demonstrating a keen awareness of a history of controversy in children's literature, he continued, "Or like Black Beauty, or Stuart Little (banned by the New York Public Library when it came out). Or it could have been thrown across the room in front of Ursula, like the Little Fur Family in the Astor Hotel (that filthy little book quotes). Or like Ferdinand the Bull (dreadful anti-war book)." Clearly on a roll, he carried on the joke:

> I am sorry that Harper & Row did not supply a little plastic envelope with ready-to-wear-stick-on-panties. These would have been designed and painted by Maurice and with a rubber-based adhesive, the children could have pulled up the pants and peeked, while parents were out of their room, and then stuck them back on again. . .
>
> Considering that Michael Angelo's painting of enormous size, behind the altar of the Sistine Chapel carries lots of nebulous panties painted by the Pope of Rome, I see no reason why we cannot say that Maurice joins Michael Angelo in censure by Pope and Louisiana Librarian of certain pictorial representations of certain anatomical parts, notwithstanding that we are in the year 1972, when for some time the theatre of the USA has been happy to see productions such as HAIR. (I haven't been lucky enough to see it myself) which has passed the censor in the matter of, panties or no panties.[361]

However, along with the praise and the jesting, Williams also expressed his sense that Sendak's work marked a turning point in the world of children's literature, the beginning of a new era. About *In the Night Kitchen*, he wrote, "[It] is most unexpected, and refreshing, you make me feel that at last I'm growing old and the generations are catching up with me and now they are passing me."[362] Williams could already see a trend that later critics of children's literature would identify as having begun with Sendak's earlier story, *Where the Wild Things Are*. Like *In the Night Kitchen*, *Wild Things* provoked controversy with its depiction of violent feeling boiling over. Its real significance, however, is pinpointed by Sheila A. Egoff:

> While the illustrations disturbed those adults who saw the "Wild Things" as ferociously threatening rather than humorously subservient to Max's will, the extreme reaction to Sendak's work intimated

that there was more at stake than a matter of interpretation of the pictures. As it turned out, this as yet unformulated anxiety was justi-fied. Sendak's underlying theme that a child has unconscious needs, frustrations, and fears unsettled society's hitherto conceived ideals of early childhood and the book itself broke the stereotypic mold that had held for almost a hundred years.[363]

Fundamental to the revolution Sendak initiated was his insistence that children are not simple naïfs, that they have complex and powerful psychic lives: "from their earliest years children live on familiar terms with disrupting emotions, that fear and anxiety are an intrinsic part of their everyday lives, that they continually cope with frustration as best they can. And it is through fantasy that children achieve catharsis. It is the best means they have for taming Wild Things."[364] That both Williams and Sendak recognized this fact is the reason Williams wrote to Sendak about the "innocent little bastards" who read their books.

Sendak's work connected children's literature to the "real" world of complexity and struggle in other ways as well. In a tribute published on the occasion of Sendak's death in the pages of *PMLA*, John Cech touched on Sendak's realism:

> *Where the Wild Things Are* not only transformed children's literature but also presaged the changes in American culture that would occur in the 1960s, when the youth movement challenged the status quo in America—in politics, in the arts, in the academy, and in our culture as a whole. To be sure, Sendak was working on his artistic hunches and impulses when he wrote and illustrated *Where the Wild Things Are*, but soon there would be young men and women on the streets of every city in America who looked uncannily like the Wild Things, and many others "made mischief of one kind and another" in a variety of Max-like disguises. Knowingly or not, he was channeling the zeitgeist.[365]

Though the most prominent, Sendak was not, of course, the only illustrator channeling the zeitgeist in that period. 1963 was also the year Ezra Jack Keats published (and won the Caldecott Medal for) *The*

Snowy Day, the story of an African American boy playing in his neighborhood after a snowfall. While Williams' brush with the American conflict over race in the 1950s had been oblique and accidental, Keats clearly was responding to the new racial climate created by the Civil Rights Movement of the 1960s. *The Snowy Day* was a radical departure for Keats, who had already had a long career of fairly conventional illustration. For one thing, he chose an entirely new medium: "The techniques that gave *The Snowy Day* its unique look—collage with cutouts of patterned paper, fabric and oilcloth; homemade snowflake stamps; spatterings of India ink with a toothbrush—were methods Ezra Jack Keats had never used before."[366] The result was boldly colorful in a way even more striking than that of *Where the Wild Things Are*.

For another thing, Keats, the son of Jewish immigrants from Poland, chose to portray an African American at a time when Nancy Larrick, in a 1965 article in the *Saturday Review*, was attacking "The All-White World of Children's Books."[367] However, *The Snowy Day* was a turning point, the recognition that race was an important element in the lives of American children. "None of the manuscripts I'd been illustrating featured any black kids," Keats recalled, "except for token blacks in the background. My book would have him there simply because he should have been there all along."[368]

Still another powerful current affecting children's literature in the 1970s was feminism, represented by works like Charlotte Zolotow's *William's Doll* (1972, illustrated by William Pène du Bois) and the children's album that famously incorporated Zolotow's story, *Free to Be . . . You and Me* (also 1972). Zolotow's account of how she came to write *William's Doll* sums up many issues. She had already felt a kind of sadness that certain unquestioned assumptions about gender roles in family life—that her husband, for all his affection for his children, had never changed a diaper, for instance—meant that both father and child were missing an emotional connection. She had also overcome her husband's resistance to giving stuffed animals to boys. Then, one day in New York's Washington Square, she overheard an argument.

I don't remember the particulars, but there was a little boy there who wanted a rag-doll. I overheard the father say, *oh get him a gun instead.* It did make me mad. It all came together: how men missed out on the pleasure of being with very young children, and how, *because* they missed it and because they had never had it with their fathers, they had no concept that war and harshness and so much unpleasantness come out of playing with guns as children, and growing up thinking it was unmanly to play with a doll or stuffed toy bear or lion.

William's Doll was written, Zolotow said, "out of a direct emotional sorrow."[369]

What Zolotow, Keats, Sendak and many another children's writers of the seventies had in common was their absorption, conscious or not, of the political, social, and cultural energies swirling through American life at the time—the intense new consciousness of the roles played by race, class, and gender in the lives of children as well as those of their parents. Williams' decision to live in Mexico, to build a walled compound, and to live insulated from the vicissitudes of the outside world had not only made it more difficult for writers and editors to communicate with him, it had also cut him off from the forces that were transforming American life. As Williams later conceded in a letter to Joan Friedberg, in Mexico he was "as good as buried."[370] Some years later, when he was doing the illustrations for Jack Prelutsky's *Under a Blue Umbrella,* the editor wrote to Williams and urged him to make some changes:

> I tried to call you just now but there is no answer so I am returning two pictures in the hopes that you will be willing to make one of the children on page nine black and maybe one of the two on page nineteen black as well. And perhaps you will be able to make someone black in the pictures you have not yet sent. I really think this is important—both to children and to the sales of the book.[371]

She was gently prodding him to do as Jack Ezra Keats had years before—to include what should have been there all along. One of the costs of Williams' idyllic life in Guanajuato was the commission for

The Trumpet of the Swan; another was the sense he expressed to Sendak that that he was growing old and the generations were catching up with him and now they were passing him.

Nonetheless, the 1970s did, to a large extent, finally resolve an issue that had long since irked—and at times, even enraged Williams: the question of royalties for work that he had labored to produce. Always an aggravation, money worries reached a critical point once he had moved to Mexico. The angry outbursts in letters to friends like Ursula Nordstrom and Maurice Sendak show just how extreme things had become and how much pressure Williams felt. But 1970 marked an important shift in Williams' fortunes, as Jeremy Nussbaum, a young attorney specializing in intellectual property, not only resolved many of the lingering questions about earlier contracts, but also negotiated much more favorable terms for Williams' new commissions and finally made Williams and his family financially secure.

From the very beginning, Williams had a careless way of agreeing to contracts without paying much attention to what they actually stipulated. He often remembered oral agreements which had never been put in writing and which no one else could or would recall. As late as 1974 Williams was still seething over his memory of the work for *Stuart Little*. Writing to Stephen de Vito, the Assistant Director of Accounting at Harper & Row, about an unrelated matter, Williams took the opportunity to bring it up again:

> One interesting thing. When I did STUART LITTLE and was given a royalty, Ursula Nordstrom told me that Mr. E. B. White had agreed to give me 15% of his royalty. She said he got a very large royalty, leaving Harper & Brothers unable to afford to give me anything. I therefore thought his 15% of his own royalty fair enough. I worked it out as 2.25%. At some time that royalty seems to have been changed to 2c per copy. which now makes .005% or half a per cent of retail??? I agreed to do Charlottes Web on the same terms; thinking it was a percentage of the retail. That is now 2c per copy, down to half a per-cent thanks to inflation. Have I worked out these figures correctly? I assumed that E. B. White got no less than 15% and possibly more.[372]

De Vito declined the invitation to rehash that argument, replying only, "Your paragraph regarding STUART LITTLE and CHARLOTTES WEB royalties is interesting, and I think it is fortunate that artist royalties are calculated on a more equable basis today even though this does not help you on the E. B. White titles."[373]

In any event, Williams' 1945 contract for *Stuart Little* had quite different and very clear terms. He was paid $1,000 for the first 30,000 copies that were sold, and then $100 for every additional 5,000 copies.[374] For *Charlotte's Web* he was given a raise: $1,500 for the first 30,000 copies. There was of course nothing about sharing in E. B. White's royalties. More importantly, there was no "escalator" in the agreement. Williams was to receive a flat fee based on the number of copies sold, no matter what the wholesale or cover price of the books. It is the kind of contract that granted immediate rewards but foresaw no future popularity for books that became children's classics and perennial best-sellers. After one of his bitter letters to her, Ursula Nordstrom reminded Williams that those payments had been appropriate for the time[375] and she was right, but she entirely missed his point, which was that in subsequent years, as inflation lifted book prices and the cost of living, those two volumes had made a great deal of money for Harper and for E. B. White while Williams' share had grown vanishingly small.

The Little House books had an even more complicated contractual history. Following the success of the E. B. White stories, Williams had signed a three-year contract with Harper & Brothers stipulating that he would receive $6,000 per year as compensation for 150 black-and-white illustrations or sixty color illustrations each year. Harper & Brothers promised to assign him work "which bears a proper relationship to his past relationship and his position as a prominent illustrator of books for children and adults," but also stipulated that "Harper & Brothers is to be permitted to withhold *all* income resulting from existing arrangements covering 'Stuart Little' and 'Little Fur Family' and any work produced during the terms of this agreement until the guaranteed $18,000 has been covered."[376] Strictly speaking, Williams never came close to fulfilling the terms of this contract.

Instead, when he was asked to illustrate the Little House books, he did all the things we have already seen: traveled to Laura Ingalls Wilder country to research the landscape and mode of life, made scores of sketches and took photographs, and then went with his family to Italy, intending to do all the artwork there. The end result was not at all what Harper and Brothers had envisioned; it was far better. But here too, as with his earlier contracts, Williams had entered into an agreement that paid him a flat fee and had no provision for him to share in the huge profits the books would make over the coming years. For the six months from July 1st to December 31st, 1958, for example, Williams' earnings on royalties were $4,002.19. He was not getting rich.

The situation became especially galling after Laura Ingalls Wilder died in 1957 and her royalties went to her heirs, who had had nothing at all to do with making or popularizing the books but who were now getting rich on them. Even after the terms of the original contract were renegotiated, Williams' share was kept low. A memo from 1960 reveals that for *Little Town on the Prairie* and *Little House in the Big Woods* Williams received a 2% royalty, while the Wilder royalty (split evenly between Harper and the Wilder estate) was 5% for the first 7,000 copies and 10% after that.

Financially, Williams was treated as if his artwork were merely decorative, an easily-wrought embellishment of Wilder's texts. At the same time, the money people at Harper knew very well that the illustrations were an extremely important part of the appeal of the Little House books. In 1981, an editor at Harper & Row responded to a request for permission to display Helen Sewell's earlier illustrations for the Little House books this way:

> Harper feels that it is important to keep the close identity between Garth Williams and the "Little House" books. It is only since the reissue of the "Little House" books with Williams' illustrations in 1953 that the series became so popular. We certainly understand your admiration of Helen Sewell and your desire to mount an exhibit of

her artwork, but we hope you understand our position, too. Should you want to include *one or two* of the Sewell "Little House" illustrations in a larger exhibit, we would need to know the exact pictures you wished to use.[377]

That an editor at Harper & Row was still defending so vigilantly the association of Wilder's texts and Williams' illustrations almost thirty years after it was established is a perfect illustration of how profitable she considered that association to be. Over most of that time, however, Williams had not shared in that profitability. As we have seen, Williams was so incensed that when Harper approached him in 1970 to illustrate a newly-discovered Wilder manuscript, *The First Four Years*, he thought seriously about refusing to do it.

The problem, always, was that Williams wanted to do business by oral agreement and mutual good feeling. When he illustrated Margaret Wise Brown's books, he did so as a friend and fellow artist. He and Brown had shared equally the 10% royalties from *Wait Till the Moon is Full*, *Little Fur Family*, and *Three Little Animals*.[378] But after Brown's death, there was no one left in the world who was willing to work on that basis, and Williams was slow to realize it. By 1970 his disappointment and frustration were pouring into the letters he was firing off to Nordstrom, Sendak, and anyone else he thought might heed.

However, Williams finally met the man who would transform his financial world: Jeremy (Jerry) Nussbaum, who was at that time a twenty-nine-year-old attorney specializing in intellectual property law. He had been born in Muskogee, Oklahoma. His parents were refugees from Nazi Germany; his father, Max Nussbaum, had been a prominent rabbi in Berlin. Within a few years the family moved to Hollywood and the world of movie stars: "It was Rabbi Nussbaum who converted Elizabeth Taylor to Judaism before her marriage to Eddie Fisher."[379] Jerry Nussbaum attended the University of California at Berkeley during the Free Speech Movement of the late 1960s and remained a staunch advocate of liberal causes his whole life. His clients over that career included not only Williams but also the authors Joseph Heller and William Gaddis, actors Kathleen Turner, Andre Gregory and Brian Stokes Mitchell, and the Nobel-prize winning neuroscientist Eric Kandel. He was exactly the man Williams needed.[380]

Within a short time Nussbaum negotiated a new contract with Harper & Row for a paperback edition of the Little House books, on much more favorable terms than any Williams had had before. "As you may recall," Nussbaum wrote him, "the original offer was phrased in terms of the wholesale price, so I think that the present percentage of retail list is a considerable improvement." Nussbaum also pointed out that the contract put Williams into an entirely new and much better relationship with Harper & Row:

> As I mentioned in my letter of November 10, the fact that you are being asked to consent to this deal at all creates a significant precedent for the future; it is not at all clear that Harper's required your permission in the first instance, but voluntary submissions such as this one will make it next to impossible for them to act without your consent in the future. Given the often difficult relationship that you have had with Harper's, I am doubly pleased that they have proceeded in this manner, and appear to have adopted a much friendlier tone than evidently was the case in the past.[381]

Nussbaum negotiated similar contracts for new editions of *Stuart Little* and *Charlotte's Web*, attended to dozens of small details—like the foreign language, British, and bookclub editions of the *Little House Day by Day* book in 1984—that Williams had never bothered with, researched the state of all Williams' previous contracts with an array of other publishers, and generally brought order to the chaos of Williams' finances. The difference was profound. In 1958 Williams had earned something in the neighborhood of $8,000. A summary royalties statement dated March 4, 1983, from after the time Nussbaum renegotiated the contracts, read like this:

1981: $125,859.55

1982: $145,370.39

1983: $209,071.05

1984: $165,638.41

The desperate money worries were over.

One person who must have been very glad that Williams' royalty issues were settled satisfactorily was Ursula Nordstrom. As we have seen, over the many years of their acquaintance, Nordstrom liked to consider herself Williams' family friend, and she tried to act, to the best of her ability, as his advocate in financial matters by finding him lucrative work and by overseeing the state of his contracts. For instance, in 1953, just after he received the three-year contract from Harpers, she wrote to him in Aspen and joked, "Are you getting rich? (If so please send a few dollars as I am very poor right now, having bought a new refrigerator.)" Telling Williams that he was "all caught up with Harper financially, with the exception of one small payment still due," she assured him "One of these days you'll make some good money on Harper Books above the $18,000," for which he had been contracted. Yet Williams' continual complaints must have proved taxing, and evidence suggests that Nordstrom struggled to retain her characteristic good humor and patience with him. In 1970, she wrote to him to confess that "your head is an utter mystery to me" and to assure Williams "I suppose we could figure up how much you have made over the years in addition to the original flat payments for those books ($1000 for Stuart and $1500 for Charlotte)—sums which look ridiculously small now but were not then." Her next statement reveals just how far she felt Williams had pushed her, yet still she could not give up on their friendship: "I probably shouldn't be writing you these personally-typed unbusinesslike letters, just turn it all over to our contract people. But I can't do that after all these years."[382]

Nordstrom had every reason to believe that she had done what she could and that all her business dealings had been clear and unequivocal—and she tried everything to convince Williams of this fact. On one occasion, she even took to playfully "firing" herself—presumably to artfully deflect some aggressive correspondence from Williams:

Dear Mr. Williams:

A letter has been received addressed to Miss Ursula Nordstrom. It is from you, and it seems to refer to some sort of operation with a razor on some drawings you allege to have submitted.

We regret to inform you that Miss Nordstrom is no longer in our employ. We have no forwarding address for her, but there is a possibility that she did apply for free-lance editorial work with a Mrs. Jane Werner Watson, the well-known writer. In any event, Miss Nordstrom is no longer with this House. She was a very fast typist, to be sure, and lately she had taught herself to operate the freight elevator. Also we must admit that apparently she helped a few of the authors in little ways—making up their laundry lists, dog-sitting for them on occasion and she was always available for midnight 'phone discussions on possible changes of titles. However, she involved this firm in so many problems connected with artists in Mexico, artists in Aspen, artists who promised to keep deadlines (and never did keep them), and also she sabotaged all the firm's efforts to add to the list a TALL BOOK OF ANIMALS. So we had to let her go. And god-damn good riddance we all say.[383]

She playfully signed the letter "(Miss) Georges Duplaix"—a reference to George Duplaix, whom Williams had accused of misleading him concerning the money he would make on the Little Golden Books. Though the letter is comic and entertaining, it contains what could be construed as legitimate complaints on Nordstrom's part—Williams had indeed missed deadlines, and he had never finished *The Tall Book of Animals.* Yet he kept the letter in his archive and he clearly valued Nordstrom as a friend who never gave up on him.

In 1975, Williams was still recovering from a series of physical, emotional, and professional setbacks. Though he was not divorced from his third wife, the couple was now separated. Yet he had never been alone for long before, and he would not be this time either. His fourth wife, Letty, remembers their courtship and marriage in vivid detail. Born on June 6th, 1952, Leticia Maria de los Angeles Vargas Arredondo was one of seven children (five daughters, two sons) born to Jose Guadalupe Vargas y Maldonado and Maria Luisa Arredondo de Vargas, a prominent family in Silao, Guanajuato. She contracted polio at the age of one, but timely medical care made it possible for her to be mobile with the help of crutches. She first met Williams on September 19th, 1975, after being introduced through a mutual friend, another Englishman living in Mexico. The serendipitous meeting would lead to their being married exactly one year later, on September 19th, 1976. Coincidentally their only daughter would later be born exactly two years later on the same date.

Letty had ventured out that evening as a "chaperone" for her older sister, who would not otherwise have been allowed to go out at night. Letty remembers that Alicia, who was garbed in traditional Mexican dress, was also in attendance, though she and Williams were not paying attention to each other. Letty was instantly attracted to Williams' cosmopolitan and cultured mannerisms, and she and a friend chatted amicably with him for most of the evening. That he was considerably older than her twenty-three years was not an issue: her own mother had been nineteen when she married her husband, who was fifty-four. (Her own mother had also not been a first wife, her father's first wife having been killed during a period of political unrest.) Williams appears to have responded to Letty's extraordinary beauty, explaining that he was most interested in her head, which he was keen to sculpt. Williams quickly made himself a regular for tea at the Vargas's home, befuddling her parents, who did not at first understand his intentions to marry Letty. Moreover, they were not pleased when his plans became clear; at the time, he seemed to have slim financial prospects and, besides, he was still married. However, as we've seen, Williams did end his marriage to Alicia with a divorce settlement that reflected how desperate he was for his third marriage to be over.

Exactly one day after the divorce, he appeared at Letty's home with legal documents in hand. When Letty's brother challenged him to state his qualifications as a husband, Williams replied, "We both have handicaps; Leticia had polio and I am too old."[384] Somehow the parents were convinced by him, but plans for marriage were derailed when Letty announced that she had no interest in cooking and the couple quarreled. Williams eventually caved in and hired a cook, but in the meantime her parents withdrew their consent for the marriage. As a result, Letty and Williams eloped. She made her escape out a bedroom window with the help of her sisters. Williams' daughter Jessica, (who was two years older than his father's fourth wife) drove the couple to the airport, stopping along the way so that Letty could obtain a visa (something easily done in those days). The couple flew to Colorado Springs, where they were married in the office of Williams' accountants. A cocktail party in an elegant hotel followed the ceremony, and then the couple went off to honeymoon for six months in Europe. Afterwards they traveled on to New York. There, as Letty remembers, she was introduced to Williams' lawyer, Lee Lurie, who was very displeased to hear that Williams had married for a fourth time. Also displeased with Williams' recent nuptials was Jessica, whose earlier support for her father was now eroded by concerns that he would withdraw from his responsibilities to his other families. The quarrel in the bar of the Algonquin Hotel bar was so heated that he and Letty were later asked to check out.

Upon their return to Guanajuato, Williams and Letty faced her family, who insisted that the couple be properly married in a Catholic ceremony. In order to accomplish this goal, over the course of one half day, Williams became a Roman Catholic. He was baptized, had his first communion, and his confirmation in one morning. What this rapid conversion meant to him is unclear, except this would not be his last foray into religion. Later, at Letty's prompting, he would also study Judaism, and he and Letty also briefly experimented with being Mormons. But the conversion to Catholicism enabled him to be married in the Templo de Tercera Orden (also known as Eglesia de San

Francisco), a stately eighteenth-century church in Guanajuato, where, after his death, Letty would later place his ashes.[385]

Thus Williams and Letty settled down to a married life that was largely pacific.

Then, September 19th, 1978, at the age of sixty-six, Williams became a father again. Certainly, at this point in his life the role of father, wage earner, and guardian was very familiar to him. He had long fretted over, tended to, and provided for his children. Now the oldest, Fiona, was nearly forty, while his youngest, Dylan, was ten. But as for other men who sometimes discover a new late-life vocation in paternity, with the birth of daughter Dilys, he would discover the pleasures of being a hands-on father. Dilys was only seventeen when her father died, but she retains clear memories of a dad who engaged in every aspect of her life. For example, she remembers Williams as a man in his early seventies who ran alongside her, encouraging her as she tottered off on her first bicycle ride. Later, when she was only eleven, he taught her to drive. (Williams got her her first car when she was fifteen.) Dilys also remembers how her father often took on the maternal role, changing her diaper and heating her bottle. On one occasion, he was left in charge of her care while her mother Leticia was in Mexico City, being refitted for the braces that she has worn for most of her life as a result of contracting polio as a child. Williams gave his small daughter multiple baths that single day, as the toddler managed to get herself into three successive messes while his back was turned—first by dousing herself in talcum powder, then by covering herself in Jello, and finally by dirtying herself with mud. Each time he carefully bathed his small daughter. Later in her life, working only at night, he would sleep while his young daughter was at school and then wake up to care for her when she returned.

Thus the final two decades of Williams' life emerge as a story of man whose overriding objective was to be husband to Letty and father to Dilys. This commitment sometimes caused friction with other members of Williams' family and a few of his acquaintances. It also contributed to the widespread impression that he was no longer active as an illustrator.

In this phase, he often traveled between Mexico, where the house in Guanajuato continued to be the family vacation home, and Santa Fe, New Mexico, and later San Antonio, Texas, where the family lived for periods of time and where Dilys was educated.

In 1979, Williams was spending much time sculpting and painting, and as he wrote in a letter to John Norbutt, a family acquaintance, writing books for children "and their adult inferiors."[386] The light tone obscures the fact that during this period, Williams was indeed experimenting with adult fiction, but of a very dark nature; his archive contains several drafts of a story set in Europe during the Holocaust. One draft attempts to capture the surreal atmosphere of a train that is slowly making its way to a concentration camp.[387] The impetus for this story might have been Williams' ongoing processing of the death of his in-laws, Dorothea's parents, at Auschwitz. In any case, as Williams wrote to an acquaintance, life in Mexico was rapidly changing, with the cost of labor escalating in particular. In the letter Williams fretted that "greed, avarice, complete lack of concern for air, water, health (or others) gives us sewer-water for a river, fumes of burning garbage for the night, and now (quite new to Mexico) bill-boards beside the highway advertising Rum, a credit-card, a very large hotel, with more threatened." Clearly Mexico was no longer the bucolic setting it had once been: "Much to develop in every direction for the good of all of us; with a crowd of money-eyed men standing to make everything profitable (for them). Sadly modeled on the old USA of the past, heedless almost of the lessons to be learnt from history, as usual."[388]

Yet Williams returned to the USA, making a family trip to Santa Fe when Dilys was only two. Williams liked the look of the place so much that he decided to stay on. He bought a house there and eventually enrolled Dilys in the Santa Fe Waldorf School. He kept the house in Mexico for vacations. Dilys remembers her father as a man who "did not know the regular rules of life." If Williams was disinclined to return to Santa Fe from Mexico after a winter break, he simply kept her out of school. When Dilys was eight, Williams fell on the ice and injured his knee, and with Williams once again sick of snow and with Letty also struggling with the cold winters in New Mexico, the family moved to San Antonio, Texas, where they were delighted to find friends of Letty's already in residence. Once they sold their house in Santa Fe, they bought a house in the suburbs of San Antonio, though at first Williams had no studio. There, at the recommendation of family lawyer and friend Richard Ticktin, Dilys was enrolled in the prestigious St. Mary's Hall.[389]

During her family's time in San Antonio, she recalls her father's ready enthusiasm for simple American pleasures—a day-long sojourn at the movies, with a lunch of hot dogs and Coke, for instance, or perhaps simply a drive around the environs to view the neighbor's homes. However, in a hand-written document from the time, Williams reveals that he still felt pressed to illustrate in order to produce income: "If we could sell our house in Mexico for two or three million dollars, I could retire from the pressure to illustrate and get back into sculpting and painting. At my age one has passed the moment of youthful worries. I have everything I ever wanted, except a huge fortune of millions of dollars, and so I only pray my health will endure and that we will not lose what we have." He ended the document with hope that Dilys would one day marry and that Letty would be secure.[390]

As he had previously done in places like New York, Aspen, and Puerto Vallarta, Williams made a large number of acquaintances in San Antonio. There his accomplishments were recognized and duly noted in a feature article in a local newspaper, *The Sunday Express News*.[391] Among those he befriended was restaurateur Cappy Lawton, a San Antonio notable and perhaps the impetus behind one of several major tributes that were to come to Williams in 1991—a "Distinguished Citizen Award," given to him and also to actor Tommy Lee Jones, on December 19th, 1991. The award recognized Williams as having made "a major contribution to the world of literature" and as being "a master of several media." Citing *Stuart Little* and the Little House series in particular, the commendation states:

A true measure of a great city rests in the strengths and talents of its individual citizens. Mr. Williams has consistently displayed those traits which identify a truly great San Antonian. The Mayor and the City Council extend grateful recognition of his contributions that make San Antonio such a great city.[392]

But Williams' health was beginning to deteriorate, and so the family returned to Guanajuato. Dilys, who was now thirteen, quickly assumed the responsibility of caring for her parents. By age fourteen, she was driving the family car to pick up groceries and other necessary items. By the time she was fifteen, Williams gave Dilys her own car.[393]

Williams had collaborated with many notable authors over the years, and, in the late 1980s, he was to find one more inspiring partnership with Jack Prelutsky, a man nearly thirty years his junior. Prelutsky had been born in 1940 in Brooklyn, New York and, after attending Hunter College, worked at a number of jobs: cab driver, furniture mover, folk singer. He had considered the possibility of working as an illustrator and had drawn a number of pictures of animals, each accompanied by a short bit of humorous verse. "I put them aside and didn't think of them for a while," he wrote.

Then a friend saw them and made me take them to his editor. She said, "You are talented." I thought she was going to love my drawings. But she told me I was a terrible artist, and she showed me the work of other illustrators—Arnold Lobel and Maurice Sendak and Tomi Ungerer—and I understood why I was a terrible artist. But she said I had a talent for verse that I didn't suspect I had.[394]

From such humble beginnings grew a splendid career—over sixty books, chiefly of clever, artful nonsensical verse full of puns, deft rhythms, and flashing wit. His first such book, *A Gopher in the Garden and Other Animal Poems* was published in 1967 with illustrations by Robert Leydenfrost. Subsequent books were illustrated by many artists, including Arnold Lobel (most famous, perhaps, for his Frog and Toad series) until Lobel's death in 1987. During his partnership with

Illustration from *Ride a Purple Pelican*.

Prelutsky, Williams couldn't hope to replace Lobel's distinctive style, but he could demonstrate that he too could still develop new techniques that were more in line with emerging styles of illustration.

Williams' approach to illustrating Prelutsky's poems in both *Ride a Purple Pelican* (1986) and *Beneath a Blue Umbrella* (1990) was to exploit new possibilities in color reproduction. As he explained in an interview with Leonard Marcus, the subdued color he had used in, for instance, *The Rabbits' Wedding* was forced on him by publishers who considered full-color printing to be prohibitively expensive. "Fortunately, nowadays you can do color." For *Ride a Purple Pelican* he mixed "a very thin oil paint, used almost like watercolor," and then added pen lines in order to create bright, bold images.[395] The result of this experiment—both its success and its limitation—can be judged by comments in two reviews of *Beneath a Blue Umbrella*. Writing in *Horn Book Magazine*, Ann Flowers noted that "Although Garth Williams' illustrations have a much rougher line than, and lack the charming detail of, his earlier pictures, the large, colorful pages and cheerfully ridiculous verse will appeal to younger listeners."[396] And Carolyn Phelan wrote, "Even the children in the back row of the classroom will enjoy Williams' illustrations, brimming with color, energy, and bright, bold design."[397] A certain subtlety and nuance that had always characterized Williams' work was lost in this technique, but in its place was a new sizzle and pop.

Around the time he was working with Prelutsky, Williams was also finally gaining the recognition he deserved for his work on the Little House series. Several decades after the death of Laura Ingalls Wilder, the books were more popular than ever. In 1971, Harper and Row (under the imprint Harper Trophy) had reprinted the series in a paperback edition that was affordable and suitable for home libraries. (Color would later be added to a box set of the stories in 2004.) Then, in 1974, the television series based on the book *Little House on the Prairie* (1974-1982) introduced an even wider audience to Wilder's books, though it made little attempt to capture in realistic terms the material conditions of pioneer life. For some viewers, the TV series initiated a nearly obsessive focus on the "true" stories, leading to increased interest in both the books and the actual historical sites. Among those responding to such interest was scholar William Anderson, who edited and reprinted a series of articles about the books under the title *The Horn Book's Laura Ingalls Wilder: Articles about and by Laura Ingalls Wilder, Garth Williams, and the Little House Books* in 1987. This collection included Williams' account of his original trip in 1953 (as discussed in Chapter Three), and it reprinted Williams' photographs from the trip.[398] Later, in 1990, Anderson was to publish *Laura Ingalls Wilder Country: The People and Places in Laura Ingalls Wilder's Life and Books*, providing further historical evidence of the sites and scenes of the stories that Williams had been the first to capture in his drawings.[399]

Against the backdrop of this keen interest in the Little House series, Williams found himself being approached as someone who had briefly known Wilder (who had died in 1957) and who was a valuable link to the world preserved in her stories. In July of 1986, he was invited back to De Smet, South Dakota, the site of several of the stories, where he had last visited in 1947. There he was lionized and treated like the celebrity he had finally become, as articles from the local newspapers attest. Although residual resentment over royalty issues with Harpers had sometimes colored Williams' memories of his earlier trip, surely the treatment he received in 1986 must have made the struggles all seem worth while.[400] A letter in Williams' archive from William Anderson to William Morris, at that time a vice president and the director of library promotion at HarperCollins, details the full extent of Williams' highly successful visit. Greeting a total of 1,100 visitors, Williams autographed books for six hours. His live presentation, captured on videotape, occurred in front of a standing-room-only crowd. He sold around $4,000 worth of books, not just from the Little House series, but also titles like *The Rabbits' Wedding* and *Charlotte's Web*.

Williams also put in an appearance at the Sioux Falls mall. When he arrived, the line stretched out of the store and snaked down past the next two stores. One woman claimed she had driven 120 miles to meet Williams. He sold $1,000 worth of books in an hour and a half. In all, Anderson calculated that Williams signed 1,000 or more books—certainly no easy feat for a man of his years. As Anderson also records, the local media were well aware of Williams' visit and they afforded him full treatment, including a television interview, coverage in five newspapers (one going out over the AP wire), and a filmed segment to be broadcast on local news. Anderson concluded his summary with these comments: "Williams is a rare commodity, a great gentleman, and his tenderness with children and all readers is in keeping with the sensitivity of his drawings."[401]

Though especially impressive in scope, this was not the only acknowledgment Williams received in his later years. He was on other occasions also invited to speak or otherwise participate in a number of events celebrating children's literature, as when he lectured on "The Contribution of the Illustrator in Children's Literature" at McGill University in 1981, following that talk with an appearance in the bookshop of his daughter, now Bettina Williams Shore, or when he visited the Marguerite de Angeli Library, Lapeer, Michigan, in1992. As the twentieth century began to wind down, literary and cultural scholars started the work of summarizing an important history of contemporary children's literature, casting a backwards eye over the postwar in particular as a rich and fruitful period. Williams' illustrative work, the production of more than forty years, was rightfully being reconsidered for the crucial contributions it had made, due in part to the efforts of scholars like Peter Neumeyer, who included extensive commentary from Williams on his illustrations in *The Annotated Charlotte's Web*.

In addition, Leonard Marcus, the author of the definitive study of twentieth-century children's literature, *Minders of Make-Believe*, as well as a highly regarded biography of Margaret Wise Brown, interviewed Williams for *Publisher's Weekly* in February of 1990. In this interview Williams started off by joking that he wondered how his daughter Fiona could be fifty when he himself was only forty-two. After covering the highpoints of his life, he reflected on the changing state of printing technology. "There is no reason I shouldn't mix a photograph into one of my pictures," he told Marcus. "I haven't done that yet."[402] In this interview, he comes across as razor sharp, energetic, and scarcely ready to retire.

An interview done by William Anderson for *The Horn Book Magazine* in 1993 offered a version of the artist who was once again reflective, but whose "tastes and interests haven't changed" (in his own words). To Anderson he recounted something of his creative process:

> To compose the pictures is very hard," he admits. "I look for all the action in the story; then I arrange forms and color. I always try to imagine what the author is seeing. Of course, I have to narrow down my ideas to the number of drawings I'm allowed, which might be as few as ten per book. I make a list of illustrations. When I see a picture, I write down the idea and a page number while I read the manuscript."
>
> "Everyone thinks, 'How nice to illustrate children's books.' But I'm pragmatic. It's a job. My inspiration is my deadline. But when I start, the work usually goes quickly. I never get tired when I'm illustrating!"

Anderson had a tour of Williams' studio (now no longer standing), which he described as having "five work tables, nine skylights, piles of props, and accumulations of art work." Anderson explained, "His family sees the studio as impossibly messy and in need of organization, but Garth's benign silence on the matter indicates that a non-artist cannot possibly understand the proper ambiance of his working surroundings." Williams and Letty were hospitable to Anderson with every kindness and courtesy, and in return Anderson painted an affectionate, intimate portrait of Williams in his waning years:

> Garth Williams retains a zest that befits his roguish, sometimes irreverent, style. He's a master raconteur who can relate wild and improbable adventures with such diverse characters as Hitler and Picasso. He's a tireless charmer when he makes personal appearances around the country, glib but tender with his admirers. He's patient but incredulous when he autographs his way through mounds of books and always gracious when he accepts the adulation he receives.[403]

Rounding out these accounts by Marcus and Anderson were two other notable publications—the first, a piece by Joan Brest Friedberg for *American Writers for Children, 1900-1960*, as part of the *Dictionary of Literary Biography*, and the second, at long last, Williams' own autobiography. The article by Friedberg paid careful attention to the variety that Williams had employed in his illustration and showed special sensitivity to his artistic skills. In this way it became a notable summary of Williams' accomplishments as an illustrator, one that he enthusiastically approved.[404] Meanwhile, in 1989, Williams finally told his own story in a short autobiography for the Gale *Something About the Author Autobiography Series*. Having amassed materials for almost seventy years, he seems to have intended to write one day the definitive narrative of his own life. In the end, he produced only this twelve-page account—hardly a full-length memoir. Left abandoned were many starts and restarts, versions and revisions of a life that, as we have described, defied an easy telling.

Yet towards the end of his life, Williams knew many who were ready to tell him what his life had been about and what he had meant to them. An especially auspicious year in Williams' life was 1991: it brought not only the aforementioned recognition by the city of San Antonio, but also a special day, October 12th, held in his honor in Mansfield, Missouri, the site of the Laura Ingalls Wilder Historic Home and Museum. Having been invited by William Anderson to participate in the Children's Literature Festival of the Ozarks sponsored by Drury College in Springfield, Williams also visited the Laura Ingalls Wilder School, where he was very popular with the children. He was then fêted with a celebration in his honor on the grounds of the Wilder Farm. Also in 1991, Williams received recognition for his contribution to American literature when he was interviewed and subsequently honored by a national program called "Mrs. Bush's Story Time." This program had been launched by Barbara Bush, wife to President George H. W. Bush, to encourage literacy. Mrs. Bush herself read notable classics in children's literature aloud over the ABC radio network, by way of encouraging parents to read out loud to their children. She sent a researcher to Guanajuato to tape an interview with Williams. An invitation to a reception at the White House celebrating the program followed, for Thursday afternoon November 21st of 1991, though Williams and Letty were unable to attend.

The last completed project of Williams' career connected back to its beginning and brought him full circle. He was approached by John Sebastian Junior, his godson and the son of one his oldest friends and a benefactor from his earliest days in Rome and then New York. Now famous as the founder of the popular rock group The Lovin' Spoonful, Sebastian Junior had written a book that was at once a tribute to his father and an ode to their parallel (though quite different) careers in music—John Senior's as a classical harmonicanist, and John Junior's as a rock musician. John Junior's manuscript, entitled *J. B.'s Harmonica*, was the story of a boy trying to forge his own identity in his father's shadow. When friends say he plays just like his father, J. B. gives up the harmonica and tries to think of a different career for himself. But eventually he learns that he can play harmonica in his own way and the family crisis is resolved.

In Sebastian's original conception of the story, the characters were human—it was, after all, essentially autobiographical—but Williams, who had always had trouble drawing people, could not get the pictures right. Finally he abandoned the attempt and made J. B. and his family bears. He still had his old facility with animals, and the new pictures were a success. *Kirkus Review* found Williams' drawings "a little dark, but his furry bears are as appealing as ever,"[405] while *Publishers Weekly* thought that Sebastian's "understated prose is comfortably bolstered by the familiar style of Williams' almost tangibly fuzzy black-and-white illustrations."[406]

The switch from humans to bears, incidentally, did not discourage John Sebastian Junior from converting *J. B.'s Harmonica* into a musical for children. In the summer of 2014, Plays in the Park, a theater program in Edison, New Jersey, advertised a fall production of *J. B.'s Harmonica*, with music and lyrics by John B. Sebastian and book by

Illustration from *J.B.'s Harmonica* courtesy of the Estate of Garth Williams.

Gary P. Cohen. The description of the show promised fun for the whole family:

> Based on the beloved children's book by singer/songwriter John B. Sebastian, *J.B.'s Harmonica* tells the delightful story of a talented family of bears, and the trials young 12-year-old J.B. faces when his father gives him a new harmonica. Featuring such classic folk-rock songs as "Do You Believe in Magic?", "What a Day for a Daydream", "Summer in the City", "Did You Ever Have to Make Up Your Mind?", "Nashville Cats" and many others. Great fun for all the Baby Boomers

and their kids, whether human or bear![407]

Still represented as bears after all these years, one of the oldest connections of Williams' life lives on in musical theater.

But Williams had struggled over this last commission. Failing health made it difficult for him to finish the project, and its completion is testimony to the kind of loyalty he often showed to his closest friends. The story of his death follows a familiar pattern for many people of advanced age: his downward spiral began with a fall that occurred when he tripped as he went to answer the phone. With two broken ribs resulting, he was never quite the same after, his daughter remembers. Sometime after this fall, he then broke his hip when he got up during the night. This time he was hospitalized for forty-three days, during which time Letty and Dilys lived at the hospital. Letty kept watch over him during the night to be sure that Williams, who often woke up disoriented, did not pull out his intravenous tubes. Dilys, who was in high school, left every morning to attend her classes. After several weeks, they brought Williams home, but he was, Dilys remembers, a "different person." Now bedridden, he was tended to by three rotating nurses.

On the night he died, the attending nurse called Dilys, then seventeen, to his room to alert her that Williams' breath had become uneven—he was "breathing funny"—taking several seconds in between each breath. Clearly the end was very near, yet Dilys was frantic to do what she could to keep her father alive. She called the doctor, and then an ambulance. When it couldn't come fast enough, she called family friends with influence to see if they might accelerate its arrival. As the intervals between each of Williams' breaths increased, Dilys next thought to take him to the hospital in her own car. Now desperate, Dilys kept urging him "please breathe!" But Williams only calmly looked at his daughter, with no apparent signs of pain or distress. He was finally taken to the hospital, where the medical staff officially declared his death by "respiratory distress." The date was May 8th, 1996. Though traumatized by the event, Dilys was comforted by the fact that her father had apparently not suffered at the end. Dilys returned from the hospital to console her mother, whose disability had kept her at home, and to make the necessary phone calls to the rest of Williams' family.[408]

For both Letty and Dilys, Williams' death was devastating. Letty in particular struggled to let go of her husband; for some time, she kept his ashes with her at home, until Dilys convinced her to put them in a suitable place. Through the intervention of an influential family member, they arranged to have Williams' ashes interned at the Templo de Tercera Orden (or the Igelesia de San Francisco), the same church where he and Letty had been married, though this honor was normally reserved only for priests and other elite members of the parish. Rumors persist that Williams is buried in Aspen, but it is both more fitting and poetic that he rests in Guanajuato, not in the United States where he once conjured himself as living the life of Huckleberry Finn, nor in anyplace in Europe, where he had originally been trained and aspired to become an artist. Surely, he belonged to all of these places—US, England, Mexico. Yet in the end, Mexico claimed him as her own.

Afterword

As a photographer for most of his life, Garth Williams took and collected innumerable pictures of his extended family and of himself. We therefore have an excellent record of what he looked like at all the stages of his life. But video footage of the live man in action is harder to come by. One notable exception is a scratchy, black and white tape currently in the possession of the Laura Ingalls Wilder Memorial Society from 1986, when Williams would have been 74. On this occasion, Williams had been invited back to De Smet, South Dakota 39 years after he first did the research for the Little House series. After a brief introduction by William Anderson, Williams presents himself to the small audience in what appears to be a library. Not a tall man, his stature is not enhanced by the typical

'80s fashion—high waisted pants, wide tie, shirt with oversized collar. His head is immediately recognizable—broad, appealing face, kind yet piercing eyes, well-defined features, a dominant brow enhanced by the now bald head ringed by longish white hair. He speaks relatively softly, almost shyly at first, with only the faintest traces of a British accent apparent in certain vowels. As he reminisces about his childhood and the circumstances that led to his career as an artist, he sometimes addresses himself directly to the children seated on the floor, off camera and at his feet. At other times, he looks out over the room and engages the adults. It isn't much to go on, this video, but the viewer is immediately drawn to the man: there is definitely some charisma here, some quality that pulls the audience in and makes them want to know this man better, to hear what he has to say.

This is, after all, Garth Williams towards the end of his life. He is conveying what he wants his audience to remember. He is leaving his legacy. In the last two decades of his life, he was preoccupied with the task of making his account, summing up, as suggested by various fragments in his archive. One undated document is entitled "MY CRITERIA FOR SELECTING A BOOK TO ILLUSTRATE AND WHAT CRITERIA I PLACE ON THE BOOKS I WRITE." In it, he describes himself as a "father" who selects books to illustrate based on whether the book is "excellent" or "tiresome or dull." About the first judgment he writes, "As an illustrator, when I read a MSS I see the story in pictures; in fact I see a movie as I read. If the pictures have been very interesting or if I feel that they will be, then that is the next point in selecting a book to illustrate." He later elaborates:

> By *good* I mean many things;—the realization of responsibility; the value of truth; that evil is undesirable; how nature is amazing; or how life is—usually with humans transposed into animals—in such a way that stories can be. I am particularly interested in the belief that humor is the most important element we should develop in the world we have to live in at any age.

Further addressing the question of how he selects the books to illustrate, he returns to the issue of collaboration with the author, only to move immediately to the question of his own original contribution:

> The author produces the most important part; the illustrator brings out the best that the author was saying in words. An illustrator can give a different meaning to the words. As an author I find myself trying to pass on the wisdom I think I have learned. I try to pass on sensations I think of value to a child. Again I am the father teaching the children what I think are the values of life, or giving them something to enjoy, perhaps to laugh at; and sometimes to love.
>
> In the end, I hope to approach some art, of literature or graphic, that will last as long as possible, and will have universal value in ages to come, like the great works of other centuries, that would by my guide in decisions of how to draw or what to say—but there is no knowing how to discover those truths. The world is always in a process of change; I hope to be aware of this at all times, and appreciate what is new when it has value.

That Williams meant for his words to be remembered can be seen in the addendum to the document: "Please return this; or make a copy for the next inquiry; Xerox, or similar."[409]

This document creates the sense that Williams was coming to closure and that he was eager to sum up a life's accomplishment and to articulate the principles that had guided his work. In another, also undated but related document, he paused to reflect on the current state of contemporary children's culture. He especially bemoaned the prevalence of violence, a trend that he describes as "positively undesirable":

> [Violence is] most frequently found in cartoon comics, on T.V. and motion pictures. When a cartoon mouse flattens to a pancake[;] a cartoon cat soon returns to normal. Then it chases again the cartoon-mouse. In reality the cat would have been completely killed, so the child gets the dubious thrill of killing. I think our society suffers as a result of these endless scenes of hittings, bashings, smashings, not to

mention space stories of only warfare, nothing else. Today if a group wants a new government they blow up a railroad station full of people. Chivalry has never been heard of, and these cowards are now heroes.

Responding to a late twentieth-century culture (and perhaps to the 1980 Red Brigade bombing of the train station in Bologna in particular?), Williams expresses a deep concern for a society in which violence is normalized and taken up as the expression of political power.

The passage is especially interesting because of the sensibility it reflects. Much more than an old person's knee-jerk reaction to "those kids today," the comment reveals an attentiveness to and interest in the lessons of representation. For Garth Williams, there was a direct connection between a visual culture that encourages the idea that violence has no material reality, no actual consequences, and a political culture that sees violence as a quick and easy means to its end. It's not hard to concede his point, or at least to wonder about the role of the representation of violence in a range of contemporary geo-political events, from drone strikes in Pakistan to the mortars in the Arab-Israeli conflict. As in the comment above, Williams revealed how he understood representation as an animated sequence of events (a movie, in effect) rendered into a static image.

Yet, although he disapproved of the fortuitous violence of the Tom and Jerry cartoon or the Star Wars movies, in his art Garth Williams had never been afraid to confront the dark side himself. His very best illustrations don't lie about the truth of our mortal being or about our ultimate fate as creatures of this world. His best art respects the child's ability to process intricate visual representations and to hold onto multiple ideas at one time. Sometimes this respect manifests itself as irony or the visual joke that says two things can be true at once: a mouse can be diminutive in stature, but majestic in his demeanor; a dog can visit a butcher's shop to buy his own dinner, but he can't resist a wild romp with his canine friends; a little girl can nurse a pig in a way that transforms her into a vision of the Madonna. With some exceptions, Williams' drawings hit just the right note, avoiding an easily accessed, one-dimensional sentimentality in favor of deeper, more complex emotions that reverberate beyond the author's words.

Having returned to American shores and having dedicated himself to the research of a vanished American rural past, Garth Williams created a unique body of distinctly American art. His illustrations and drawings for the Laura Ingalls Wilder books in particular served to illuminate another obscure past. In a similar vein, though animals claim no nationality, Williams' creatures can nonetheless also be said to express a distinctly American sensibility. Certainly their boundless energy, their creativity, and their sense of endless possibility mark them as the products of a new world. This is not to suggest, however, that he created an art that could not travel. To the contrary, his illustrations have been frequently enjoyed and published abroad—in English, French, Italian, Dutch, Finnish, Slovene, and South Afrikaans editions, among many others. And Garth Williams' art is especially popular in Japan.

On the one hand, a keen interest in all things Laura Ingalls Wilder drew attention to Williams' work during the 1980s. Japanese readers avidly sought both translations of the Little House series and information about Williams himself. At the same time, the Japanese have long had a special fondness for all of his animal drawings, and for *The Rabbits' Wedding* in particular, as can be seen in the 2002 Japanese publication of *The Picture Book World of Garth Williams* by Motoo Ito, with an introduction by Leonard Marcus. The wide-spread popularity of Williams' animals may have something to do with his tendency to draw "neonatized" portraits, as discussed in Chapter Five: his large-eyed creatures could certainly find themselves home in a world of anime. Yet their allure also belies any simple explanation: could his unique representation of the natural world also speak to a Japanese sensibility? There does seem to have been something in both the man and his art that attracted a Japanese audience, so much so that in 1987 Hiromi Nakahira, writing on behalf of the Gandarufu, Inc., contacted Williams with a proposal for an entire "Year of Garth Williams" campaign. Pending Williams' approval, department stores were poised to display original drawings alongside merchandise, including letter sets and postcards with images from the books. In the end, the plan did not come to fruition, though some tie-in merchandise was eventually produced and sold. To this day, in certain Japanese toy stores you can buy a toy version of the small bear who makes his appearance in *Little Fur Family*, and many of Williams books are on sale. In addition, Williams' work has been of interest to Japanese scholars, with a recent publication about his work appearing in 2009.[410] In this way, Williams' art seems destined to live on, both in the United States and across the world, and it can be said to have fulfilled his own stated ambition—to create works "that will have universal value in ages to come, like the great works of other centuries."

Acknowledgements

We want to thank the team at Beaufort Books, especially our dynamic editor, Megan Trank, and our designer, Michael Short.

This biography could not have been written without the kind and generous assistance of the Williams family. We thank Dylan Williams (Brooklyn and Guanajuato), who first agreed to meet with us and to introduce us to the other members of the family; Bettina Williams Shore and Bruce Shore (Montreal), who have been an invaluable source of information, as well as extraordinarily welcoming and hospitable; the late Gunda Lambton, whom we were honored to meet through the kind efforts of Bettina and Bruce Shore; Eystn Williams (Newport, R.I.) who shared many of her memories with us; Fiona Williams Hulbert

(Edinburg), who gave us a clear perspective on her father's years in New York and afterwards; and Leticia and Dilys Williams (Queretero) for allowing us access to Garth Williams' papers.

From the time of his earliest professional ambitions until the last days of his life, Williams filed away important documents, letters, unpublished manuscripts, contracts, financial statements, and other records. These files are currently stored in Queretaro, Mexico, and have made it possible for us to piece together the story of his personal life.

Thanks also to Humberto Manuel Soto Camargo for his hospitality in Mexico and to Rodrigo Marcocchio Romero for showing us Garth's property in Guanajuato.

Many other individuals provided assistance with our research. Thanks to William T. Anderson, Alessandra Giovenco (archivist, British School at Rome), Terry Heard (Archivist for the City School of London), Spencer Howard (Archives Technician, Herbert Hoover Presidential Library), Tara Jackson (Laura Ingalls Wilder Historic Home & Museum), Peter Leach, Craig Murray (Imperial War Museum), Peter Neumeyer, the late George Nicholson, Cheryl Palmlund (Laura Ingalls Wilder Memorial Society), Neil Parkinson (Archives & Collections Manager, Royal College of Art, London), Mark Pomeroy (Archivist, Royal Academy of Arts, London), Anna Scott (Archivist, Aspen Historical Society), Madelin Terrazas (Archives Assistant, Churchill Archives Centre, Cambridge, UK), Richard Ticktin, Deanne Urmy, and Toyoko Yamamoto. Thanks also to our readers, Katherine Harris, David Mitchell, and George O'Har.

Boston College provided generous research funds to support the writing of this biography. Special thanks to our Chair, Suzanne Matson, our Provost, David Quigley, and our Dean, Gregory Kalscheur.

Garth Williams Bibilography

YEAR	TITLE	AUTHOR	PUBLISHER
1945	*Eastward in Eden*	Claude Silve	Creative Age Press
1945	*I Married Them*	Janet Van Duyn	Howell, Soskin
1945	*Stuart Little*	E. B. White	Harper
1945	*Tux 'n Tails*	Raymond Andrieux	Vanguard Press
1946	*In Our Town*	Damon Runyon	Creative Age Press
1946	*The Great White Hills of New Hampshire*	Ernest Poole	Doubleday
1946 – 1969	*The Chicken Book*		Howell, Soskin
1946	*Every Month Was May*	Evelyn Eaton	Harper
1946 – 1968	*The Little Fur Family*	Margaret Wise Brown	Harper
1948	*Robin Hood*	Henry Gilbert	Lippincott
1948	*Wait Till the Moon Is Full*	M. W. Brown	Harper
1948	*Tiny Library* (I)	Dorothy Kunhardt	Simon & Schuster LG
1948	*The Golden Sleepy Book*	M. W. Brown	Simon & Schuster LG
1949	*Flossie and Bossie*	Eva Le Galienne	Harper
1949	*Tiny Library* (II)	Dorothy Kunhardt	Simon & Schuster
1950	*The Tall Book of Make Believe*	Anthology	Harper

1951	*Elves and Fairies*	Anthology	Simon & Schuster
1951	*The Adventures of Benjamin Pink*	Garth Williams	Harper
1952	*Charlotte's Web*	E. B. White	Harper
1952	*Mister Dog*	M. W. Brown	Simon & Schuster LG
1952	*Baby Animals*	Garth Williams	Simon & Schuster LG
1953	*Baby Farm Animals*	Garth Williams	Simon & Schuster LG
1953	*Animal Friends*	M. W. Brown	Simon & Schuster LG
1953	*The Sailor Dog*	M. W. Brown	Simon & Schuster LG
1953	*Little House in the Big Woods*	Laura Ingalls Wilder	Harper
	Little House on the Prairie		
	On the Banks of Plum Creek		
	Farmer Boy		
	By the Shores of Silver Lake		
	The Long Winter		
	Little Town on the Prairie		
	These Happy Golden Years		
1954	*The Friendly Book*	M. W. Brown	Simon & Schuster LG
1954	*The Cat Who Thought He Was a Mouse*	M. W. Brown	Simon & Schuster LG
1955	*The Golden Name Day*	Jenny Lindquist	Harper
1955	*Baby's First Book*	Garth Williams	Simon & Schuster LG
1956	*Three Little Animals*	M. W. Brown	Harper
1956	*Home for a Bunny*	M. W. Brown	Simon & Schuster LG
1957	*My First Counting Book*	Lilian Moore	Simon & Schuster LG
1957	*Over and Over*	Charlotte Zolotow	Harper
1957	*The Happy Orpheline*	Natalie Carlson	Harper
1957	*Animal A.B.C.*	Garth Williams	Simon & Schuster LG
1958	*The Rabbits' Wedding*	Garth Williams	Harper
1958	*Three Bedtime Stories*	Traditional	Simon & Schuster LG
1958	*The Family Under the Bridge*	Natalie Carlson	Harper
1958	*Do You Know What I'll Do?*	Charlotte Zolotow	Harper
1959	*Little Silver House*	Jenny Lindquist	Harper

1959	*Emmett's Pig*	Mary Stolz	Harper
1959	*The Rescuers*	Margery Sharp	Little, Brown
1959	*A Brother for the Orphelines*	Natalie Carlson	Harper
1960	*The Cricket in Times Square*	George Selden	Farrar, Strauss & Co.
1960	*Bedtime for Frances*	Russell Hoban	Harper
1962	*A Tale of Tails*	Elizabeth MacPherson	Simon & Schuster LG
1962	*Miss Bianca*	Margery Sharp	Little, Brown
1963	*The Turret*	Margery Sharp	Little, Brown
1963	*Amigo*	Byrd Baylor	Macmillan
1963	*The Little Giant Girl and the Elf Boy*	Else Holmelund Minarik	Harper & Row
1963	*The Sky Was Blue*	Charlotte Zolotow	Harper & Row
1964	*My Bedtime Book*	M. W. Brown and JaneWatson	Simon & Schuster LG
1964	*The Gingerbread Rabbit*	Randall Jarrell	Macmillan
1964	*Bread-and-Butter Indian*	Anne Colver	Holt, Rinehart & Winston
1965	*The Whispering Rabbit and Other Stories*	M. W. Brown	Simon & Schuster LG
1966	*Miss Bianca in the Salt Mines*	Margery Sharp	Little, Brown
1967	*Push Kitty*	Jan Wahl	Harper & Row
1968	*The Laura Ingalls Wilder Songbook*	ed. Eugenia Garson and Herbert Haufrecht	Harper & Row
1969	*Tucker's Countryside*	George Selden	Farrar Straus Giroux
1970	*Bread-and-Butter Journey*	Anne Colver	Holt,Rinehart & Winston
1973	*The First Four Years*	Laura Ingalls Wilder	Harper & Row
1973	*Lucky Mrs. Ticklefeather*	Dorothy Kunhardt	Simon & Schuster LG
1974	*Harry Cat's Pet Puppy*	George Selden	Farrar Strauss Giroux
1977	*Fox Eyes*	M. W. Brown	Pantheon
1979	*The Little House Cookbook*	Barbara M. Walker	Harper & Row
1981	*Chester Cricket's Pigeon Ride*	George Selden	Farrar Strauss Giroux
1981	*Chester Cricket's New Home*	George Selden	Farrar Strauss Giroux

1982	*Self-Portrait*	Garth Williams	Addison-Wesley Longman
1985	*The Little House Diary*	Barbara M. Walker	Harper & Row
1986	*Ride a Purple Pelican*	Jack Prelutsky	HarperCollins
1987	*The Old Meadow*	George Selden	Farrar Strauss Giroux
1990	*Beneath a Blue Umbrella*	Jack Prelutsky	HarperCollins
1993	*J.B.'s Harmonica*	John Sebastian, Jr.	Harcourt

Endnotes

1 "E.L.B." "For Ages 8 to 12: Animal Stories: Barnyard Duo Flossie and Bossie," *The New York Times Book Review*, November 13, 1949, p. 20. http://search.proquest.com.proxy.bc.edu/hnpnewyorktimes/docview/105928223/fulltextPDF/9F90C3ACFE68459DPQ/3?accountid=9673

2 "Original 'Charlotte's Web' art fetches big money at auction," October 16, 2010, CBS Local Boston website, http://boston.cbslocal.com/2010/10/16/original-charlottes-web-art-fetches-big-money-at-auction/

3 "Margaret Wise Brown" by Garth Williams. April 1968. Unpublished document in the Garth Williams Archive.

4 In the Williams' papers, the earliest attempt at an autobiography is dated 1960. This is followed by versions in 1970, 1977, and three revisions in 1981. There may have been additional attempts. On February 26, 1987, he wrote to Harper that he intended to revise his "self-portrait" once again.

5 "Garth Williams (1912-)." *Something about the Author Autobiography Series*. Ed. Joyce Nakamura. Vol. 7. Detroit: Gale Research, 1989. 313-327. <http://galenet.galegroup.com.proxy.bc.edu/servlet/SATA_Online/mlin_m_bostcoll/BH2179075021>. Accessed 26 July 2012. Page 312.

6 *Something About the Author*, p. 313.

7 Email correspondence with Denise Williams, July 1, 2012.

8 *Something About the Author*, p. 313,

9 Gunda Lambton, *The Frankenstein Room: Growing Up in Germany Between the Wars* (Ottawa: Voyager Publishing, 2000), p. 150.

10 Lambton, *The Frankenstein Room*, p. 151.

11 State of New York, Certificate and Record of Birth for Garth Williams. Record Number 20969 April 20, 1917.

12 Hand written notes found in the Garth Williams Archive.

13 Lambton, *The Frankenstein Room*, p. 149.

14 Lambton, *The Frankenstein Room*, p. 154..

15 *Something About the Author*, p. 313.

16 Undated manuscript in the Garth Williams Archive.

17 S.S. *Cedric* passenger list from Ancestry.com, consulted September 15, 2013.

18 *Something About the Author*, p. 313.

19 *Something About the Author*, p. 313.

20 Lambton, *The Frankenstein Room*, p. 149.

21 Lambton, *The Frankenstein Room*, p. 150.

22 Email correspondence with Terry Heard, Archivist for the City School of London, August 9, 2012.

23 Lambton, *The Frankenstein Room*, p. 155.

24 *Something About the Author*, p. 314.

25 *Something About the Author*, p. 314

26 Anthony Anderson, *The Man who was H. M Bateman* (Exeter, England: Webb and Brower, 1982), p. 18.

27 Email correspondence with Neil Parkinson, Archive and Collection Manager. Royal College of Art. February 17, 2012.

28 *Something About the Author*, p. 314.

29 Hilary Cunliffe-Charlesworth, "The Royal College of Art: Its Influence on Education, Art, and Design 1900-1950" (Unpublished Doctoral Thesis. Sheffield City Polytechnic, 1991), p. 52.

30 *Something About the Author*, p. 314.

31 *Something About the Author*, p. 314.

32 Letter in the Garth Williams Archive.

33 Timothy Peter Wiseman, *A Short History of the British School at Rome* (London: British School at Rome, Regent's College, 1990), p. 12.

34 Gunda Lambton, *Sun in Winter: A Toronto Wartime Journal* (Montreal: McGill-Queens University Press, 2003), pp. 2-3.

35 Lambton, *The Frankenstein Room*, pp. 137-38.

36 Lambton, *The Frankenstein Room*, p. 139.

37 Lambton, *The Frankenstein Room*, p. 140.

38 Undated manuscript in the Garth Williams Archive.

39 Lambton, *The Frankenstein Room*, p. 141.

40 Lambton, *The Frankenstein Room*, p. 160.

41 In fact the situation was less clear: up until 1923, wives were required to reside outside the school. Under the liberal directorship of Bernard Ashmole (1925-28), the rule had been relaxed. In 1926, painter Winifred Knights remained after her scholarship ended after marrying Tom Monnington, another resident. Also, sculptor Barbara Hepworth was allowed to reside as the wife of John Skeaping (whom she later divorced). In any case, Williams' residency was due to expire in the spring of 1938, so the couple probably needn't have worried about Williams' status as a married man (*The British School at Rome 100 Years,* pp. 14-15).

42 Lambton, *The Frankenstein Room*, p. 160.

43 Undated manuscript in the Garth Williams Archive.

44 *Something About the Author*, p. 315.

45 Lambton, *The Frankenstein Room*, p. 165.

46 Lambton, *The Frankenstein Room*, p. 166.

47 Undated manuscript in the Garth Williams Archive.

48 Interview with Gunda Lambton, July 2012. *The Frankenstein Room*, p. 168.

49 Lambton, *Sun in Winter*, p. 78.

50 Lambton, *The Frankenstein Room*, p. 316.

51 Lambton, *Sun in Winter*, p. 2.

52 Lambton, *The Frankenstein Room*, pp. 171-72.

53 Lambton, *The Frankenstein Room*, p. 174.

54 *Something About the Author*, p. 315.

55 *Something About the Author*, p. 316.

56 Undated manuscript in the Garth Williams Archive.

57 Raymond Peat, "British civilian bicycle messenger and relief worker with Air Raid Precautions in Hull, GB, 1940-1942." Interviewed by Jim Peat. Imperial War Museum Catalogue number 13651.

58 Undated manuscript in the Garth Williams Archive.

59 *Something About the Author*, p. 316.

60 *Something About the Author*, p. 318

61 "*Something About the Author*, 318.

62 This is according to Madelin Terrazas, Archive Assistant to the Churchill Archive Centre at Cambridge. According to Terrazas, had Churchill written a letter to Roosevelt on Williams' behalf, a copy should have been filed and catalogued under Williams name. (Email correspondence, April 5, 2012). The letter may have been informal and therefore not recorded.

63 Lambton, *Frankenstein Room*, p. 182.

64 Lambton, *Frankenstein Room*, p. 182.

65 Lambton, *Sun in Winter*, p. 98.

66 *Something About the Author*, p. 320.

67 *Something About the Author*, pp. 320-321.

68 http://discovery.nationalArchive.gov.uk/SearchUI/Details?uri=C3505186#. Accessed 1/7/2013.

69 Connery Chappell, *Island of Barbed Wire: Internment on the Isle of Man in World War Two* (London: Robert Hale, 1984).

70. http://discovery.nationalArchive.gov.uk/SearchUI/Details?uri=C3505186#. Accessed January 7, 2013.

71 http://www.geni.com/people/Dr-Heinrich-Dessauer/6000000007014454472. Accessed January 8, 2013. The record of the death of Dr. Dessauer's wife has not been recovered.

72 Lambton, *Sun in Winter*, p. 4.

73 Lambton, *The Frankenstein Room*, p. 190.

74 Lambton, *Sun in Winter*, p. 1.

75 *Something About the Author*, p. 316.

76 *Something About the Author*, p. 321.

77 Gunda Lambton, *Sun In Winter: A Toronto Wartime Journal 1942-45* (Montreal & Kingston: McGill-Queen's UP, 2003), p. 99.

78 Library and Archive Canada Web Site (www.collectionscanada.gc.ca): The Canada Gazette 21 June 1940, 1. (http://www.collectionscanada.gc.ca/databases/canada-gazette/093/001060-119.01-e.php?document_id_nbr=8406&f=g&PHPSESSID=h62bjsqq9jmh0ccibjiq32rl87)

79 *Sun in Winter*, p. 4.

80 *Sun In Winter*, p. 78.

81 "Garth Williams (1912-)." *Something about the Author Autobiography Series*. Ed. Joyce Nakamura. Vol. 7. Detroit: Gale Research, 1989. 313-327. <http://galenet.galegroup.com.proxy.bc.edu/servlet/SATA_Online/mlin_m_bostcoll/BH2179075021>. Accessed 26 July 2012. p. 318.

82 *Something about the Author*, p. 318.

83 Curriculum Vitae in the Garth Williams Archive.

84 In the *New Yorker* on January 4, 1941, a piece appeared by a Professor C.C. Briggs of the Pratt Institute. Briggs was at that time teaching a course called "Program of Defense Buildings." Briggs was also investigating whether the New York City Subway system could serve as suitable bomb shelters. (He found them "far from ideal," though he also declared New Yorkers better protected against bomb threats than people in Europe because of the many steel-frame skyscrapers.) It is possible that Williams got his idea about serving to help identify bomb-safe structures from Briggs.

85 Correspondence between the authors and the U. S. Department of Justice.

86 Certificate and letter from Williams Archive. "Something About the Author," p. 319.

87 The Garth Williams Archive.

88 "Wheeler Sees US 'Rushing' into War," The New York *Times*, 28 April 1941.

89 "The Text of Colonel Lindbergh's Address at Rally of the America First Committee Here," *The New York Times* 24 April 1941, 12.

90 *The First ABAC Exhibition: Paintings and Sculpture from England, Canada & America.* 44 West Fifty-sixth Street New York January-February 1941. (MOMA Queens)

91 *New York Times,* February 22, 1942.

92 *Exhibition of Painting by Members of the American British Art Center and Sculpture by Jacob Epstein*, March 17 to April 4 1942 (In Artists Scrapbook Chadwyck Healy MOMA reference N 6490 .M856 1986 v2 Fiche # 1.191).

93 *New York Times* February 22, 1942.

94 "Suites on East Side Leased to Doctors; Other Rentals Range From the Heights to Greenwich Village," *The New York Times,* 6 June 1941.

95 Personal Interview with Fiona Williams Hulbert, August 13, 2013.

96 *Sun In Winter,* p. 45.

97, *Sun In Winter,* p. 99.

98 James Thurber, *The Years With Ross* (Boston: Little Brown Company, 1959), p. 44.

99 Leonard Marcus, "Garth Williams" *Publishers Weekly.* 237.8 (Feb. 23, 1990): p. 201.

100 *Something about the Author,* p. 320. *The New Yorker* has not responded to requests to confirm this story.

101 *Something about the Author,* p. 319.

102 Correspondence with Bettina Williams Schor, July 2012.

103 *Sun in Winter,* p. 189.

104 *Sun in Winter,* p. 190.

105 *Something about the Author,* p. 318.

106 *Sun in Winter,* p. 219.

107 *Sun in Winter,* p. 223.

108 *Sun in Winter,* p. 98.

109 *Sun in Winter,* p. 160-161.

110 *Sun in Winter,* pp. 240-41.

111 *Sun in Winter,* p. 243.

112 *Sun in Winter,* p. 251.

113 William Kehoe, "Waiters and Diners" *New York Times* Nov. 25th, 1945.

114 Ursula Nordstrom, "Stuart, Wilbur, Charlotte: A Tale of Tales" *New York Times* May 12, 1974.

115 *Letters of E. B. White.* Revised edition. Edited Dorothy Lobrano Guth, revised by Martha White (New York: Harper Collins, 2006), p. 541.

116 Roni Natov and Geraldine DeLuca, "Discovering Contemporary Classics: An Interview with Ursula Nordstrom" *Lion and the Unicorn,* 3:1/2 (1979/1980) p. 119.

117 Leonard Marcus, editor, *Dear Genius: the Letters of Ursula Nordstrom,* (New York: Harper Collins, 1998), pp. 8-9.

118 *Something about the Author,* p. 320.

119 Correspondence with Fiona Williams Hulbert, July 2012.

120 Cited in Scott Elledge, *E. B. White, A Biography* (New York: W. W. Norton and Company, 1984), p. 253.

121 *E. B. White,* p. 254.

122 *E. B. White,* p. 254.

123 Jill Lepore, "Lives and Letters: The Lion and the Mouse" in *The New Yorker.* http://www.newyorker.com/reporting/2008/07/21.

124 Lepore.

125 *E .B. White,* p. 264.

126 *E. B. White,* p. 264.

127 *Letters of E. B. White,* p. 255.

128 "Garth (Montgomery) Williams (1912-)." *Something About the Author.* Ed. Donna Olendorf. Vol. 66. Detroit: Gale, 1991. 228-235. *Something About the Author.* URL http://go.galegroup.com/ps/i.do?id=WBTPOV454845089&v=2.1&u=mlin_m_bostcoll&it=r&p=SATA&sw=w&asid=9d2170a4cec702c5787ebaeed98acea1 p. 233. Accessed Web. 27 June 2015.

129 Margaret Blount, *Animal Land: The Creatures of Children's Fiction* (New York: Avon 1974), p. 244.

130 *Dear Genius,* p, 9.

131 *Dear Genius,* pp. 8-9.

132 E. B. White, *Stuart Little* (1947; New York: Harper & Row, 1973), p. 86.

133 White, pp. 86-87.

134 Leonard S. Marcus, "Garth Williams: His Career Spanning Almost Half a Century, the Artist's Illustrations for Children's Books Have Become Classics," *Publishers Weekly* 237.8 (Feb. 23, 1990), p. 201.

135 *The Letters of E. B. White,* p. 250.

136 Katherine White, "Children's Books: Fairy Tales and the Postwar World" *New Yorker* December 8, 1945, p. 120.

137 Charles Poore , *The New York Times* October 27, 1945.

138 Paul H. Fry, "Animal Speech, Active Verbs, and Material Being in E. B. White" in *Animal Acts: Reconfiguring the Human in Western History,* edited by Jennifer Ham and Matthew Senior. New York: Routledge, 1997, p. 199.

139 Malcolm Cowley, "Stuart Little: Or, New York Through the Eyes of a Mouse" *The New York Times,* October 28, 1945.

140 Marah Gubar, "Species Trouble: The Abjection of Adolescence in E. B. White's Stuart Little" *The Lion and The Unicorn* 27 (2003), p. 102.

141 Gubar, p. 101.

142 Gubar, p. 105.

143 Gubar, p. 106.

144 Marcus, *Publishers Weekly* (1990), p. 201.

145 "Garth (Montgomery) Williams (1912-)," p. 233.

146 Jason Britton and Diane Roback, "All-Time Bestselling Children's Books," *Publishers Weekly* 248.51 (Dec. 17, 2001), 24; Elledge, *E. B. White,* p. 264.

147 Interview with Fiona Williams Hulbert, October 25, 2012.

148 Ancestry.com - UK, Outward Passenger Lists, 1890-1960. Consulted January 3, 2013.

149 David Wyman, *The Abandonment of the Jews: America and the Holocaust 1941-45* (New York: New Press, 1984), p. 127.

150 The document can be viewed at: http://www.jewishvirtuallibrary.org/jsource/Holocaust/truman_on_dps.html. Accessed January 17, 2013.

151 Garth Williams, "Illustrating the Little House Books" in *The Horn Book's Laura Ingalls Wilder* edited by William Anderson (1943 and 1953; rpt. The Horn Book, Inc. 2000), pp. 27-28.

152 Interview with Gunda Lambton, August 13, 2013.

153 Leonard Marcus, editor, *Dear Genius: the Letters of Ursula Nordstrom*, (New York: Harper Collins, 1998), p. 233.

154 Leonard Marcus, "Garth Williams; his career spanning almost half a century, the artist's illustrations for children's books have become classics." *Publishers Weekly* 237.8 (February 23, 1990), p. 201.

155 *Dear Genius,* p, 233.

156 *Dear Genius*, p. 17.

157 *Dear Genius*, p. 32.

158 William Anderson "Introduction" to *The Horn Book's Laura Ingalls Wilder*, p. 5.

159 Anderson, p. 5

160 John E Miller, *Becoming Laura Ingalls Wilder: the Woman behind the Legend* (Columbia, Mo: University of Missouri Press, 1998), p. 250.

161 Anderson, p. 35.

162 Note in the Garth Williams Archive.

163 Laura Ingalls Wilder to Ursula Nordstrom, November 3, 1947. Letter from Garth Williams Archive.

164 Garth Williams, "Illustrating the Little House Books," p. 30.

165 Garth Williams, "Illustrating the Little House Books," p. 30. See Anita Clare Feldman, *Little House, Long Shadow: Laura Ingalls Wilder's Impact on American Culture* (Columbia: University of Missouri Press, 2008), p. 206.

166 Garth Williams, "Illustrating the Little House Books," p. 32.

167 Garth Williams, "Illustrating the Little House Books," p. 36-37.

168 Garth Williams, "Illustrating the Little House Books," p. 33.

169 Garth Williams, "Illustrating the Little House Books," p. 34.

170 Garth Williams, "Illustrating the Little House Books," p. 35.

171 *Pioneer Girl* by Laura Ingalls Wilder. Edited by Pamela Smith Hill (South Dakota State Historical Society, 2014).

172 Caroline Fraser, "The Prairie Queen," *New York Review of Books*, December 22, 1994.

173 John E. Miller. *Becoming Laura Ingalls Wilder: The Woman Behind the Legend* (Columbia, MO: University of Missouri Press, 1998,) p. 186.

174 Anne T. Eaton, "Books for Children." *New York Times Book Review*, 24 April 1932, p. 9.

175 Anne T. Eaton, "New Books for Boys and Girls," *New York Times Book Review*, 3 October 1935, p. 10.

176 Katherine S. White, "Books," *The New Yorker* (25 November 1939), p. 89.

177 Miller, p. 215.

178 Anita Clair Feldman, p. 161.

179 Anderson, p. 5.

180 Joan Brest Friedberg, "Garth Williams" on-line resource *Dictionary of Literary Biography. http:// galenet.galegroup.com,* p. 10. Accessed February 1, 2013.

181 Passenger list for S. S. *de Grasse* from Ancestry.com, consulted on September 15, 2013.

182 Garth Williams, "Self-portrait." (2nd version). The Garth Williams Archive.

183 Nordstrom, p. 32.

184 Garth Williams, "Self-portrait." (2nd version). The Garth Williams Archive.

185 Unpublished memoir of Margaret Wise Brown, April 1968, p. 2. The Garth Williams Archive.

186 William Holtz, *The Ghost in the Little House* (University of Missouri Press, 1995).

187 One notable exception is an unpublished paper entitled "The *Little House* of Helen Sewell and Garth Williams" by Louisa Smith, Mankato State University and George R. Bodmer, Indiana University Northwest, delivered at Children's Literature Association Conference, Springfield, Missouri, 3 June 1994.

188 My Criteria for Selecting a Book to Illustrate." The Garth Williams Archive.

189 According to Sewell, the influence of the tropics dominated her art for years (*The Horn Book* October 1957, p. 371).

190 Louise Smith and George Bodmer, "The Little House of Helen Sewell."

191 Louise Smith and George Bodmer, "The Little House of Helen Sewell."

192 Ann Romines, *Constructing the Little House Books: Gender, Culture, and Laura Ingalls Wilder* (Amherst: U Mass Press, 1997), p. 264n.

193 John E. Miller, p. 212.

194 Laura Ingalls Wilder, *By the Shores of Silver Lake* (1939; rpt. New York: Harper and Row, 1953) pp. 71-2.

195 Miller, p. 257.

196 Laura Ingalls Wilder, *On the Way Home* (New York: Harper and Row, 1962).

197 "Little House on the Prairie" (1974-1982). NBC.

198 Gabrielle Mitchell-Marell, "Little House Under Renovation," *Publisher's Weekly*, December 4, 2006. http://www.publishersweekly.com/pw/print/20061204/3266-little-house-under-renovation.html. Accessed May 31, 2013.

199 Passenger list for the S. S. *Nieuw Amsterdam* from Ancestry.com, consulted on September 15, 2013.

200 Betty Pepis, "A Mining Shack Becomes a Mountain Retreat," *The New York Times*, August 19, 1955. http://select.nytimes.com/gst/abstract.html?res=F10F11FA3B5E127A93CBA81783D85F4 18585F9 Accessed June 11, 2013.

201 "Garth Williams (1912-)." *Something about the Author Autobiography Series*. Ed. Joyce Nakamura. Vol. 7. (Detroit: Gale Research, 1989), 322.

202 Leonard Marcus, *Margaret Wise Brown: Awakened by the Moon* (Boston: Beacon Press, 1996), p. 279.

203 "Margaret Wise Brown" by Garth Williams. April 1968. Unpublished document in the Garth Williams Archive.

204 "Margaret Wise Brown" by Garth Williams. April 1968. Unpublished document in the Garth Williams Archive.

205 Bruce Berger, A *Tent in the Meadow: Celebrating 50 Years of the Aspen Music Festival and School, 1949-1999* (New York: Time Warner, 1999), pp. 25-26.

206 Robert L. Perkin, "Book Illustrator Contributes to Culture" *Rocky Mountain News* (Denver, Colorado), Thursday, September 29, 1955, p. 36

207 Berger, p. 14.

208 Berger, pp. 32-33.

209 Perkin, p. 36.

210 Interview with Estyn Williams, June 17, 2013.

211 Peter F. Neumeyer, *The Annotated Charlotte's Web* (New York: Harper Collins, 1994), p. xix.

212 Eudora Welty, "Along Came a Spider: Charlotte's Web" by E. B. White." *The New York Times*, October 19, 1952. http://www.nytimes.com/books/98/11/22/specials/welty-charlotte.html. Accessed June 12, 2013.

213 "All-time bestselling paperback children's books," *Publishers Weekly* 243.6 (Feb. 5, 1996): p. 29. http://go.galegroup.com.proxy.bc.edu/ps/retrieve.do?sgHitCoun... Accessed June 3, 2013.

214 E. B. White, "The Death of a Pig" *Atlantic Monthly* January 1948.

215 Quoted in *E. B. White: A Biography by Scott Elledge* (New York: W.W. Norton and Company, 1984), p. 294

216 Michael Sims, *The Story of Charlotte's Web* (New York: Walker and Company, 2011), p. 178.

217 Sims, p. 186.

218 Ursula Nordstrom, "Stuart, Wilbur, Charlotte" A Tale of Tales," May 12, 1974. *The New York Times.* http://www.nytimes.com/books/97/08/03/lifetimes/white-tales.html. Accessed June 9, 2013.

219 Neumeyer, p. 121, note 6.

220 Leonard Marcus, editor. *Dear Genius: The Letters of Ursula Nordstrom* (New York: Harper Collins), pp. 35-36.

221 Scott Elledge, *E. B. White: A Biography* (New York: W. W. Norton, 1986), 300.

222 *Dear Genius*, p. 43.

223 *Dear Genius*, pp. 43-44.

224 Neumeyer, p. 199.

225 *Dear Genius*, p. 45.

226 *Dear Genius,* p. 45.

227 *Dear Genius,* p. 46.

228 Neumeyer, p. xxxiv.

229 Dorothy Lobano Guth, *The Letters of E. B. White*, Revised by Martha White (New York: Harper Collins, 2006), p. 533.

230 *The Letters of E. B. White*, p. 440.

231 Interview with Fiona Williams Hulbert, July 9, 2013.

232 *Dear Genius,* p. 44

233 *Dear Genius*, p. 45.

234 Neumeyer, p. 200.

235 Neumeyer, p. 15, n. 5.

236 Neumeyer 83, n. 11.

237 Neumeyer, p. 132, n. 5.

238 Neumeyer, p. 50, n. 7.

239 Neumeyer, p. 50, n. 7.

240 Perry Nodelman, *Words About Pictures: The Narrative Art of Children's Picture Books* (Athens: University of Georgia Press, 1988), 219.

241 Nodleman, p. 202.

242 Neumeyer, p. 95, n. 4.

243 Neumeyer, p. 88, n. 5.

244 Neumeyer, p. 202.

245 Neumeyer, p. 202.

246 E. B. White, *Charlotte's Web* (New York: Harper & Row, 1952), p. 7.

247 Neumeyer, p. xxxiii.

248 Quoted in Neumeyer, p. 249.

249 Quoted in Neumeyer, p. 246.

250 Sims, pp. 223-24.

251 Garth Williams, "Illustrating the Little House Books," *The Horn Book Magazine* 29 (1953), 421. See above, Chapter 3, page xx.

252 Nodelman, p. 70.

253 Our friend and colleague, Alston "Stoney" Conley, very kindly helped us to understand the importance of the concept of "line" in drawing.

254 Sims, p. 238.

255 Robert L. Perkin, "Book Illustrator Contributes to Culture," *Rocky Mountain News* (Denver, CO), September 29, 1955, p. 36.

256 Perkin, p. 36.

257 Perkin, p. 36.

258 Ernest Poole, *The Great White Hills of New Hampshire* (Garden City, NY: Doubleday and Company, 1946), pp. 171-72.

259 Damon Runyon, *In Our Town* (New York: Creative Age Press, 1946), 50; 2-3.

260 *Something About the* Author, p. 319.

261 Gillian Avery and Margaret Kinnell, "Morality and Levity 1780-1820," in Peter Hunt, ed., *Children's Literature: An Illustrated History* (New York: Oxford University Press, 1995), p. 73.

262 See, for example, M. F. Ashley Montague, "Time, Morphology, and Neoteny in the Evolution of Man," *American Anthropologist* N.S., 57 (1955), pp. 13-27.

263 Leonard S. Marcus, *Margaret Wise Brown: Awakened by the Moon* (Boston: Beacon Press, 1996), p. 195.

264 Garth Williams, "Margaret Wise Brown," typescript dated April 1968, in the Garth Williams Archive.

265 Margaret Wise Brown, *Little Fur Family*, illustrated by Garth Williams (New York: Simon and Schuster, 1946), p. 1.

266 Anna Panszcyk, "This Is Not About Picture Books: From 'Here and Now' to Surrealism in Margaret Wise Brown's *Little Fur Family* and *The Important Book*," *Children's Literature Association Quarterly* 36 (2011), pp. 359-60.

267 Marcus, *Margaret Wise Brown*, p. 199.

268 Panszcyk, p. 360.

269 Garth Williams, "Margaret Wise Brown," typescript dated April 1968, in the Garth Williams Archive.

270 Marcus, *Margaret Wise Brown*, p. 230.

271 Margaret Wise Brown, *Wait Till the Moon Is Full* (1948; New York, HarperCollins, 1976), n.p.

272 Leonard S. Marcus, *Golden Legacy: How Golden Books Won Children's Hearts, Changed Publishing Forever, and Became an American Icon Along the Way* (New York: Golden Books, 2007), p. 119.

273 Marcus, *Golden Legacy*, p. 93.

274 Marcus, *Golden Legacy*, p. 115.

275 Marcus, *Golden Legacy*, p. 122.

276 Garth Williams to Ursula Nordstrom, Guanajuato, Mexico, Sept. 12, 1970, in the Garth Williams Archive.

277 Garth Williams to Ursula Nordstrom, Guanajuato, Mexico, Sept. 12, 1970, in the Garth Williams Archive.

278 Garth Williams to Lee Lurie, January 24, 1958, in the Garth Williams Archive.

279 Royalty Statement, Artists and Writers Press Inc., January 28, 1964, in the Garth Williams Archive.

280 Royalty Statement, Artists and Writers Press Inc., August 6, 1964, in the Garth Williams Archive.

281 Margaret Wise Brown, *The Golden Sleepy Book*, illustrated by Garth Williams (New York: Golden Books, 1948), n.p.

282 Marcus, *Golden Legacy*, p. 122.

283 Unpublished notes on "Margaret Wise Brown" April 1986, in the Garth Williams Archive.

284 Margaret Wise Brown, *Mister Dog*, illustrated by Garth Williams, in *A Garth Williams Treasury of Best-Loved Golden Books*, introduction by Leonard S. Marcus (New York: Golden Books Publishing Company, 2001), p. 147.

285 Joan Brest Friedberg, "Garth (Montgomery) Williams," in *American Writers for Children, 1900-1996*, ed. John Cech, *Dictionary of Literary Biography, Vol. 22* (Detroit: Gale Research, 1983), p. 370. http://go.galegroup.com.proxy.bc.edu/ps/i.do?&id=GALE%7CH1200002272&v=2.1&u=mlin_m_bostcoll&it=r&p=LitRC&sw=w Accessed August 5, 2011.

286 Letter to Ursula Nordstrom, 1956. Garth Williams Archive.

287 Leonard Marcus, *Dear Genius*, (New York: HarperCollins, 1988), p. 112.

288 Charles Isherwood, "Parisian Hobo and Urchins from Kathy Lee, Lyricist," *The New York Times*, January 7, 2005; http://www.nytimes.com/2005/01/07/theater/reviews/07brid.html?ref=kathieleegifford

289 Tim Willoughby, "Garth Williams: Aspen's Most Famous Artist," *Aspen Times Weekly*, January 14, 2009; http://www.aspentimes.com/article/20090118/ASPENWEEKLY/901149958

290 George A. Woods, "Pictures for Fun, Fact and Fancy," *The New York Times Book Review* (June 8, 1958), p. 42.

291 "Children's Best Sellers," *The New York Times Book Review* (November 2, 1958), p. 48.

292 "Children's Book Stirs Alabama: White Rabbit Weds Black Rabbit," *The New York Times* (May 22, 1959), p. 29.

293 *The New York Times* (May 24, 1959), E1.

294 "Children's Book Stirs Alabama," p. 29.

295 "Southern Action on Book," letter from Victor G. Fourman, *The New York Times* (May 28, 1959), p. 30.

296 Friedberg, p. 371.

297 Display Ad 29—No Title, *The New York Times* (June 5, 1959), p. 25.

298 Karla Kusking, "Femalechuvinistmousemaker," *The New York Times Book Review* (May 7, 1972), p. 2.

299 Werner Sollors, "Can Rabbits Have Interracial Sex?" in Monika Kaup and Debra Rosenthal, eds., *Mixing Race, Mixing Culture: Inter-American Literary Dialogues* (Austin: University of Texas Press, 2002), pp. 14, 16.

300 Friedberg, p. 370.

301 Letter to Urusla Nordstrom, September 9, 1958, Garth Williams Archive.

302 Margery Sharp, *The Rescuers* (1959; New York: New York Review Book, 2011), p. 4.

303 "Margery Sharp" in *Something About the Author*, ed. Anne Commire, Vol. 29 (Detroit: Gale Research, 1992), 179. *Something About The Author Online*. http://galenet.galegroup.com.proxy.bc.edu/servlet/SATA_Online?dd=0&locID=mlin_m_bostcoll&d1=SATA_029_0122&srchtp=b&c=2&typ=All&docNum=BH2176295122&b0=margery+sharp&vrsn=1.0&srs=ALL&b1=KE&ste=10&d4=0.25&dc=tiPG&stp=DateDescend&n=10&tiPG=0 Accessed December 4, 2013.

304 "George Selden Thompson (1929-1989)." *Something about the Author*. Ed. Diane Telgen. Vol. 73. Detroit: Gale Research, 1993. 217-221. *Something About The Author Online*. Gale. <http://galenet.galegroup.com.proxy.bc.edu/servlet/SATA_Online/mlin_m_bostcoll/BH2176735098>. Accessed 11 December 2013.

305 Lesley S. Potts, "George Selden," in *Dictionary of Literary Biography, Volume 52: American Writers for Children Since 1960: Fiction*. A Bruccoli Clark Layman Book. Edited by Glenn E. Estes, Graduate School of Library and Information Science, University of Tennessee. The Gale Group, 1986. pp. 325-333. http://galenet.galegroup.com.proxy.bc.edu/servlet/GLD/hits?r=d&origSearch=true&o=DataType&n=10&l=d&c=1&locID=mlin_m_bostcoll&secondary=false&u=DLB&t=KW&s=4&NA=george+selden. Accessed December 11, 2013.

306 See Chapter Three, p. xx above.

307 Stephen Roxburgh, "George Selden," in Diane Roback, "Colorful Characters," www.publishersweekly.com/colorfulcharacters. Accessed December 11, 2013.

308 Polly Goodwin, review of *The Cricket in Times Square*" in the *Chicago Sunday Tribune Magazine of Books*, December 25, 1960, p. 6; quoted in "Introduction to Thompson, George Selden (1929-)." *Children's Literature Review*. Ed. Gerard J. Senick. Vol. 8. Detroit: Gale Research, 1985. *Literature Criticism Online*. Web. http://go.galegroup.com/ps/i.do?id=GALE%7CUWZMSD496605546&v=2.1&u=mlin_m_bostcoll&it=r&p=LCO&sw=w&asid=172698b99a535a8254f8691d73ee2822 Accessed December 4, 2013.

309 Court Document from Jefferson County, Colorado Civil Action Number 15868. Garth Williams Archive.

310 "Garth Williams (1912-)." *Something about the Author Autobiography Series*. Ed. Joyce Nakamura. Vol. 7. Detroit: Gale Research, 1989. 313-327. <http://galenet.galegroup.com.proxy.bc.edu/servlet/SATA_Online/mlin_m_bostcoll/BH2179075021>, p. 323. Accessed 26 July 2012'

311 Interview with Fiona Williams Hulbert, July 9, 2013.

312 "Ruslatado del Analisis Toxicologico enviado por el Sr. F Williams," the Garth Williams Archive.

313 Letter to Lucille Ogle, July 26, 1974, the Garth Williams Archive.

314 *Something About the Author*, p. 323.

315 *Something About the Author*, p. 323.

316 Interview with Alicia Rayas, August 12, 2014.

317 The Garth Williams Archive.

318 Letter to Lucille Ogle Oct. 6, 1963, Garth Williams Archive.

319 Letter to Lucille Ogle August 20, 1963, Garth Williams Archive.

320 Letter to Lucille Ogle, September 11, 1964, Garth Williams Archive.

321 Letter to Ursula Nordstrom, May 15, 1964. Garth Williams Archive.

322 Letter from Ursula Nordstrom, May 12, 1964, Garth Williams Archive.

323 Interview with Estyn Williams, July 17, 2012.

324 *Something About the Author*, p. 323.

325 This book was reissued, with new illustrations by Javaka Steptoe depicting an African American family in 2000.

326 Copy of letter from Charlotte Zolotow to Ursula Nordstrom, 1963, in the Garth Williams Archive.

327 Letter to Ursula Nordstrom, 1963, in the Garth Williams Archive.

328 Sally Lodge, "Three Randall Jarrell Books Come Home to Michael di Capua," *Publisher's Weekly* 242.9 (Feb. 27, 1995), p. 41.

329 Mary Jarrell, "Introduction" in Jerome Griswold, *The Children's Books of Randall Jarrell* (Athens: University of Georgia Press, 1988), p. 7.

330 Letter from Michael Di Capua at The MacMillan Company, June 27, 1963, in the Garth Williams Archive.

331 Sally Lodge, "Three Randall Jarrell Books Come Home to Michael di Capua," *Publisher's Weekly* 242.9 (Feb. 27, 1995), p. 41.

332 Randall Jarrell letter to Michael di Capua, quoted in Richard Flynn, *Randall Jarrell and the Lost World of Childhood* (Athens: University of Georgia Press, 1990), p. 104.

333 The quotation is from the Cinco Puntos web page: http://www.cincopuntos.com/authors_detail.sstg?id=5

334 Bonnie Henry, "Desert Druid Writes On," *Arizona Star*, May 17, 2009. http://azstarnet.com/lifestyles/bonnie-henry-desert-druid-writes-on/article_44bb6c9b-de27-5a91-b402-259727e10e17.html Accessed June 26, 2015.

335 Letter to Lucille Ogle, May 13, 1961, in the Garth Williams Archive.

336 Letter to Lucille Ogle, March 26, 1964, in the Garth Williams Archive.

337 Letter to Lucille Ogle, April 23, 1964, in the Garth Williams Archive.

338 Letter to Ogle July 26, 1964, in the Garth Williams Archive.

339 Interview with Estyn Williams, July 17, 2012.

340 Letter from Garth Williams to Estyn Williams, courtesy of Estyn Williams.

341 Letter to Ursula Nordstrom, January 30, 1970, in the Garth Williams Archive

342 Correspondence to the Chase Manhattan Bank, May 11, 1977 and postscript of a letter to Richard Ticktin, dated August 22, 1977, in the Garth Williams Archive.

343 Letter to Ursula Nordstrom, September 25, 1970, in the Garth Williams Archive.

344 Letter from Jeremy Nussbaum, October 8, 1970, in the Garth Williams Archive.

345 Ursula Nordstrom to Garth Williams, April 1, 1969, in the Garth Williams Archive.

346 Ursula Nordstrom to Garth Williams, April 29, 1969, in the Garth Williams Archive.

347 Ursula Nordstrom to Garth Williams, November 10, 1969, in the Garth Williams Archive.

348 Ursula Nordstrom to Garth Williams, November 25, 1969, in the Garth Williams Archive.

349 Garth Williams to Ursula Nordstrom, December 18, 1969, in the Garth Williams Archive.

350 Garth Williams to Peter Neumeyer, October 2, 1983, in the Garth Williams Archive.

351 E. B. White to Garth Williams, December 31, 1969, in the Garth Williams Archive.

352 Garth Williams to Peter Neumeyer, October 2, 1983, in the Garth Williams Archive.

353 John Updike, "The Trumpet of the Swan," *The New York Times*, June 28, 1970, http://www.nytimes.com/books/97/04/06/lifetimes/updike-r-swan.html Accessed June 26, 2015.

354 Garth Williams to Harriet F. Pilpel of Greenbaum Wolff & Ernst, August 25, 1970, in the Garth Williams Archive.

355 Williams Anderson "Garth Williams After 80" *The Horn Book Magazine* 69.2 (March-April 1993), p. 181

356 Letter to Ursula Nordstrom 1970, in the Garth Williams Archive.

357 *In the Night Kitchen* was number 24 on the ALA's "Top 100 Banned/Challenged Books: 2000-2009." http://www.ala.org/bbooks/top-100-bannedchallenged-books-2000-2009 Accessed June 26, 2015.

358 At that time Spiro Agnew, Vice-President in the Richard Nixon administration, was the voluble spearhead of conservative political values in the United States.

359 The "Cock-a-Doodle Doo!" page is, of course, the one on which Mickey's penis is on full display.

360 Garth Williams to Maurice Sendak, November 14, 1970, in the Garth Williams Archive.

361 Letter to Ursula Nordstrom and Maurice Sendak April 29, 1972 in the Garth Williams Archive.

362 Letter to Maurice Sendak November 14, 1970.

363 Sheila A. Egoff, *Thursday's Child: Trends and Patterns in Contemporary Children's Literature* (Chicago: American Library Association, 1981), p. 250.

364 Maurice Sendak, "Caldecott Award Acceptance," quoted in Egoff, p. 251.

365 John Cech, "Maurice Sendak and *Where the Wild Things Are*: A Legacy of Transformation," *PMLA: Publications of the Modern Language Association*, 129.1 (2014), p.105.

366 "Ezra's Life" from the Ezra Jack Keats Foundation Web page, http://www.ezra-jack-keats.org/ezras-life/ Accessed June 26, 2015.

367 Larrick noted Keats's "sympathetic picture" but expressed reservations that it was about "just one child" and clearly disapproved of the stereotyped portrayal of the boy's mother, "a huge figure in a gaudy yellow plaid dress, albeit without a red bandanna." Nancy Larrick, "The All-White World of Children's Books," *The Saturday Review*, (Sept. 11, 1965), p. 65.

368 "Ezra's Life."

369 "About *William's Doll*" on The Official Charlotte Zolotow Web Site, http://charlottezolotow.com/
willilams_doll.htm (The misspelling of "willilams" is indeed in the page's url.) Accessed June
26, 2015.

370 Garth Williams to Joan Friedberg, November 8, 1981, the Garth Williams Archive.

371 Susan Hirschman to Garth Williams, March 16, 1989, the Garth Williams Archive.

372 Garth Williams to Stephen de Vito, October 30, 1974, the Garth Williams Archive.

373 Stephen de Vito to Garth Williams, December 3, 1974, the Garth Williams Archive.

374 Harper & Row royalties statement, June 1, 1945, the Garth Williams Archive.

375 Ursula Nordstrom to Garth Williams, September 27, 1970, the Garth Williams Archive.

376 Contract dated "1947" in pencil, the Garth Williams Archive.

377 Elizabeth Gordon to David N. Sterling, November 9, 1981, the Garth Williams Archive.

378 Barbara Dicks (secretary to Ursula Nordstrom) to Garth Williams, March 24, 1959, the Garth
Williams Archive.

379 Irene Silverman, "Jeremy Nussbaum, Attorney and Activist," obituary in *The East Hampton Star*,
June 21, 2012. http://easthamptonstar.com/?q=Obituaries/2012621/Jeremy-Nussbaum-Attorney-
and-Activist Accessed June 26, 2015.

380 Silverman, Op. Cit. Robert Simonson, "Jeremy Nussbaum, Entertainment Lawyer, Dies at
70," *Playbill*, June 19, 2012. http://www.playbill.com/news/article/167212-Jeremy-Nussbaum-
Entertainment-Lawyer-Dies-at-70- Accessed November 12, 2013.

381 Jeremy Nussbaum to Garth Williams, December 17, 1970, Garth Williams Archive.

382 Letter from Ursula Nordstrom, 1953, the Garth Williams Archive.

383 Letter from Ursula Nordstrom, January 25, 1962, the Garth Williams Archive.

384 "Garth Williams (1912-)." *Something about the Author Autobiography Series*. Ed. Joyce Nakamura.
Vol. 7. Detroit: Gale Research, 1989. 313-327. <http://galenet.galegroup.com.proxy.bc.edu/servlet/
SATA_Online/mlin_m_bostcoll/BH2179075021>, p. 324. Accessed 26 July 2012.

385 Interview with Leticia Williams, Guanjuato, Mexico, March 3-4, 2014.

386 Garth Williams to John Norbutt, March 24, 1979, the Garth Williams Archive.

387 Unfinished manuscript, the Garth Williams Archive

388 Garth Williams to John Norbutt, March 24, 1979, the Garth Williams Archive.

389 Interview with Dilys Williams, Guanajuato, Mexico, March 3-4. 2014.

390 Handwritten document, November 1988, marked "Texas," the Garth Williams Archive.

391 "Young at Heart: Illustrator spins web of classics" by Nora Lopez *The Sunday Express News*, December
17, 1989, Section F, pp. 1-2.

392 Untitled document, the Garth Williams Archive.

393 Interview with Dilys Williams, Guanajuato, Mexico, March 3-4. 2014.

394 Jack Prelutsky, "In Search of the Addle-pated Paddlepuss," 1990. Rpt. *Children's Literature Review*
vol. 115 (2006), p. 62. http://go.galegroup.com.proxy.bc.edu/ps/retrieve.do?sgHitCountType=N
one&sort=RELEVANCE&docType=Biography&prodId=LCO&tabID=T002&searchId=R8&
resultListType=RESULT_LIST&searchType=AdvancedSearchForm&contentSegment=&curr
entPosition=1&searchResultsType=MultiTab&inPS=true&userGroupName=mlin_m_bostcoll
&docId=GALE|YWNRVH366930254&contentSet=GALE|YWNRVH366930254# Accessed
November 12, 2013.

395 Leonard S. Marcus, "Garth Williams: His Career Spanning Almost Half a Century, the Artist's Illustrations for Children's Books Have Become Classics," *Publishers Weekly*, vol. 237, no. 8 (Feb. 23, 1990), 201. http://go.galegroup.com.proxy.bc.edu/ps/retrieve.do?sgHitCountType=None&so rt=RELEVANCE&inPS=true&prodId=LitRC&userGroupName=mlin_m_bostcoll&tabID=T0 02&searchId=R2&resultListType=RESULT_LIST&contentSegment=&searchType=AdvancedS earchForm&currentPosition=1&contentSet=GALE%7CA8541967&&docId=GALE|A8541967& docType=GALE&role=LitRC Accessed November 12, 2013.

396 Ann A. Flowers, Review of *Beneath a Blue Umbrella*, *Horn Book Magazine* 66, no. 2 (March-April, 1990), p. 216.

397 Carolyn Phelan, Review of *Beneath a Blue Umbrella*, *Booklist* 86, no. 17 (1 May 1990): p. 1701.

398 William Anderson, *Horn Book's Laura Ingalls Wilder: Articles About and by Laura Ingalls Wilder, Garth Williams, and the Little House Books* (Anderson Publishing, 1987).

399 William Anderson, *Laura Ingalls Wilder Country: The People and Places in Laura Ingalls Wilder's Life and Books* (1990). This was a reprint of a Japanese version of the same book, published in 1988. See discussion below.

400 For example, in a letter to Sendak on November 11th, 1970, he had groused, "I spent six months travelling around the miserable west looking at the frightful people there, and the grimness of life without any meaning except survival. . . . all that was paid for by me out of my advance 'royalties.'" But Williams was capable of many moods, and this one, like others, seems to have passed quickly.

401 William ("Bill") Anderson to William ("Bill") Morris, July 17, 1986, the Garth Williams Archive.

402 Leonard Marcus, "Garth Williams; his career spanning almost half a century, the artist's illustrations for children's books have become classics." *Publishers Weekly* 237.8 (February 23, 1990), p. 201.

403 William Anderson, "Garth Williams after Eighty" *The Horn Book Magazine*. 69.2 (March-April 1993): p181.

404 Joan Brest Friedberg, "Garth (Montgomery) Williams," in *American Writers for Children, 1900-1996*, ed. John Cech, *Dictionary of Literary Biography, Vol. 22* (Detroit: Gale Research, 1983), p. 370. http://go.galegroup.com.proxy.bc.edu/ps/i.do?&id=GALE%7CH1200002272&v=2.1&u=m lin_m_bostcoll&it=r&p=LitRC&sw=w Accessed August 5, 2011.

405 *Kirkus Review*, April 1, 1993. https://www.kirkusreviews.com/book-reviews/john-sebastian/jbs-harmonica/ Accessed June 26, 2015.

406 *Publishers Weekly*, April 1, 1993. http://www.publishersweekly.com/978-0-15-240091-0 Accessed June 26, 2015.

407 http://www.playsinthepark.com/index.php/season/Archive/item/childrens-show-tbd. Accessed April 4, 2014.

408 Interview with Dilys Williams, Guanajuato, Mexico, March 3-4. 2014.

409 Undated document, Garth Williams Archive.

410 See *Ku:nel* Magazine, 2009. Volume 7, no. 3.

Permissions

All photographs, unless noted, appear courtesy of the Estate of Garth Williams and with the kind permission of the Williams family.

The drawing on page 97 and the photograph on page 102 appear courtesy of the Aspen Historical Society.

Williams's wedding announcement on page 60 appears courtesy of Dilys Williams.

Amigo. Reprinted with the permission of Aladdin, an imprint of Simon & Schuster Children's Publishing Division, from AMIGO by Byrd Baylor, illustrated by Garth Williams. Illustration copyright (c) 1963 by Garth Williams; illustration copyright renewed 1991 by Garth Williams. All rights reserved. (Pages 159 and 171)

By the Shores of Silver Lake by Laura Ingalls Wilder. Text copyright 1939, 1967 Little House Heritage Trust. Illustration by Garth Williams used by permission of HarperCollins Publishers. (Page 89)

Charlotte's Web by E. B. White. Copyright 1952 by E.B. White. Text Copyright renewed 1980 by E. B. White. Illustrations by Garth Williams used by permission of HarperCollins Publisher. (Pages 7, 107, 110, 112, 113, 114, 115, and 116)

Cricket in Times Square from *Cricket in Times Square* Copyright 1960 by George Selden. Reprinted by permission of Farrar, Straus, and Giroux, LLC. All Rights Reserved. (Page 157)

Great White Hills of New Hampshire. Poole, Ernest. *The Great White Hills of New Hampshire*. Garden City, NY: Doubleday, 1946. (Page 123)

In Our Town. Runyon, Damon, and Garth Williams. *In Our Town*. New York: Creative Age Press, 1946. (Pages 124 and 125)

J.B.'s Harmonica. Sebastian, John, and Garth Williams. *J.B.'S Harmonica*. San Diego: Harcourt Brace Jovanovich, 1993. (Page 211)

Little Fur Family by Margaret Wise Brown. Copyright 1946 by HarperCollins Publishers. Text Copyright renewed 1947 by Robert Brown Rauch. Illustration by Garth Williams used by permission of HarperCollins Publisher. (Pages 131, 132, and 134)

Little House on the Prairie by Laura Ingalls Wilder. Text copyright 1935, 1963 Little House Heritage Trust. Illustration by Garth Williams used by permission of HarperCollins Publishers. (Page 176)

Little Town on the Prairie by Laura Ingalls Wilder. Text copyright 1941, 1969 Little House Heritage Trust. Illustration by Garth Williams used by permission of HarperCollins Publishers. (Pages 82, 83, 91, 92, and 93)

Index